Anne Walbank Buckland

Our Viands

Whence they come and how they are cooked, with a bundle of old recipes from

cookery books of the last century

Anne Walbank Buckland

Our Viands
Whence they come and how they are cooked, with a bundle of old recipes from cookery books of the last century

ISBN/EAN: 9783744797504

Printed in Europe, USA, Canada, Australia, Japan

Cover: Foto ©ninafisch / pixelio.de

More available books at **www.hansebooks.com**

OUR VIANDS

WHENCE THEY COME AND HOW THEY ARE COOKED

WITH A BUNDLE OF OLD RECIPES FROM COOKERY BOOKS OF THE LAST CENTURY

By ANNE WALBANK BUCKLAND

MEMBER OF THE ANTHROPOLOGICAL INSTITUTE. AUTHOR OF
'ANTHROPOLOGICAL STUDIES.' 'THE WORLD BEYOND
THE ESTERELLES,' ETC.

'*Tell me what thou eatest and I will tell thee who thou art.*'
OLD PROVERB.

'*Viands of various kinds allure the taste*
Of choicest sort and savour; rich repast.'—POPE.

LONDON
WARD & DOWNEY
12 YORK STREET COVENT GARDEN W.C.
1893

CONTENTS

PART I

INTRODUCTION

THE art of cookery is no new thing, yet the tastes of mankind are so diverse, that the proverb, 'One man's meat is another man's poison,' becomes a truism. There still exist savages who prefer raw meat to cooked, as did the Fuegians who were lately exhibited in London, but even they had acquired a taste for hard boiled eggs, which they devoured with great relish.

There may also be found in the heart of savage Africa, in Australia, and in some of the South Sea Islands, tribes who prefer human flesh to any other, but these all like their meat, whatever it may be, cooked; and following the custom of the most ancient of men, will sit round a fire broiling their bones, cutting off bits by degrees just scorched, and repeating the process till nothing but the bare bone remains. But even then the feast is not ended, for all the bones are broken, and the marrow, which is highly esteemed, is sucked out as a concluding *bonne bouche*.

In this mode of cooking and eating, the modern savage closely follows the ancient cave-dwellers, amongst whom marrow seems to have been always esteemed a prime delicacy.

This we know, because many of the bones found in the kitchen middens of these early people are partly charred, and all the marrow-bones are broken. But these troglodytes were not extravagant cooks, nothing was thrown away which might prove useful. Having split the bones and devoured the marrow, they proceeded to make spear and arrow heads from the splinters, for the capture of fresh game to furnish future feasts, and it is more than probable that they crushed and ate the smaller bones, for this is still the custom among savages. Mr. Borcherds, an early South African traveller, describes a feast among some Bushmen to whom a sheep had been given : he says, 'Each bone was separated from the flesh as cleanly as possible, the bones were crushed, and together with the raw kidneys, distributed amongst the children, who seemed to enjoy the delicacy as much as ours do cakes. The meat was laid on the fire, and when half cooked devoured.' Mr. Lumholtz, in his travels 'Among Cannibals' in Australia, describes a feast of snakes, in which the bones were also crushed and eaten ; and in that singularly interesting legend, denominated 'The Mountain Chant,' given in the *Smithsonian Reports*, the hero is represented as killing two rabbits, and pounding them up bones and all with seeds, for food. So that here we have from three parts of the world evidence of the use of crushed bones, and may reasonably infer that the custom was universal, especially in times of scarcity.

Sitting at our well-appointed tables, we smile at the primitive devices adopted by savages, yet some of them have hit upon a mode of cooking which may fairly be termed scientific, so well is it calculated to retain the juices of the meat ; as for instance, in Australia, the snakes which furnished the feast described by Lumholtz, were coiled up, tied together, and baked in an oven scooped out of the earth, in which a large fire was made, serving to heat several stones. Some of these were removed, and upon the others a large quantity of green leaves or grass was laid, and upon this the snakes, which were covered with more green leaves and more hot stones, and then the earth was pressed down tight over the whole, no steam being allowed to escape. When done, the meat, tender and juicy, was taken out in the leaves which served as a dish. Mr. Lumholtz extols this method of cooking for salt beef and pork, especially when ginger leaves are used,* but the natives reserve it for snakes and human flesh, cooking other things by throwing them on the hot embers like the Bushmen, and eating them half raw. The New Zealanders cook their potatoes in the same kind of earth-oven, which, probably, in cannibal times also served for the *long pig* in which they delighted.

The art of baking in ovens is of great antiquity; the ovens of ancient Egypt are frequently represented in contemporary paintings; and the African savage will scoop out the adhesive earth of ants' nests, or the clay of river courses, to form an oven wherein to bake bread, stopping up the opening with wood and clay or cow dung, just as our cottagers used to do with the earth-ovens made at the end of most cottages, at a time when it was the wholesome custom among farm-labourers to make and bake their own bread.

Boiling is another primitive mode of cooking, and the method which is still employed in some uncivilised countries, is to take the hide of the slaughtered animal, tie it up so as

---

* Years ago it was the custom in some parts of England to bake bread rolls wrapped up in cabbage leaves. This imparted a peculiar and, to many palates, agreeable flavour to the bread. In a description of a recent Chinese dinner, we find among the delicacies, a knife fish, rolled in banana leaves, and baked between hot stones.

to form a bag, place the meat in this bag with some water, and then drop in stones, heated in the fire to a white heat, until the meat is cooked. It must be a very tedious process, and not particularly appetising, but the only one available where pottery and metal are alike unknown. The alternative method of placing the meat on hot stones and covering it with the ashes was doubtless that most generally practised, and is still adopted by hunters and by the gipsies in our own country; one of the dainties of the latter being a hedge-hog thus roasted, whilst the hunter in Africa will regale himself with the foot of the elephant, or a porcupine cooked in the same manner. Then of course there is the tripod of sticks, upon which the meat is hung over the flame, and it is doubtful whether meat thus cooked is not of finer flavour than that which we dry up in ovens, or boil to death in ordinary saucepans.

In very hot countries the sun turns cook, and the hunter has only to place his steak on heated stones exposed to the mid-day sun, and it will soon be sufficiently cooked, or he may cut his game in slices and hang the pieces on a thorn-bush to be thoroughly dried in the sun, and then carry it away with him as *biltong* in South Africa, or jerked beef (*charki*) in America.

We have heard of nests of eggs cooked by the heat of the sun in South Africa, whilst in Iceland and some other countries it is possible to cook by means of the boiling springs.

We are apt to experience a feeling of disgust in reading of the Eskimo crowded in their snow houses, regaling themselves with great pieces of seal-blubber, and washing down the feast with train oil, but we do not consider the disadvantages under which these poor people labour in a country where it would be impossible to indulge in gastronomic luxuries, not only on account of the scarcity of food, but also because of the scarcity of fuel, their only cooking apparatus consisting of that simple oil lamp, which serves the treble purpose of fire, candle, and cooking-stove. Yet French and Italian cooks achieve most of their culinary triumphs by the aid of a cooking-stove only once removed from that of the Eskimo, being heated by charcoal only.

Luxury has now taken such hold upon us that we wonder how it could ever have been possible to eat comfortably without silver forks, yet our grandmothers knew them not, but used forks of steel, at first with only two tines or prongs, which they managed as deftly as the Chinese do their chop-sticks, although they did not scruple to put the knife in the mouth on occasion, and, in fact, the knives were made rounded at the end for that purpose. Forks, indeed, are but a late invention, and our Saxon ancestors cut their meat from the spit with their hunting knives, not only when engaged in the chase, but when seated at table in their great banqueting halls, as witness a curious old drawing in the Cotton Manuscript, in which two serving-men or cooks are represented kneeling holding a spit in one hand and a platter in the other, whilst three guests—seated at a table covered with a heavy cloth, upon which are various dishes, and cakes of bread marked with a cross—cut from the spit presented to them such meat as they please, apparently letting it fall into the platter held to receive it. Yet we are told that the Anglo-Saxons possessed forks, some having been found with coins of Cænwulf, King of Mercia and Athelstan,* but these are supposed to have

* See Chambers's ' Book of Days.'

been mere toys, for forks certainly did not come into general use in England before the end of the seventeenth century, although they appear to have been used in Italy at an earlier date. They have now penetrated into the heart of savage Africa, and Mr. A. A. Anderson * describes an interview with Lo Bengula, in which 'a little Mashona boy brought, on a piece of grass matting, four large pieces of bullock's lights, that had been broiled over a fire, and a fork; advancing on hands and knees to his dreaded master, he placed them on the grass in front of his majesty, who took the fork, and transfixing one after the other they disappeared from sight in his capacious mouth.'

The table appointments of ancient Egypt are familiar to us from the paintings. We see the guests seated at table in gala dress, be-wigged and be-jewelled, holding the lotus-lily in their hands by way of nosegay, whilst attendants in the very scantiest of attire, naked except for a girdle and a necklace to show that they are slaves, serve them with meat and wine, evidently in too great profusion, for that disgusting practice, which prevailed also among the epicures and gluttons of ancient Rome, of taking emetics when satiated † in order to be able to renew the feast, is most realistically depicted.

That which is remarkable in these Egyptian feasts is the

---

* 'Twenty-five Years in a Waggon.'

† It may be of interest here to give the receipt of Apicius for digestive salts from Soyer's ' History of Food : '—take 1 lb. of common salt pulverised, mix with 3 oz. white pepper, 2 oz. ginger, 1 oz. lamoni, 1½ oz. thyme, 1½ oz. celery seed, 2 oz. wild marjoram, 1½ oz. rocket seed, 3 oz. black pepper, 1½ oz. holy thistle, 2 oz. hyssop, 2 oz. spikenard, 2 oz. parsley, 2 oz. aniseed. Take a small quantity after a too plentiful dinner.

preponderance of women represented. It is evident that in those remote times ladies were not consigned to the galleries to look on whilst their lords and masters enjoyed the good things provided by Egyptian cooks, but were allowed their full share both of the comestibles and of the table talk.

The ancient Greeks were studiously simple in their habits, and their cookery in early times appears to have partaken of this simplicity. The famous black broth of the Spartans, which was the national dish, and of which they were so fond that they seldom ate anything else, appears to have been a horrible compound of pork broth, with vinegar and salt. Of this dish it is related, that Dionysius, the elder, having had it carefully prepared by a Lacedæmonian slave, just tasted it and threw it from him in disgust, demanding of the slave whether that was the broth of which the Spartans were so found—'No,' replied the slave, 'it lacks one ingredient, that of violent exercise before partaking of it.'

In Attica the common people lived almost entirely upon vegetables, but among the wealthy there was great profusion as soon as luxuries began to be introduced from abroad. At entertainments a king of the feast was chosen by lot, whose duty it was to fix the quantity of wine to be drunk by the guests, and to determine in what manner they were to pass the evening; this was often by music and singing patriotic songs, although the king of the feast frequently proposed a subject which all present were expected to discuss. The guests at the dinner parties of the Athenians seem to have been limited to nine, for it was an Athenian saying that a convivial meeting should not consist of fewer than the Graces or more than the Muses, and before sitting down they were accustomed to use the warm bath, and to anoint themselves with oil.

The institution of ' King of the Feast' appears to have descended to the Romans, for this functionary is mentioned with approbation both by Plutarch and Cato. His office somewhat resembled that of the chairman or president of to-day, although he would appear to have had more to do with the general conduct of the feast, regulating the quantity of wine to be drunk, and who should sing or tell a story, or in any other way amuse the guests.

The Romans in Republican times were as frugal in their diet as the Spartans, seldom tasting meat, but living chiefly upon milk, eggs, and vegetables, and a kind of pudding somewhat resembling our batter pudding; but this simple mode of life was quickly abandoned, and the luxury of the wealthy Romans exceeded anything known in the present day. Nero's banqueting-room was wainscotted with ivory, and the panels were so constructed as to turn on pivots and shower down flowers and perfumes on the guests, whilst the circular roof imitated the movements of the spheres, representing a different season of the year as each course was placed on the table. 'The supper-rooms of Elagabalus,' we are told, 'were hung with cloth of gold and silver, enriched with jewellery; the frames of the couches were of massive silver, with mattresses covered with the richest embroidery; and the tables and table services were of pure gold ;* whilst even of private individuals Horace writes—

> ' Where ivory couches overspread
> With Tyrian carpets glowing, fed
> The dazzled eye.'

* ' Sketches of Manners and Institutions of the Romans,' p. 164.

The guests reposed upon elegant couches placed round the tables, and only sat in sign of mourning; each was provided with a special robe, generally white, by the host, a custom alluded to in the New Testament; whilst a bill of fare, or, as we should say now, a *menu* was placed before every guest. As for plate, Crassus is said to have possessed some, of which the workmanship alone cost about fifty-two shillings the ounce. Sylla had silver dishes of sixteen hundred ounces; and a freedman of the Emperor Claudius had one which weighed five hundred pounds, forming the centre dish of eight others, each weighing fifty pounds. But in the midst of all this luxury it is amusing to read that every guest was expected to bring his own napkin, which he generally sent home by a slave filled with some of the good things from the table *—a custom which, perhaps, some of us would not be sorry to see revived.

Small figures of Mercury, Hercules, and the penates were placed on the table, and libations were poured to them at the beginning and end of a feast; whilst the salt placed beside them was regarded as sacred. We find, too, the superstitions regarding the spilling of salt, and the unlucky number thirteen, in full force among the Romans. Pliny says the purchase of a cook cost as much as the expense of a triumph, and no mortal was so valued as the slave who was most expert in the art of ruining his master. Hosts seemed to vie with each other in the costliness of feasts, and of Apicius it is related that, after having wasted half a million sterling on the pleasures of the table, he committed suicide because, having only eighty thousand pounds left, he could not continue his extravagances.

* ' Sketches of Manners and Institutions of the Romans,' p. 164.

And yet, during the early part of the Empire, sumptuary laws were in force regulating the expenses to be incurred at banquets, and even the number of dishes, and it is said that Julius Cæsar frequently sent lictors to suspected houses, and had the dishes carried off from the tables if they exceeded the number permitted by law; whilst Augustus decreed that an ordinary repast should not cost more than 200 sesterces (about £1, 12s. 6d.), or 300 on feasts or days of solemnity, and 1000 at a wedding. If we compare this with the luxury of Nero and Elagabalus and later emperors, when a single fish cost fifty guineas, when pearls were dissolved in vinegar and drunk, not for pleasure, but only to add to the cost of a feast; and when the senate was convened to consult as to the best manner of dressing a turbot for the emperor's table, we shall hardly be surprised at the decline and fall of Rome.

Yet this excess of luxury was a great incentive to commerce, for merchants who scoured the seas for things rare and costly were sure of a market on their return; whilst they carried with them in their wanderings to distant shores not only many useful wares by way of barter, but also those germs of civilisation, destined to grow up and bear fruit when the pomp of the Roman emperors which had caused their transplantation had withered and fallen into an untimely grave.

PART I

BREAD

WHEAT, BARLEY, RYE, OATS

'𝔅etter halfe a loafe than no bread.'

CHAPTER I

BREAD

MAN is an omnivorous animal: nothing comes amiss to him. When hunger impels he will eat the vilest refuse, but in times of prosperity bread, meat, and vegetables form the staple of his diet. 'Doctors differ' as to the original food of mankind. It varied probably, as now, according to climate, consisting of fruit and seeds where these grew spontaneously and in abundance, and of animal food where fruit, etc., could not be readily obtained; but with the dawn of civilisation man began to cultivate plants for food, and particularly the several grains still used for making bread. Of these, wheat, barley, and rye seem to have been the earliest cultivated, oats being later, whilst it is doubtful whether maize was known except on the American continent.

We are so accustomed to look upon bread as the 'staff of life,' the food above all others necessary for our sustenance, that the term, 'without bread,' has long been in our language synonymous with 'starvation.' Hence we find it hard to realise the fact that, if we restrict the term bread to that which is generally so called, that is food prepared from the farina or flour of various grains, not only individuals, but entire nations have lived, and continue to live to this day without bread; nay, that we may trace the history of mankind back to a time when bread was utterly unknown.

The early men who hunted the mammoth, the rhinoceros, and the bear through the forests which now lie beneath the waves of Torbay and Cromer, and sheltered themselves in Brixham caverns, Kent's Hole, and the Victoria and Welsh caves, knew nothing of bread; they may indeed, and probably did, as savages do now, eat such roots and fruits as came in their way, but it is abundantly evident that they did not cultivate the soil, nor prepare grain for food. They have left us their rude stone tools, and later the bone harpoons with which they caught their fish, the needles with which they sewed their skin garments, and the shell, bone, and stone ornaments in which they delighted, but they evidently lived like the hyenas, their contemporaries, upon flesh and marrow, and it is doubtful whether they even knew how to light a fire, or to cook in any way the game they fed upon. There is, at all events among the older relics, no trace of fire, no implements for grinding corn, and no calcined grains, such as are so abundant in those singularly interesting deposits of much later date, the Swiss Lake dwellings, where corn and fruits of different kinds, calcined and thus rendered indestructible, have been found beneath the mud of lakes where they have lain for at least two thousand years, so little injured by time that even the seeds of the raspberry can be identified. We can prove that these ancient lake-dwellers were advanced agriculturists, because we can distinguish among these remains cereals of various kinds, two or three sorts of wheats, one being that kind denominated Egyptian, two or three barleys, millets,

and peas, also apples, pears, raspberries, blackberries, hazel
nuts, and beech nuts, but no trace of any agricultural imple-
ment has been found, and we do not know how they turned
over the soil, planted their seed, and gathered their harvest.
Probably their chief agricultural implements were pointed
sticks, such as are still used by many semi-civilised peoples,
and they ground or crushed their corn by means of such
mullers or hand-mills as are found so frequently among
remains of the later Stone (Neolithic) age; certain it is that
they made bread, or at least unleavened cakes of the imper-
fectly ground corn; they also stored the crushed corn in
coarse earthenware pots, and ate it either roasted, boiled, or
moistened, as it still is sometimes in Germany and Switzerland.   Many of these relics are of a people wholly un-
acquainted with the use of metal, yet they knew how to
weave linen, to make nets for fishing, and pottery similar to
that often discovered in tumuli in Great Britain.   It is not,
however, till we come to the Bronze age that *oats* are found
among the cereals in use, thus indicating progress, not only
in the art of tool-making, but also in that of agriculture.
Between the age of the earliest cave-dwellers and the earliest
of the Swiss Lake dwellers archæologists place the well-
known 'kitchen-middens' of Denmark, upon which Sir
Charles Lyell based so strong an argument in favour of the
antiquity of man, but although these relics show a decided
advancement upon those of the primitive cave-men here and
elsewhere, no trace can be found in them of even the
rudiments of agricultural knowledge.   It may indeed be
said by some, that difference of climate may account for
this want of agricultural knowledge in the Danish savages,
who have left their refuse heaps to show us what they ate

and what were their occupations, and that whilst these kitchen-middens were accumulating in Denmark, and the stalagmite slowly sealing down the records of early man in Kent's Cavern and elsewhere, that in other more favoured spots men were tilling the soil, gathering in their harvests of wheat and barley, grinding their corn, and making their bread; and undoubtedly this may have been the case, because the beginning of agriculture cannot be traced, and the first glimpses we get of the art in the Swiss Lake dwellings show it already in an advanced stage; and since it seems certain that man did not originate either in England or Denmark, but made his way thither by slow degrees, at a period when the conformation of land and sea differed widely from that with which we are now so familiar; therefore during this slow advance of mankind from his primeval home to the utmost bounds of the universe, those remaining in the original cradle of the race would have had time to progress in civilisation, and to attain skill in those arts which can only be successfully practised in settled communities; nevertheless, the extreme antiquity of the art even in Britain, is testified by traces of furrows found beneath peat-bogs in Scotland where now corn will not grow, and may be seen in Cornwall also, among those heaps of metallic waste which are now looked upon as hopelessly barren; but who these early agriculturists were, and at what time they lived, is an unsolved problem.

If, however, we turn to Eastern lands, to the records of the earliest of historians, we shall find agriculture in a state of great advancement. Before the days of Moses, not only was wheaten bread in common use, but the art of leavening it was also well known. At that period Egypt was the storehouse of the world, and had been so, at least, from the days of Abraham; for, although we know from the monuments that corn was grown abundantly in Assyria, yet it was to Egypt that the patriarchs always resorted during those times of famine, which would appear to have been as frequent then in Mesopotamia as they have unfortunately been of late years in India, and it is worthy of remark that Egypt owed her comparative immunity from these terrible visitations, not only to the fertility caused by the annual overflow of the Nile, but to the wisdom of her rulers in instituting vast irrigation works, whereby that overflow was regulated and equalised by means of great reservoirs, wherein surplus water was stored, in order that it might be distributed over the land, through a network of canals when the rise of the Nile was deficient. The first direct mention of meal and bread in the Bible is in Genesis xviii. 5, 6, where Abraham invites the angel to take a morsel of bread, and tells Sarah to 'make ready quickly three measures of fine meal, knead it, and make cakes upon the hearth.' This, it may be observed, was subsequent to the time when famine had driven them into Egypt, and although we are told that Adam was sent forth from Paradise to till the ground from whence he ' was taken, and also find it recorded that Cain was a tiller of the soil, yet it is abundantly evident that the patriarchs were pastoral nomads like the Arabs of the present day, and in no sense of the word agriculturists, and that if we wish to trace the early history of cereals we must look rather to archæological than to Biblical records.

We know what the bread of ancient Egypt was like,

for it has been found in tombs, and may be seen in the British Museum.   The authorities say it was chiefly barley cakes, but we learn from the Bible, as well as from the records of the tombs, that wheat was largely grown, and also that leaven was used in the making of bread, for the children of Israel, when they departed out of Egypt, took their 'kneading troughs with the dough before it was leavened.'   This was the origin of the Jewish feast of unleavened bread.   The leaven employed was doubtless a piece of stale dough, 'hidden in the meal till the whole was leavened,' and this is still used in some countries, but it causes an unpleasant sourness, very unpalatable to those unaccustomed to it.   The Jews, however, evidently made cakes upon the hearth, of meal mixed with oil, but it does not seem quite clear whether the meal was of wheat or barley.

We know, also by actual specimens, what sort of bread was used by the old Swiss Lake dwellers, who built their pile houses out into the lakes, but who cultivated wheat, barley, and rye on the mainland, and, as time went on, oats also.   When their houses were burnt by some enemy to the water's edge, the food they had stored in them was burnt also, and, with a lot of articles of domestic use, sank down to the bottom of the lake, where it lay unheeded and unknown for many centuries, until discovered by accident only a few years ago.

Another specimen of bread comes down to us after having been buried for centuries—this time by the ashes of a volcano; for among the relics of Pompeii we find loaves of bread, as put into the oven on the day when the rain of fiery ashes fell and caused the baker to fly for

his life, leaving his loaves to await customers until this
nineteenth century, when they have been withdrawn from
the oven to prove to admiring antiquaries that Pompeian
bakers knew how to set up a batch of bread almost in the
same form as those of London; but bread was often baked
in moulds, which have been found in Herculaneum, and
these loaves were all divided into portions by a cross, like
scones at the present day. Doubtless, all these ancient
breads were what we should now call of whole meal, for
there were no millers in those early days to sift away the
most nutritious portion of the meal. The corn was mostly
crushed on a hollow stone by means of another stone,
as we know by the many specimens of these primitive
mills which have been found; or it was passed between
two stones fastened together to form what is called a quern,
with two sticks to serve as handles, which two women
sitting passed round to each other from hand to hand,
thus grinding the corn as it was poured in through a hole
in the centre, as in a coffee-mill. References to this kind
of hand-mill are frequent in the Bible. Even now hand-
mills are in use in India and in many Eastern countries;
whilst the primitive form of winnowing the grain—in which
a woman stands in a doorway and pours the grain down
from a vessel held as high as she can, the wind carrying
away the chaff, the heavier corn falling to the ground—is
still retained in some parts of Europe, as, for example,
among the dwellers in Alpine valleys; but water-mills are
said to have been invented in the reign of Augustus, and,
long after that, in Rome, mills were turned by asses and
sometimes freemen, who worked thus for a living, whilst
slaves were sometimes punished by being sent to work

in the mills, being afterwards known as *asinus*. The poor donkeys enjoyed a holiday during the summer festival, being then turned loose and adorned with garlands.

The variety of bread at present in use is astonishing, every country has some peculiarity, but I only purpose here to mention a few of the *wheaten* breads of Europe, leaving others to be treated of later.

The bread of Great Britain and Ireland is too well known to need description, but in Scotland the white bread is too white and deficient in crust to please our palate, whilst the brown is superior to anything we get in London. The bread of Devonshire and Cornwall calls also for a passing notice, being baked in an iron pot, which makes it rather close and of a peculiar shape. It is, however, very sweet and good. When we cross over to France, we find wheaten bread of various qualities and forms, but characterised chiefly by *length*, so that to buy bread by the yard is not a mere *façon de parler*. The finer French rolls are well known, but the waiter in a restaurant frequented by the poorer classes does not present such luxuries to his customers. With two or three yards of coarse bread under his arm, he slices off thick rounds to serve with each plate of *bouilli*. Journeying on to Spain, we find the bread excellent, and used alike by rich and poor. It is very white, and fashioned something like a door-knocker—thick in the centre, and tapering off so as to be fastened together with a kind of knob. In Italy the native bread is not good, although it looks tempting. Made in the shape of a ball, and covered with crusty knobs, it is as the apples of Sodom, so dry and sour that none but natives can eat it with relish. There is, however, a bread peculiar to North Italy which is palatable enough, but too fanciful for everyday use. This bread is called *grizzini,* and is made in long tubes a little larger than macaroni, and baked quite brown. When placed before you it resembles a bundle of sticks, and when fresh and crisp is very good, although not very satisfying. The best is made in Turin and Genoa. It is not known in South Italy, where macaroni may be said almost to take the place of bread, especially among the lower orders, who beg for money to eat macaroni instead of asking for bread. Macaroni is a stiff paste of flour and eggs, forced through holes so as to form long pipes; it is then hung across strings in the porches or windows of the houses to dry. In Naples it is eaten boiled in oil, and always with grated Parmesan cheese.

In Germany the best white bread is everywhere made in small rolls of different shapes, very delicious when quite new, but the Germans have an almost superstitious belief in the medicinal virtues of aniseed, and all the ordinary household bread is plentifully sprinkled with these seeds, the flavour of which is far from pleasant to an English palate. The Germans, also, eat rye bread, but of that anon. All through Europe at the present day the finest wheaten bread —chiefly in the form of rolls—is consumed by the upper classes, whilst the poorer people eat rye or barley bread. Probably little wheaten rolls were early in use in England when the ordinary household bread was of rye or barley. Shakespeare alludes to these delicate wheaten cakes when, in his song of the fairies, he says :—

A grain o' the finest wheat
Is manchet that we eat.

But we must not enter into fairy lore, lest our subject should drift into something too ethereal for mortal appetite.

The bread of ancient Greece is said to have been of dazzling whiteness and exquisite taste, but they soon began to mix ingredients with the paste which altered its character, and seventy-two kinds of bread were introduced. Some of these, according to Soyer's 'History of Food,' were made with milk, honey, oil, cheese, and wine, mixed with best flour, and all were known as *artos* bread. Women sold this bread in an open market, as also *azumos*, a kind of biscuit made without leaven; *artologanos*, in which wine, pepper, oil, and milk were introduced; and *escarites*, made of light paste with raw sweet wine and honey. The poorer people had *dolyres*, made of rye and barley; whilst ladies of fashion ate puff-cakes called *placites* or *melitutes*, and the workmen bought *tyrontes*, a bread mixed with cheese.

Amongst the Romans, porridge appears to have been the national dish until wheaten bread was introduced from Greece; they had also a very coarse bread made of bran and a little coarse flour, which was made expressly for dogs and slaves. Their leaven, according to Pliny, was made from millet or wheat-bran, soaked in wine and dried in the sun, or of a dish of barley paste placed on red-hot coals till it boiled, and then put into vessels till it became sour.

Barley bread is now so entirely discarded, that it is hard to realise that even up to the beginning of the present century, it was the common food of the English peasantry, even as it was in ancient times the bread of Egypt, and of the Jews in the days of Christ, as we learn from the miracle wrought upon the lad's five barley loaves. We remember once talking to an old man, who grumbled at the hardness of the times and the difficulty of getting a living. 'But,' we said, 'you get a great deal more wages now than when you were young.' 'Oh, ay,' he said, 'but it don't seem to go so fur.' 'That's because you live better, perhaps?' said we. 'For instance, you didn't get white bread and butter every day then.' 'Noa, noa,' said he, 'that we didn't; barley bread as black as my hat and a bit of thin cheese was what we did get mostly, and a slice of fat bacon and cabbage now and then—that's what we did live upon when I were young.' 'Well,' we answered, 'if you would eat the same now, you'd soon be quite rich.' But he only shook his head, repeating, 'Barley bread as black as my hat—noa, noa, couldn't eat it now: teeth baint so good as they wer.'

In truth, it must have been hard, dry stuff, and we are not surprised that it should have been superseded by wheaten bread as soon as wheat became sufficiently cheap to be used in common. In like manner oat cake is now discarded, even in Scotland, 'the land of cakes,' except in some few districts, and it is more difficult to get oat cake in Edinburgh than in London, in which latter city it is consumed as a luxury by the rich, instead of forming the staple food of the working classes. Yet it is good wholesome fare, and might be eaten advantageously, especially by children, instead of the much-adulterated and unsatisfying white bread now so largely, and, indeed, exclusively eaten by the English poor, for they will not eat whole-meal bread if it is offered them, partly, perhaps, owing to the price, which is always higher than that of white bread, but chiefly because of its traditional use by poor people, so that white bread has come to be regarded as a luxury by the poor, and therefore preferred.

When, however, we come to rye bread, we find that,

although it is now unknown in this country, it still forms
the principal food of the peasantry of the greater part of
Europe. Often have I seen the German peasant toiling
along the dusty road by the side of his horse, cutting huge
slices from what resembled a great black ham tucked under
his arm, and feeding therewith himself and his horse alter-
nately. This black bread does not look very appetising,
but if you buy a sandwich of it, with German sausage, at
the railway stations, as you can do, you will find it far from
despicable. The Russian peasants also eat rye bread only,
and a slice is always served at the tables of the wealthy, and,
when eaten hot and quite new, is very good and nutritious.

But the most peculiar, and we should imagine the least
palatable, of these rye breads, is that consumed in Norway
under the name of Fladbröd, which is made only twice a
year, in a hut constructed for the purpose. The rye-meal
paste is spread as thin as possible on a large flat round
gridiron, the size of a small table, turned very deftly by
means of a wooden stick, and when sufficiently baked is
stored for use in heaps 8 feet high; but it is coarse and
indigestible.

It is hardly to be supposed that any of my readers will be
tempted to return to this food of our ancestors, especially as,
according to our old friend quoted above, ' Teeth baint as
good as they wer '—a fact which many of the wise attribute
in no small degree to the consumption of fine wheaten
bread instead of the whole-meal bread, or the barley, oaten,
and rye bread formerly in common use.

We have lately seen rye bread exposed for sale in a few
London shops, so, probably, there is a limited sale for it,
although chiefly among the Germans; but in early times the

bread consumed by men in our own country must have
been as unpalatable as the rye bread of Germany or the
Fladbröd of Norway, for in seasons of scarcity it was sometimes made of acorns steeped in water to destroy the bitterness; and even as late as 1546 Du Bellay, Bishop of
Mans, in representing to Francis I. the misery existing in
the provinces, assured him that in many localities the people
had nothing to eat but bread made of acorns.*

There was also a sort of bread sold known as *horse bread*,
in which beans and peas were the chief ingredients, nevertheless, even in the fourteenth century there would appear
to have been different kinds of wheaten bread made and
sold by bakers, the finest being the simnel bread before
mentioned; the next quality was known as *wastel*, then
came *French bread* called also *puffe* or *cocket;* after that
came *tourte*, which must have resembled our whole-meal
bread, and which was in use by the common people and in
monasteries. Of this there was also an inferior sort known
as *trete*, from which some of the fine flour had been sifted;
and lastly there was *black bread* made of barley and rye.†

Some of us are old enough to remember when every

* In Tyndale's ' Sardinia,' p. 191, we read: ' The acorn-bread, which
forms the general food of the people of Cagliari, is thus prepared. The
acorns when shelled are put into a large seething-pot with water which
has been strained through the ashes of burnt vegetable matter and clay.
This lye extracts the bitterness of the acorn, and gives a consistency to
the mixture, which is boiled down till it assumes a reddish-brown colour,
when it is taken out, dried in the sun, and cut into cakes.'

† The ordinary food of the Russian peasant consists of black rye
bread and cabbage broth thickened with oatmeal, but the famine has
lately deprived them of even this meagre fare, and they have been
compelled to eat bread largely composed of bark of trees, unwholesome
herbs, earth, and sometimes a handful of rye.

household, at least in the country, made its own bread ; very delicious bread it was, too, sweet and wholesome, brown, without a lot of indigestible bran, and leavened with barm from home-made beer, sometimes rather difficult to procure, so that the family baking had to be put off till the yeast was forthcoming, and then it was necessary to borrow loaves of the neighbours, or to make unleavened cakes upon the hearth, using soda and tartaric acid or buttermilk by way of rising.   Then, too, there was a friendly interchange among neighbours of newly-baked loaves, and not only so but of the use of the oven, Mrs. M. heating her oven one week and Mrs. N. the next ; or sometimes the dough would be sent to a bakehouse, the tidy servant carrying it wrapped up in a blanket and sundry cloths, and making it up at the baker's, putting her mistress's name on it, according to the old nursery rhyme—

> ' Prick it, and dawk it, and mark it with D,
>   And pop it in the oven for baby and me,'

and paying a small sum for the accommodation. The baker's toll was regulated by law in the days of King John, and according to the 'Book of Days' was to be 'for his own labour, three pence and such bran as might be sifted from the meal,' whilst he was allowed to add 'to the prime cost of the wheat for fuel and wear of the oven the price of two loaves ; for the services of three men, he was to add to the price of the bread three halfpence ; and for two boys, one farthing ; for the expenses attending the seal, one halfpenny ; for yeast, one halfpenny ; for candle, one halfpenny ; for wood, threepence ; and for wear and tear of the bolting-sieve, one halfpenny.' *

* See Chambers's 'Book of Days,' p. 119, etc.

There would seem to have been a great many regulations as to the making and selling of bread, and adulteration was common then as now, for sometimes the bakers would put fine bread on the outside and coarse inside, till an enactment was made forbidding the practice, and also the sale of bran loaves or of flour mixed with bran, whilst the bakers of brown bread were forbidden to sell white, and every loaf had to be sealed so as to certify to the buyer its quality.

C

CHAPTER II

MAIZE AND MILLET

It has fallen to my lot more than once to be told by Americans 'You have no corn in England.' At first I felt somewhat insulted by this assertion—especially as we were at the time journeying by rail through a part of the country where the yellow corn, in the ear and in the sheaf, gladdened the eye and made one rejoice in a plentiful harvest. But, of course, according to American notions, we *have* no *corn* in England, for they confine the term corn to the one cereal *maize*, which is believed to have been indigenous in America, and unknown to Europe before the time of Columbus. The Americans are, undoubtedly, wrong in limiting the term corn to maize, because long before the discovery of America corn was the generic term for wheat, barley, oats, and rye, and maize received its name of Indian corn from the first European settlers in America, who found it growing there, and in use by the natives as the only bread-stuff. We all know Longfellow's charming description of the birth of this beautiful plant in 'The Song of Hiawatha.' After the hero had buried Mondamin, who was the maize personified—

> Day by day did Hiawatha
> Go to wait and watch beside it,

Kept the dark mould soft above it,
Kept it clean from weeds and insects
Drove away with scoffs and shoutings,
Kahgahgee, the king of ravens;
Till at length a small green feather
From the earth shot slowly upward.
Then another and another,
And before the summer ended
Stood the maize in all its beauty,
With its shining robes about it,
And its long, soft, yellow tresses.
And in rapture Hiawatha
Cried aloud, 'It is Mondamin !
Yes, the friend of man, Mondamin !'
Then he called to old Nokomis,
And Iagoo the great boaster;
Showed them where the maize was growing;
Told them of his wondrous vision,
Of his wrestling and his triumph,
Of this new gift to the nations,
Which should be their food for ever.

Well may this plant be called 'the friend of man,' for since its first introduction it has spread more rapidly than could have been supposed possible, being cultivated in every land where the climate will allow it to ripen; but when we find savages in the heart of Africa, who apparently have never met with a white man, cultivating this plant, we become somewhat sceptical as to its introduction by white men since the days of Columbus.

It is undoubted that agriculture was known very early in some parts of America, and that maize was the chief cereal grown, although millet and beans were also cultivated. Now, although maize was found by Darwin in a raised beach on the coast of Peru, 85 feet above sea-level, and must therefore have been of vast antiquity in America, yet all the American legends relating to it tell of its introduction or cultivation by foreigners, coming from the sea. Quetzalcoatl in Mexico, Manco Capac in Peru, Hiawatha among the wild Indian tribes of North America, are some of these legendary introducers of this great boon to man.

The existence of these legends with regard to maize is curious, because no similar legends, except in China, exist in the Old World with regard to the first cultivation of wheat, barley, and rye; and the American legends have not found their way to those remote parts of Asia and Africa where maize has certainly been grown for centuries, although legends are generally caught up eagerly and passed from mouth to mouth among savages, who are ever ready to invest that which is new with some marvellous attribute.

Botanists all assign an American origin to maize, and believe its native home to be Paraguay, or some region of Central America, and therefore it is assumed that it was unknown in the Eastern Hemisphere before the days of Columbus, who is said to have introduced it into Spain in 1520. But it is reported to have been found growing at the Cape at the time of its first discovery by the Portuguese in 1493, and we are told it is figured in an old Chinese book of botany in the national library of Paris; and grains of maize are said to have been found in ancient houses in Athens, as well as in the wrappings of Egyptian mummies, whilst some have supposed that this was the 'corn of Egypt.' This, however, is hardly possible, seeing that it has never yet been found figured on the monuments of Egypt, whilst wheat is frequently represented.

The first notice of this corn is found in 'The Nieue Herball,' published in London in 1578, where it is described as

Frumentum Turcicum or *Frumentum Asiaticum*, in French, *Blé de Turquie* or *Blé Sarazin;* in English, *Turkey corn* or *Indian wheat;* and the author says of it, 'This grayne groweth in Turkie wher as it is used in time of dearth,' adding, 'There is as yet no certain experience of the natural vertues of this corne. The bread that is made thereof is drie and harde, having very small fatnesse or moysture, wherefore men may easily judge that it nourisheth little, and is evill of digestion.'

One thing is certain, whatever may have been the origin of maize, and the date of its first cultivation in America and in the Old World, it is now grown very extensively in all parts of the world in which the climate is suitable, even in the heart of savage Africa and in Madagascar, forming every-where one of the staple foods of man. It does not ripen always with us, but might, I believe, be grown advantageously to supply the market with that delicious vegetable so highly esteemed in America and South Africa (*green corn*), which we now only get in tins from America. Tinned green corn and succotash, which is a mixture of green corn and beans, have of late years found their way into English households, and very good they are, but the corn on the cob, as eaten in America, is better, as all who have tasted it will testify.

Although maize appears to have been early known in China, it is not named among the five sorts of corn culti-vated by the Chinese in the days of Chin-Nong, their second emperor, or the head of the second dynasty—some historians placing seventeen emperors between him and Fohi, who, according to the Chinese annals, reigned over a people differing little from brutes. Fohi taught the people to fish, and to domesticate animals for food, and Chin-Nong

instructed them in agriculture, inventing the necessary implements of husbandry, and teaching the people to sow five
sorts of grain, hence his name, which signifies Heavenly
Husbandman.   On the fifteenth day after the sun enters
Aquarius, which is the commencement of Spring, a feast is
held in honour of husbandry and celebrated husbandmen,
numerous figures in connection with this art are carried in
procession, and among them a huge cow of clay, so large
that forty men can with difficulty carry it.   Behind this cow,
whose horns are gilt, is a young child with one foot naked
and one covered, representing the genius of labour and
diligence.   The child strikes the earthen cow without
ceasing with a rod, as if to drive her forwards.   She is
followed by all the husbandmen with musical instruments,
and by companies of masquers.   At the governor's palace
this cow is broken in pieces, and the fragments, with a
number of small cows taken from the larger one, are distributed to the multitude, whilst the governor makes a
discourse in praise of agriculture.

The Chinese, who have always been diligent agriculturists,
attach great importance to the influence of the moon upon
vegetation, and have a table of those plants which invariably
flower in the night, and their great religious agricultural
festival, at which the emperor ploughs a furrow with his
own hand and sows the five kinds of grain, is always
regulated by the moon.   The five kinds of grain sown by
the emperor are those introduced by Chin-Nong, and consist of wheat, rice, millet, beans, and caoleang, probably
Holcus sorghum, which is widely cultivated in Asia and
Africa, and was formerly well known in Greece and Rome,
and which is now called Guinea corn or Caffre corn, although

it may possibly have been maize, which, as I have pointed out, was known early in China. A festival very similar to that of China took place in ancient Egypt and in Peru, in both of which countries the monarch held the plough and sowed the grain, which, of course, in Peru consisted of maize, and at the close of the maize harvest some of the corn was made into an image called a 'Pirva,' which was held in great veneration.

A writer in the *Monthly Packet* (November 1877) has pointed out the great resemblance between this ancient Peruvian festival and some harvest customs which still exist in Great Britain. Thus in Northumberland it was formerly the custom to dress an image, crowned with flowers and holding a sheaf of corn and a sickle, and to fix it to a pole in the fields, whence it was brought home on the last day of harvest by the reapers with music and dancing; in some villages a kern or corn baby is still kept. Devonshire farmers make a kind of image of the last ears of corn twisted together, which is brought in with great rejoicings at every harvest home, and called a *knack*, which it is very unlucky to part with till the next harvest. In Scotland the last handful of corn reaped used to be called the *Maiden*, and was formed into a cross and carefully kept, the supper following being called the *Maiden Feast*.

It will be observed that not only is maize absent from the five kinds of grain sown by Chin-Nong, but also barley and oats, so that we may conclude that all three were alike unknown in China at that early period, although barley was certainly very anciently known and cultivated in Egypt.

Maize is hardly used for the making of *bread* in the sense in which we use the term, although in America it was doubtless from time immemorial ground and made into cakes resembling oat cake. The Mexican, Peruvian, and Central American graves of very ancient date contain numbers of grinding stones, made something like a stool with short legs, the top sloping and somewhat hollowed out. These are always accompanied by large stones resembling short rolling-pins, with which the Indian women crushed the maize and made it fit to boil into porridge or make into cakes. The Kaffirs generally take maize—I do not know the Kaffir name, but the Colonists call it *mealies* (a term, by the way, which the generality of English people take to mean *potatoes*) —and put a quantity into a jar or pot of water, pile burning fuel round it, and let it stew all day: it thus swells and becomes tender, and is eaten in this form as their staple food. Sometimes the women stamp it in a wooden mortar with one, or sometimes two, long pestles to get off the outer husk, and occasionally they grind it on stones in the same manner as the ancient American Indian did, and make cakes of the flour.

It is only of late that our English cooks have deigned to make use of this foreign bread-stuff. When first introduced, it was deemed only fit to feed pigs and poultry: we are so exceedingly conservative, especially with regard to food, that it requires at least half a century to acclimatise a new comestible, but at last we have accepted maize in its various forms as passably good food for John Bull and his family. Brown & Polson's corn flour is perhaps the best known and most extensively used of all, and this is not a flour ground in a mill, but a precipitated starch. Maizena, hominy, Oswego, and other preparations of Indian corn are also now in common use, and doubtless enter into the composition

of sundry cakes, biscuits, etc., which formerly were
compounded solely of wheat flour, and are extensively
used for thickening soups, gravies, blancmanges, and
custards, instead of the far more expensive isinglass,
eggs, etc., which are recommended in cookery books.
But we have not yet attained to the full knowledge
of the capabilities of this useful cereal, and cannot compound the endless variety of corn cakes and crackers in
use in America. Doubtless, in time we shall come to
appreciate all these foreign delicacies, but at present we
are content to make wheat our staple cereal, and to use
maize merely as an adjunct, except as cattle and poultry
food, for which it has come into general use, being cheap
and abundant, although I am still conservative enough
to believe that poultry fed by the old method—that is,
upon barley-meal and potatoes—are far better than those
fattened upon Indian corn, which, if used exclusively,
is apt to make more yellow fat than that firm, white meat
so much appreciated by the cook and housekeeper.

There are innumerable varieties of this useful cereal,
some being almost black, some quite white, others red,
and the commonest variety yellow. The size of the grain
also varies greatly from large kernels, pressed tightly
together on the cob so as to form a compact mass difficult
to separate, to very small grains of opal-like lustre scarcely
larger than a good grain of wheat, and so arranged on the
little cob as to retain a rounded egg-like form, pointed at
the extremity. This is the kind which is grown especially
for eating as green corn, being peculiarly tender and
delicate. Parched Indian corn is much eaten by the natives,
and it is said that an Indian will subsist a long time on

six or eight ounces per day of parched corn mixed with water. The dried leaves also form an excellent forage for horses and cattle, and in Mexico the green stalks are cut and eaten as a sweetmeat, there being a large amount of sugar in them.

The tortillas of Mexico, so often mentioned in books of travel, are made, according to Captain Lyon, of crushed maize formed with water into unleavened cakes, baked on the hearth, and eaten with a sauce compounded of chilies. 'In the houses of respectable people a woman, called from her office, Tortillera, is kept for the express purpose of making these cakes; and it sounds very oddly to the ear of a stranger, during meal-times to hear the rapid patting and clapping which goes forward in the cooking-place until all demands are satisfied.'

It may be observed that among the cereals regarded by the Chinese as of the first importance, the two millets are almost unknown among ourselves. They never figure among the grains in common use, and, although frequently used on the Continent as a thickening for soups, and sometimes in England for making milk-puddings, they are seldom found in English kitchens. Yet under the name of Dourah one of the millets forms the chief food of the Egyptians; and Guinea or Kaffir corn is almost as much used as maize or wheat all over the African continent, where three harvests of it may be reaped yearly. It is also largely consumed in Arabia, Syria, and in the West Indies among the negroes. It was doubtless much more used anciently than at present, being especially suited to countries where little rain falls, and the soil is too poor and sandy for the cultivation of wheat or maize.

Buck-wheat, which is much grown on the Continent as food for cattle and poultry, is not used for human food, except among the very poor, who sometimes mix it with a little flour and make of it a black bitterish bread, not at all appetising or nourishing; but all kinds of birds and animals are very fond of it, and it is grown for feeding pheasants in England, and also for bees, who collect much honey from the blossoms. Pigs are said to become intoxicated by eating buck-wheat, and are quickly fattened upon it, whilst it causes cows fed upon it to yield a larger quantity of rich milk.

CHAPTER III

VARIOUS BREAD-STUFFS

WE have passed in review the bread-stuffs used in Europe and America, but there remains a very important class of bread-making material very little known to us, but affording nourishment to many thousands in some of our Colonies.

Those who visited the West Indian court of the Colonial and Indian Exhibition—and especially that part devoted to British Guiana—must have noticed a number of flat white cakes hung up in nets and labelled *Cassava Bread*, but the greater number of those who saw probably went away as wise as before.   They might also have seen, in this same court, glass jars filled with a white substance, cut in thin slices, and labelled sweet and bitter cassava, and, at the entrance, they might probably have been attracted by the figure of an Indian woman, with a child on her back, sitting on a piece of wood attached to a very curiously-shaped long basket, but, unless they had lived in the West Indies, it would never have occurred to them to connect this basket and the woman with bread-making in any form ; yet this basket forms an important adjunct to the art of bread-making in the West Indies, for the cassava is the root of a plant known as *Jatropha manihot*, or, shortly, manioc, which when fresh is a deadly poison, but

44

when properly prepared is an excellent and very nourishing food. The mode of preparation is to take the root and rasp it on tin or wooden graters : the raspings are then placed in the long plaited basket, which is hung to a tree, and drawn down by means of a weight attached to a pole at the bottom. Sometimes, as represented at the Exhibition, a woman sits on the pole to drag the basket out to its full extent, thus squeezing all the juice from the rasped root, which, when sufficiently squeezed, is emptied out on raw hides and dried in the sun. It is then baked on smooth plates made of clay. The coarse flour is spread out quite dry on the hot plates, and made into very thin, flat, round cakes by the women, who turn it very dexterously by means of two pieces of split cane. When baked it will keep any length of time. The starch precipitated from the poisonous juice of the manioc forms that excellent and nutritious food known as tapioca, and the dried root itself is also eaten, and is very excellent food, so that in nothing is the old adage that ' one man's meat is another man's poison' better exemplified than in this plant *Jatropha manihot*, for whilst it supplies good and wholesome food for thousands, the extracted juice is so poisonous that it was used by the Indians to poison their enemies the Spaniards, and it is said to cause death in a few minutes. Nevertheless, not only is the prepared root eaten with impunity and used in making several fermented liquors, but the leaves also are boiled and eaten.

Cassava or manioc, prepared in the same way—that is, by extracting the poisonous juice—is used as food not only in the West Indies, but in West Africa, Madagascar, and many of the South Sea Islands, but it is being gradually superseded by maize and wheat, although it seems a pity that it should be thus superseded, for we are told that an acre planted with *Jatropha manihot* will yield nourishment to more people than six acres planted with wheat.

It is a curious fact that not only manioc, but other roots of a poisonous nature, have been used for food by uncivilised peoples from time immemorial, and it must have required a considerable amount of thought and observation to enable men in such a low state of culture to convert such plants into wholesome food. The root of the Arum lily is one of the plants thus utilised, and we must not forget that the potato, now so universally eaten and esteemed, belongs to the most poisonous order of plants, being cousin-german to the deadly nightshade.

Maize may be regarded as the connecting link between cereals used for bread-making, and roots like the arum and manioc, since like these it becomes more palatable by being steeped in water to precipitate the starch, and using this for baking or boiling, instead of simply pounding or grinding the grain and mixing the flour with water, as is done with wheat, barley, oats, and rye.

The Italians use maize in large quantities to make that which seems the chief food of the poor, and is known as *polenda*, being a kind of porridge of ground Indian corn, and you can scarcely enter a cottage without seeing the padrona stirring the rich yellow mess destined for the family meal, which is always slowly simmering in a huge brass vessel hung over the charcoal fire in the common apartment. Sometimes this porridge is made of chestnuts, and is then known as *polenda dolce*.

There was a grain formerly much cultivated in Cornwall which is said to have made excellent porridge, and with potatoes a splendid food for pigs and poultry; this is a kind of oat (*avena nuda*) known locally as pilez or pellas, which grows readily in black moorland moist soils, and which might probably be grown advantageously in Ireland, for it is said that a gallon of ground pilez, mixed with twenty gallons of potatoes, makes an excellent fattening food for pigs and poultry; whilst the straw, which is very fine, is capital fodder for cattle and horses.

Rice, which may be reckoned as one of the most important of the cereals, is not used for making bread, although the grain boiled, or ground and mixed with other materials, forms an excellent food.

It is the fashion of the present day to ignore or deny the value of rice as an article of food, and it is, perhaps, true that its nutritive properties are less than those of other cereals; nevertheless, it affords support to untold millions of Asiatics, forming the principal food of the natives of India, China, Japan, and many other countries; whilst in Europe, Africa, and America—in fact, in the whole civilised world—no store closet would be complete without a bag of rice for use in curries, puddings, cakes, and a variety of dishes too numerous to mention. In fact, this cereal—notwithstanding the dictum of doctors and analytical chemists —seems to enter more largely into our cookery books than any of the others, with the exception of wheat, which, in the form of flour, is now a prime necessary of civilised life.

It is somewhat singular that rice, so highly esteemed by the *poor* in Asia, is used chiefly by the *rich* in other parts of the world. Even in times of famine, our poor would think themselves very badly used if charity doled out to them the rations which the mild Hindoo or John Chinaman would think all sufficient. Even as food for pigs and poultry, rice is despised among us, and it is a singular fact that fowls fed on rice for a week only, will grow very fat, but if the diet is continued longer they will lose flesh instead of gaining it.

Rice would seem to be indigenous in Asia, although in modern times it has spread widely through the tropical regions of America, where, indeed, it has also been found in a wild state. It is never likely to be grown extensively in Europe, as it requires a combination of heat and moisture; and it seems strange that it should have become such a favourite and almost universal crop in India seeing its necessity for water. In China, we are told, a variety is grown which is not so dependent upon moisture, and which is called imperial rice, because it was discovered by one of the emperors, who, in walking through a rice field, noticed one stalk much taller and finer than the rest; this he marked, and when it was ripe it was taken and planted in the imperial gardens, cultivated with care, and became a new species. It would seem advisable to cultivate this imperial or mountain rice in such countries as India, but probably there are disadvantages attending its cultivation not noted by the historian.

According to Pliny, linseed meal was used fried and mixed with honey for bread among Asiatics, and also by the Lombards and Piedmontese, and hempseed was also fried and served for dessert. Gruel, which with us is reckoned as food for invalids only, was a national dish among the Romans. Two of the favourite invalid foods of the present day must be mentioned here, for although in very general use few people know their origin. Sago, so much in favour among the sick, and in the nursery,

is the pith of the sago palm, growing in marshy land
in the East Indies. One tree will produce from 500
to 600 lbs. of sago, but the tree takes fifteen years to
come to maturity. Arrowroot, on the contrary, is, properly
speaking, a product of the West Indies, the best coming
from Bermuda, but, strange to say, very little is known
of the plant which produces it, and probably it is extracted
from several roots, in the same manner as cassava from
the *Jatropha manihot*, by rasping and . soaking in water
till the starch is precipitated, which forms a white powder
when dried in the sun. The *Maranta arundinacea* is the
chief plant thus employed, but a spurious kind of arrowroot
has been made from the root of the Cuckoo Pint.

But of all foods in ordinary use among uncivilised
peoples, the bread-fruit of South Sea Islands deserves
especial notice; this is the fruit of *Artocarpus incisa*,

‘ That tree which in unfailing stores
The staff of life spontaneous pours,
And to those southern islands yields
The produce of our labour’d fields.’

The mode of cooking the bread-fruit is thus described
in Murray’s ‘Encyclopædia of Geography:’ ‘Sometimes
the natives of a district assemble to prepare it in a large
and common oven, when it is called *opio*. This is done
by digging a large pit, 20 or 30 feet round, and filling it
with firewood and large stones, till the heat almost brings
the latter to a state of liquefaction, when the covering
is removed, and many hundreds of ripe bread-fruit are
thrown in, with a few leaves laid over them; the remaining
hot stones are placed above them, and the whole covered

D

with leaves and earth.*   It remains in this state a day or
two, when the parties to whom the fruit belongs dig a
hole and take out what they want.   Bread-fruit baked
in this way will keep good for several weeks after the
oven is opened.'   In the Sandwich Islands the bread-fruit
is eaten raw, or cooked by throwing it on the fire till
the outer rind becomes charred and the inner opens out
like a smoking loaf of bread; the taste is said to resemble
hard-boiled egg.   There is another way of preparing bread-
fruit, by throwing it in a heap and allowing it to ferment,
it is then beaten into a kind of paste called *mahi*, and will
keep for months, but is sour and indigestible.

The South Sea Islanders also make a kind of bread
of the root of the Pia (*Tacca pinnatifida*), which is beaten
to a pulp and subjected to repeated washings, when it
forms a sort of arrowroot.

Taro, of which we often read in books of travel in the
South Seas, is the root of *Arum esculentum*, which, like
the manioc, requires steeping and boiling or baking to
make it wholesome.   It is cooked in the same way as
the bread-fruit, and then beaten into a paste-like dough
called Poë, which is eaten by being scooped out with
the forefinger of the right hand and placed in the
mouth, a practice which has caused that finger to be
named the Poë finger.

In West Africa Pea-nut bread is eaten.   This is made
by roasting and crushing the nuts and pressing the paste
into the skin of a banana.

In Abyssinia Teff-bread, made from *Poa Abyssinica*, is

* This is precisely the process adopted by the Australians for
cooking snakes, as described later.

commonly eaten. This is made by placing the pounded grain mixed to a paste with water in a jar, and placing it at some distance from the fire until it begins to ferment, it is then made into large circular cakes and baked. The taste although sour is not disagreeable, and it is used at their banquets of raw meat, the meat being cut up small, seasoned with salt and cayenne pepper, and wrapped in the bread which is soft and spongy, and is often used as a table napkin, for Bruce says every man wipes his fingers on a piece of this Teff-bread, and leaves it for the next comer, which, he says truly, is a disgusting custom.

The native Australians have no bread, but they crush and eat the seed of the nardu plant, so well known as having formed the sole food of the explorers Burke and Wills until they died of starvation, the seeds being inadequate to support life.

The Chinese make a bread, eaten by all from the emperor to the meanest peasant, of a paste of kidney beans made into great flat cakes like cheeses, it is very white, and is eaten raw or boiled with fish and herbs, and sometimes fried in oil, or dried and smoked and mixed with carraway seeds.*

* See 'Empire of China,' 'Navarette' Pinkerton's *Travels*, vol. i.

CHAPTER IV

CAKES AND PUDDINGS

WE have never met with an explanation of the reason
why all the principal events in human life should require
to be celebrated by different kinds of cakes. We have
cakes for christenings, weddings, birthdays, schooldays, and
funerals. Almost all the festive seasons have their special
cakes—such as Twelfth Day, Easter, Mid-Lent, etc.—and
even such solemn seasons as Good Friday and the Jewish
Passover have their appropriate cakes; but perhaps the
most singular of all these cakes are those sold in Northern
Italy on All Souls' Day (November 2), and known as *Pane
dei morte*—that is, 'bread of the dead.' These are made
chiefly at Brescia, and resemble in form parts of the human
body. Rough pieces of flesh are represented by a reddish
compound something like toffee, but highly flavoured with
cinnamon and other spices, whilst the bones are simulated
by a lighter-coloured compound, or by almonds. Thus you
may purchase a jaw, in which the teeth are formed of
almonds, etc. The most singular part of this All Souls'
custom is that the superstitious appear to fancy some real
connection between these cakes and the parts of the dead
which they resemble. We do not know the origin of these
cakes, but they would seem to be a survival from the days

of cannibalism, when, as among some savages even now, it was considered respectful to partake of the dead bodies of relations. At all events, whatever may be their origin, they are very delicious and highly appreciated.

In many parts of England there is an approach to the Italian *Pane dei morte* in the distribution of funeral cakes, which sometimes are served only at the house of the deceased, but in some counties they are sent round to the neighbours after the funeral. The following lines refer to this custom in Yorkshire :—

> ' Roundlegs to Wadsley went,
> Wi' burying cakes he was sent,
> He knocked at our alehouse door—
> " Does any dead folk live here ? " '

These ' burying cakes ' do not appear to have any especial form, but they are generally slightly bitter.

One of the most celebrated of English cakes, and which would seem to have originally had some religious significance, is that known as the ' Simnel.' This is a cake resembling a rich plum-pudding enclosed in a crust, like a raised pie, and its great peculiarity is that it is boiled first and baked afterwards. The season appropriate to it is Mid-Lent Sunday, known as ' Mothering Sunday,' because on that day it was formerly the custom of families to assemble and to join in a little feast. The popular story as to the origin of this cake is that an old couple, named Simon and Nellie, in preparing the Mid-Lent feast for their children, found a remnant of Christmas plum-pudding and a piece of unleavened Lenten dough, which they resolved to convert into a cake, but a violent quarrel ensued as to whether it should be baked or boiled. At last, after much altercation, ending in blows, a

compromise was arrived at, by which the cake was first boiled
and then baked, and this turned out so very satisfactorily
that cakes thus prepared became famous under the name of
'Simnels,' from the first syllables of the names of the old
couple.   The tradition has been embodied in the following
poem :—

'THE CAKE OF SIMONELLIE.'*

' Where Girlith village looks adown
        To birlie Morecambe Bay,
Old gammer Nell did blythelie dwell
        With Simon Halliday;
And the good God keepit them both from bale,
        As the worthie paire did pray.

' Three sonnes had they, lustie, strong ;
        The elder at the sea,
The mid one for a prentis bond,
        Youngest at mother's knee,
" Too young is he to earn his bredde,
        And I wonna spare all three,"
                        Quoth she.

' The Christmasse-tyde goes by apace,
        And Lenten time is here ;
Bob-crabbes are forbidden taste,
        The jollie boule goes drere.
" Cheere thee, good gaffer," then sayd Nell ;
        " It is but once a year :

' " A sennight and sen days are past,
        Another sennight in—
And now draws on the rorie feste
        Yclepèd Motherin,
When the bairn draws nere to the mother deare,
        And when festing is no sin,"
                        Quoth she.

* Walcott (Bodl.), No. 173.

' " Full long for the Mid-Lent time, I ween,
  Hath thy stomach, Simon, cryde.
Our good ladye will bless the feste
  We shall hold upon this tyde ;
With our sailor ladde, and our prentis eke,
  And the bairnie by my syde.

' " The rorie pastie, and baken pie,
  The flytche of bacon broil,
And the lustie boule with the roasten crabbe
  Shall glad the bairnies' oyle ;
For my laddies' sake a callant callant cake
  On the weeke's end will I boil,"
     Quoth she.

' " Ye be daft, good woman, your boarde to spoil :
  What faerie doth ye take ?
Your flytche ye may broil, but your cake not boil—
  A clout for a boilen cake !
A brawer good wife am I than ye,
  In the ovenne let it bake,"
     Quoth he.

' " A braw good wife ! now, by Lordie's life——."
  " Now, by Lordie's death," quoth he,
" Ye shall bake your cake, or no cake I take,
  When the ladde comes home from sea."
They wrangled so that the gossips gaped
  To see what thing might be.

' Then uppe and spake the youngest ladde,
  That stood by his mother's knee,
" Nay, father, were it awell that strife
  The good God here shoulde see.
When Motherin Sunday draws anear
  Each home at peace shoulde be.

' " The mother dear the cake shall boil,
  And the father bake it dree ;
And not Simon's cake be the baken cleped,
  Nor the boilen Nellie's be,

But the virtues twain of the boil and bake
In the cake of Simonellie,"
            Quoth he.

' Then ho, ho, ho, for the rarie showe,
    When gaffer and gammer agree ;
    And boil and bake the Motherin cake—
    The cake of Simonellie.'

It would, however, appear that this is a modern tradition to account for a very ancient name, which is found in French as well as in English, and in mediæval Latin, and which is supposed to be derived from *simila*, fine flour ; and we find the name given to the finest white bread in mediæval times.* Herrick the poet, writing early in the seventeenth century, speaks of the custom of young people in Gloucester carrying simnels to their parents on Mid-Lent or Mothering Sunday—

' I'll to thee a simnel bring
'Gainst thou go a-mothering ;
So that when she blesses thee,
Half that blessing thou'lt give me.'

These simnels were usually marked with the figure of Christ or the Virgin Mary, showing that they had some religious significance. The poem quoted above places the origin of the simnel legend at Girlith, on Morecambe Bay ; but Shrewsbury has long been famous for the cakes, although until lately they were hardly known except in the western counties, now, however, they can be bought in London, and not only at Mid-Lent but at Christmas.†

* See Chambers's 'Book of Days,' p. 336.

† At the Congress of the Folk Lore Society, held in October last at Burlington House, a great number of local feasten cakes were exhibited, and among them simnels, differing greatly in form, from Lancashire, Gloucestershire, Shropshire, Norfolk, and Yorkshire.

Probably the best known cake of religious significance is the hot cross bun, sold everywhere in England on Good Friday. The number of these cakes consumed yearly must be reckoned by many millions. It has also been a custom in Scottish towns for the last forty years.

'One a penny, two a penny, hot cross buns,' is the one street cry on Good Friday, and whilst all other shops are closed, the bakers and confectioners drive a thriving trade. The cross marked upon these buns has now, of course, a reference to the solemn event commemorated on the day; but the cake itself has a very ancient history, and is supposed to be the lineal descendant of those cakes offered in worship to the queen of heaven, as denounced by the prophet Jeremiah :—' The children gather wood, and the fathers kindle the fire, and the women knead their dough to make cakes to the queen of heaven,' which cakes, according to antiquaries, were also marked with a cross. In the Museo Borbonico at Rome there is a sculpture representing the miracle of the five barley loaves in which the loaves are marked by a cross.

Consecrated cakes, probably all similarly marked, were offered to the gods on different occasions in many countries, as in China, Egypt, and Mexico; and the Saxons, before they were converted to Christianity, ate them in honour of the goddess Eastre. In Egypt these cakes were made in the shape of horns in honour of Isis, and their name—*bons* or *boun*—is supposed to be the origin of our word *bun*.

A curious survival of these offerings to heathen gods existed not many years ago in the Isle of Man, when a herdsman, representing a Druid, on May-Day took a piece of bread, covered with a custard of eggs, milk, and butter, and breaking it, threw pieces over his shoulder, exclaiming, 'This I give to thee, O Fox, and this to thee, O Eagle, spare thou my lambs,' etc., etc. A similar ceremony existed, I believe, in Sicily, whilst in Sardinia a quantity of raisin-bread, *Pane di zappa*, is hidden in three cart-loads of wood, which are drawn round the village by oxen specially fattened, after which the wood is piled up and burnt before the churches.

Honey-cakes were offered in Rome to the serpent representing the god Esculapius, and the shew-bread of the Jews, consisting of unleavened cakes composed of fine flour and oil, was an offering to the Deity, afterwards consumed by the priests.

We read of a Roman Catholic ceremony on Good Friday in Pre-Reformation days, in which the figure of Christ being deposited in a tomb the people came to worship and present gifts of corn or eggs, after which there was a ceremonial burial of the image, and with it the 'singing-bread,' but what this singing-bread was is not specified; it was, however, probably a cake marked with a cross—apropos of which must be recorded the old superstition that bread baked on Good Friday would never get mouldy, and formerly a piece of Good Friday bread was kept in every house, and a little of it grated was supposed to be a sovereign remedy for many ailments, but especially for diarrhœa.

In modern times the bun appears to have become an almost exclusively English cake, and in the last century there were special houses to which the *élite* resorted to consume this delicacy. Two of these are historically famous, the Chelsea bun-house and its rival the Royal.

At Easter cakes of a different kind appear; they are generally very thin and sweet, and have a certain affinity with the unleavened Passover cakes of the Jews, but they vary considerably in different counties. In Dorsetshire the Easter cakes contain currants and spices, and are sprinkled with white sugar. These were formerly carried round by the clerk of the parish, who expected for them a small Easter offering. In Durham at one time the clergy and laity used to play ball in the churches at Easter for *tansy* cakes, which are still esteemed in some parts.

In many places endowments exist for the distribution of cakes at Easter. There is one of these at Biddenden, in Kent, consisting of twenty acres of land, to provide cakes for all attending the parish church on Easter Sunday, the parishioners each receiving, in addition, a loaf of bread and a pound and a half of cheese. All the boys of the Blue-Coat School receive a bun and a new shilling from a fund of this kind, and probably endowments of a similar character exist also on the Continent, for in some churches on certain days huge baskets of small cakes are carried round and distributed to the congregation.

To turn from cakes of a semi-consecrated character to those of festal use, the first place must be given to the twelfth cake, formerly everywhere seen, of gigantic size and elaborate decoration on every festal board on Twelfth Day, and which was used as a sort of lottery or medium of divination, a bean being concealed in it. The one to whom this fell was 'King of the Bean,' and was considered especially lucky, and sometimes we read that this 'King of the Bean' was lifted up, in order that he might mark crosses on the rafters to preserve the house from evil spirits. This custom of choosing a 'King of the Bean' seems to have descended to us from pagan times, and is not peculiar to England, for

in France the proverb exists for a peculiarly lucky fellow—
Il a trouvé la fève au gateau.

Twelfth-Day cakes and Twelfth-Day observances have,
however, faded almost into oblivion in these utilitarian days,
when even children begin to say, ' What is the use of this
and that?' but in Ireland many of the old customs are still
kept up, and a thimble, a crooked sixpence, and a wedding
ring are baked in cakes, the first for the old maid, the second
for wealth, and the ring, of course, for a wedding; but, if
memory serves aright, these fortune-telling cakes are eaten
on Halloween instead of Twelfth Day, and I do not know
whether the Twelfth-Day ' King of the Bean' is still elected.
We read that in 1613 the gentlemen in Gray's Inn were
permitted by Lord Bacon to perform a Twelfth-Day masque
at Whitehall, in which a character called Baby Cake was
attended by an usher bearing a great cake with a bean and a
pease.*

The ' King of the Bean' is supposed to have been derived
from the Roman Saturnalia, in which lots were drawn with
beans as to who should be king.

There is, however, one cake that seems to grow in favour
year by year, and that is the bridecake, upon which all
the confectioner's art is lavished, until it seems almost
a sin to cut it and destroy its beauty. In fact, some
of the more elaborate specimens are so made that the
cake may be abstracted without injuring the external case.
The monster cake presented to the Queen on her Jubilee
was thus made, so that the exterior was on view intact
among the other presents, although the kernel was gone.

Lawn-tennis has created a new cake, which is highly

* Chambers's ' Book of Days,' vol. i., p. 63.

appreciated. We believe this originated in Bath, famous for many confectioners' *chefs d'œuvres*, which can hardly be met with elsewhere, such as the Sally Lunn, which is quite a different thing there to the cake known under that name elsewhere, and the Bath bun, which can only be eaten in perfection in Bath. The lawn-tennis cake is a rich plum cake, made rather thin and flat, with a good covering of almond paste, iced, and with a sprinkling of sweetmeats or green angelica cut very fine on the top.

In Cornwall many peculiar cakes may be met with, but almost all of them contain saffron, which does not commend them to all palates.

Scotland is known as 'the land of cakes,' and the variety to be met with there is astonishing. The best known is the shortbread, which is now sold largely in London— especially at Christmas—daintily put up in boxes and with a motto in candied peel on the top; but this short-bread varies greatly: that made in Aberdeen is the best, especially that sent to Balmoral, which is said to be made of crushed macaroons.

There is a well-known cake which should rather be classed under the head of puddings; this is the pancake, still religiously eaten on Shrove Tuesday, which the old riddle has, in consequence, designated as the greatest *fryday* of the year. The custom of eating pancakes on Shrove Tuesday dates back to very remote times, and the tossing them in the pan was the occasion of much merriment. For-merly the master of the house was always called upon to toss the first pancake, which was generally so clumsily done as to cause it either to ascend the chimney, or to find a place on the kitchen floor, for which the cook demanded a fine.

Chambers's 'Book of Days' contains an interesting account of tossing pancakes in Westminster School, the cook being obliged to toss the cake over the bar which divides the upper from the lower school, which being done the boys scramble for the cake, and the one who secures it unbroken, and carries it to the Deanery, receives an honorarium of a guinea.

The same article gives the following quaint description of the pancake by the poet Taylor :—

'There is a bell rung, called the Pancake Bell, the sound whereof makes thousands of people distracted, and forgetful either of manners or humanity. Then there is a thing called wheaten flour, which the cooks do mingle with water, eggs, spice, and other tragical magical enchantments, and then they put it by little-and-little into a frying-pan of boiling suet, where it makes a confused dismal hissing (like the Lernian snakes in the reeds of Acheron) until at last, by the skill of the cook, it is transformed into the form of a flip-jack called a pancake, which ominous incantation the ignorant people do devour very greedily.'

Eggs, as a great ingredient in the pancake, are much in request on Shrove Tuesday, which, in Cornwall, gave rise to a very barbarous sport, for the hens, which had not laid an egg before Shrove Tuesday, were placed on the barn floor and beaten to death, or sometimes a hen, with some bells hung round it, was tied to a man's back, and others blindfolded and armed with boughs, ran after him and struck at the bird, guided by the bells, and when the bird had been killed in this manner it was boiled with bacon, and eaten with the pancakes.

The British pancake has been transformed in France

into the omelette, the vol-au-vent, the soufflé, supplemented by delicate tartlets of extreme lightness, very sweet and full of cream, iced and ornamented with dried cherries and pistachio nuts. All these things have been elaborately evolved from the inner consciousness of many generations of French *chefs*, but primitive puddings doubtless consisted simply of grain of different kinds boiled in water or milk, to which various ingredients were added, according to taste, after the fashion of the national dish of Barbary called *cuscosco*, which consists of a sort of paste or porridge made of crumbled bread and enriched with small pieces of meat, vegetables, and condiments. This is placed in a large wooden or earthen bowl set in the middle of the company, each one thrusting their fingers in the bowl, stirring its contents, and helping themselves to such tit-bits as they may fancy.

This cuscosco reminds one of a famous dish of our ancestors known as furmity, furmante, or frumenty, formerly indispensable at Christmas, but now relegated to Mid-Lent or Mothering Sunday, when the lesson for the day read in the churches, is of Joseph and his brethren, for this dish is popularly supposed to be that wherewith Joseph regaled his brothers, giving a double portion to Benjamin. The name comes probably from *froment* (wheat), in French, which would point to its introduction by the Normans. In Bath the wheat is sold in basins, boiled ready for use. In Chambers's 'Book of Days' the following recipe is given as the most ancient known :—'Take clean wheat, and bray it in a mortar that the hulls be all gone off, and seethe it till it burst, and take it up and let it cool; and take clean fresh broth and sweet milk of almonds,

or sweet milk of kine, and temper it all; and take the
yolks of eggs. Boil it a little, and set it down, and mess
it forth with fat venison or fresh mutton.' Venison was
seldom served without this accompaniment; but furmity,
sweetened with sugar, was a favourite dish of itself, the
'clean broth' being omitted when a lord was to be the
partaker.*

There was also an indispensable Christmas dish known
as plum porridge, of which the old nursery rhyme
relates :—

> ' The man in the moon came down too soon †
> To ask his way to Norwich;
> The man in the south he burnt his mouth
> Eating cold plum porridge.'

This plum porridge, always served as a first course at
Christmas, was made by boiling beef or mutton with broth
thickened with brown bread; when half boiled, raisins,
currants, prunes, cloves, mace, and ginger were added, and
when the mess had been thoroughly boiled, it was sent to
table with the best meats. This is supposed to have been
the origin of the plum-pudding, which in its present form
does not appear in cookery books earlier than 1675, and
then not as a Christmas dish. Mince pies, shred pies, or
Christmas pies are, however, much older, and figure in Ben
Jonson's 'Masque of Christmas.' These pies seem to have
been particularly obnoxious to the Puritans, as savouring of
superstition, the crust which encloses them being supposed

* A more modern recipe for the making of Frumenty will be found
among those at the end of this section, and I can strongly recommend
it to those who like to try the dishes so much prized by our forefathers.
† Antiquaries say for 'too soon' should be read 'to Sion.'

to represent the manger in which the infant Saviour was laid. There is a rhyme which runs thus :—

> ' The high-shoe lords of Cromwell's making
> Were not for dainties—roasting, baking;
> The chiefest food they found most good in
> Was rusty bacon and bag pudding;
> Plum broth was popish, and mince pie—
> O, that was flat idolatry ! '

Soyer's book, 'The History of Food,' gives us two recipes worth reproducing. The first is for making the Athenian national dish :—'Dry near the fire, in the oven, twenty pounds of barley flour; then parch it; add three pounds of linseed meal, half a pound of coriander seed, two ounces of salt, and the quantity of water necessary.' This does not read particularly appetising, and the same may be said of the next—the famous Carthaginian pudding. 'Put a pound of red-wheat flour into water, and when it has steeped some time transfer it to a wooden bowl. Add three pounds of cream cheese, half a pound of honey, and one egg. Beat the whole together, and cook it on a slow fire in a stewpan.' Both these appear to have been something between porridge and hasty pudding, and in the same category may be placed the fermity or frumenty described above; and from these were doubtless derived the far-famed hasty pudding of Jack the Giant-Killer, and our batter and custard puddings, as well as that king and pride of British cooks, the Christmas plum-pudding, which foreigners vainly attempt to imitate.

The Egyptians had learned to make pastry much as we do now, and figures in the temples and tombs, and on the papyri are represented kneading dough with their feet, rolling the paste, cutting it into various forms, and carrying it

E

to the oven. The cakes thus made were of various forms, often resembling animals. One of these in the British Museum is in the form of a crocodile's head; and others have been found deposited in tombs in the form of rings, or rolled over like Swiss-roll, and sprinkled with seeds after the manner of the Jew's bread of the present day.

Whether the Egyptian pastry consisted simply of bread dough we do not know, but it probably contained oil or fat of some kind, for it is certain that the cakes of the Hebrews were composed of fine flour and oil, with probably honey sometimes added; but none of the Egyptian pastry has been found containing fruit like our pies, although cakes consisting entirely of dates are known to have been made, and called date bread.

Our fruit puddings are simply pies boiled instead of baked. Who is there who fails to appreciate a pudding or pie of fresh fruit, whether of green gooseberries in the early spring, or of black and red currants and raspberries or cherries in summer, and all the delicious plums, damsons, and greengages of autumn! Happily, the art of bottling fruits has attained to such perfection that we may now get fruit pies and puddings all the year round, instead of, as in former times, having to depend upon apples and jams only, during the winter months. The thrifty housewife, it is true, used to bottle gooseberries for her own winter use, but they could not be purchased; whereas now, for a few pence, we may indulge in pies of currants, cherries, and greengages at Christmas.

PART II

MEAT

'A piece of a Kid is worth two of a Cat'

CHAPTER V

ON thousands of tables at Christmas-tide the roast beef of Old England smokes with appetising odour. From the lordly baron which always graces the Queen's table, and the goodly sirloin of aristocratic renown, to the humble but far from despicable aitch-bone, all is toothsome, wholesome, and highly esteemed alike by high and low, rich and poor. The wretched inmates of gaol and workhouse look forward to the feast of roast beef and plum-pudding, which is almost sure to be given by the charitable for their delectation at Christmas, and in almost every parish the same substantial fare is provided for the poorer parishioners. At the tables of the rich, it is true, the time-honoured sirloin is now relegated to a subordinate position, its place being usurped by the turkey, which has superseded also the stately peacock, formerly at this season, adorned with all its feathers, introduced with something approaching to religious ceremony, as was also the great boar's head, with its chaplet of rosemary and a lemon between the teeth; but then, as now, the loin of beef, knighted in due form by Charles II., was always the *pièce de résistance*, and from time immemorial the double loin, known as the *baron*, has always been a royal dish, and one specially selected is always sent from Windsor to Osborne to grace the Queen's dinner table, being accompanied by that other famous Christmas dish, a boar's head, sent of late from Germany.

In olden times great rejoicings were generally accompanied by an ox roasted whole, huge fires and monster spits being required for the purpose; and once history relates that an ox was thus roasted whole on the Thames. This was during the great frost in 1715-16, when the river was frozen over for several weeks. This somewhat barbarous mode of rejoicing is now almost obsolete, yet during the severe frost of the winter of 1890, in which the Thames was again frozen over in places, we heard of sheep being roasted whole on the river at Christmas; but in these days of refinement people in general prefer having their portion of meat to cook in their own way, instead of each slicing a half-cooked morsel from a burning carcase.

The practice of cutting meat from the spit seems to have been common before the invention of forks, and many old Saxon drawings show the cooks, or servers, kneeling by the king's table, holding spits from which the monarch cuts a portion with a huge knife; nor must the cook's useful drudge be forgotten, who, as late as 1800, when smoke-jacks came into fashion, had the chief share in roasting the meat in large establishments—we mean the 'turnspit,' a bandy-legged dog, somewhat resembling the modern dachshund—who was set to turn the spit by means of a wheel, somewhat after the fashion of a squirrel in a cage, and was probably beaten and sorely worried by the cooks whenever the jack stopped. There are many stories told of these useful dogs, who knew their proper turn, and would not be persuaded to work out of it; and if one of their companions got out of the way when it was his day for turning the spit, the one unjustly set to work has been known to find the truant and kill him. The poor turnspits must have hated Christmas, with its huge joints of roast beef, its peacocks and game, all entailing hard work upon the poor kitchen drudges.*

Beef was known and appreciated from the very earliest times, the wild cattle having been hunted and slaughtered long before they were domesticated, and the skulls of many, of a species now extinct, are found all broken in the same way, evidently by a blow with a very heavy stone hammer. But as soon as men began to keep flocks and herds and to till the ground, the ox became doubly valuable, not only as a food but as a beast of burden, and it is continually alluded to by the most ancient writers in this capacity, whilst the earliest of paintings represent the patient kine dragging the plough or wheeled cart, yoked together even as in the present day by a heavy piece of wood bound over the necks of both. The humane laws of Moses forbade the muzzling of the ' ox that treadeth out the corn,' and in several passages of the Bible the yokes of oxen are spoken of. Elisha was ploughing with twelve yoke of oxen when Elijah cast his mantle upon him, and it seems to have been a common act of worship in those days to slay a yoke of oxen and burn them with the implements in use, as a sacrifice of thanksgiving or propitiation. ' Behold,' said Araunah the Jebusite to David, ' here be oxen for burnt sacrifice, and threshing instruments and other instruments

---

* A very interesting article upon the turnspit may be read in Chambers's ' Book of Days.'

of the oxen for wood.' Nor was it only among the Jews that oxen were used for sacrifices: the Greeks and Romans sacrificed white bulls to Jupiter, whilst the cow was sacred to Juno, as it was to Isis in Egypt. In the latter country the bull Apis was, as is well known, an object of idolatry, being distinguished by special marks, and numerous mummies of this sacred bull may be seen in the British. Museum. In India, Siva the destroyer rides upon a bull, and the cow is as much venerated among the Brahmins as it was in ancient Egypt, some of the Indian princes being obliged to pass through a golden image of a cow in order to become regenerated, and raised to the Brahminical caste.

There is evidently something of a sacrificial origin in the eating of beef at Christmas, for it has undoubtedly a reference to the birth of Christ in the cow-shed, in remembrance of which event, the old superstition says, all oxen kneel in adoration at twelve o'clock on Christmas Eve.

All through Africa the ox is much in favour as an article of food, and also as a beast of burden. James Bruce's assertion that the Abyssinians sometimes cut steaks from the living animal has been verified by later travellers, but it is to be hoped the practice is not general.

Cattle in vast numbers are slaughtered apparently as sacrifices among the Zulu tribes on great occasions; thus we are told that on the election of Lo Benguela, whose name has been so prominently before the world of late, as king of the Matabele, his first act of sovereignty was to superintend the slaughter of cattle brought as an offering to him. 'Each tribe contributed a small troop, and from each lot six, ten, or a dozen were selected. The black were killed first; then the black and white speckled; and lastly, the coloured ones. The first were offered to the *manes* of his father; the second, to the Molimo or Great Spirit; and the rest for other purposes. The king made a short speech as he pointed out each victim; and then the sacrificer, holding his assegai just as one would hold a pin, placed its point low down behind the shoulder blade, where it does not spoil the skin for a shield, assuring himself by a gentle titillating motion that it was rightly directed.' *

What a coronation ceremony, and what an idea it gives us of the sanguinary character of these dusky kings and the despotic power they wield over their subjects. 'Of course,' Baines continues, 'the slaughter of so many oxen in so confined a space was a work of difficulty, especially when some had fallen, and the rest maddened by the sight and smell of blood, made frantic efforts to escape, but there was no confusion. The place where the king had dismounted was kept clear by a circle of Majokkas, bound in honour to die upon the spot rather than let him be incommoded; others formed rings round each lot of cattle, and when two heaps had fallen, and there was no room for more in the kotla, the rest were killed outside, as the king successively devoted them. In the evening the carcases were skinned and cut up, and next day the king distributed the meat to his newly-acquired subjects.'

Mr. Baines has also given us the mode of cooking and serving the slaughtered oxen. 'A couple of earthen cauldrons were simmering on the fire, and a stalwart warrior approaching these, took off the lids, drove a sharp stick into a filthy-looking mass, and finding it sufficiently cooked, harpooned and hauled out the contents, and heaped them on

* Baines's ' Gold Regions of South-Eastern Africa,' p. 35.

two great wooden dishes, laying on each some twigs that had been boiled with the meat as charms against evil influence. The cook now intoned the praises of the king, the hungry warriors joining in the chorus. One of these vessels shaped its course towards us, steered by the kneeling functionary, and he, drawing his knife, cut off large slices from which we pared the filthy outside, and found the remainder excellent. The king's supper was now ready, his "plate" was laid on the waggon chest, and his knife and fork, supplied only for himself. He invited us to draw out our own and use them freely.'*

The hecatombs of this African despot throw into the shade the sacrifices of more civilised peoples, for these might be counted by units, as for example Æneas says :—

> ' The sacrifices laid
> On smoking altars to the gods he paid.
> A bull to Neptune, an oblation due,
> Another bull to bright Apollo slew,
> A milk-white ewe the western winds to please,
> And one coal-black to calm the stormy seas.'

In the sacrifices of the Hebrews also one or two bullocks sufficed, but it would seem from the account of Josephus, that the table of Solomon was supplied almost as liberally as that of Lo Benguela. Speaking of the tributes collected by his officers, he says: 'Now these contributed to the king's table, and to his supper every day, thirty cori of fine flour, and sixty of meal; as also ten fat oxen, and twenty oxen out of the pastures, and a hundred fat lambs; all these were besides what were taken by hunting harts and buffaloes, and birds and fishes which were brought to the king by foreigners day by day.'

* Baines's ' Gold Regions of South-Eastern Africa,' p. 36.

By this it may be seen that men of all colours and in all ages have thought the ox a fit offering for the gods, probably because they have themselves loved the savoury meat, for as Livingstone says of the Makololo, 'They have abundance of game, but in their opinion, which I am sure every Englishman will endorse, there is nothing equal to roast beef.'

At present it must be allowed that as an article of food beef is better understood and more appreciated among English people than on the Continent, where the tasteless pieces of beef which have been used to make the bouillon are invariably served with sauce of various kinds, and the *bifsteak*, so called in honour of the famous English dish, is often a piece of very coarse buffalo, or of some tough old ox which has fulfilled his term of days at the yoke. Beefsteak, or to speak more correctly, rumpsteak, is only to be had in perfection in London, for it would seem as though country butchers had not learnt the secret of the proper cut. A rumpsteak grilled in a London eating-house is not to be surpassed as a savoury dish, and may be eaten with fried onions or oyster sauce, according to taste. It often surprises colonists that they cannot obtain here the piece especially prized by them, and known in South Africa as *the hump*, but either our oxen are destitute of that appendage, or our butchers cut the carcase differently.

The consumption of beef is now so great that our native supply has to be largely supplemented by the cattle reared on ranches in America and New Zealand, either brought over frozen or in tins. Chicago, the chief tinning manufactory, is supplied with oxen in such profusion that they are described as forming a constant stream moving ever

onwards up an inclined plain to be killed when they reach
the top; being skinned, cut up, and tinned immediately,
almost entirely by machinery.

Since the introduction of *diner à la Russe*, the great
joints which formerly appeared on our dinner, supper, and
breakfast tables have almost disappeared. We no longer
see, except in cooks' shops, the great salted rump, formerly
a famous breakfast dish; and the baron is reserved for the
Queen's table, whilst the sirloin no longer appears entire,
but is cut into several pieces to suit the requirements of the
household. Doubtless, we lose much of the juices and
flavour of the meat in these small joints, but the national
taste has become of late more assimilated to that of the
French, and prefers made dishes to the simple cut-and-come-
again joints of our ancestors. It would appear that at
Christmas in the olden days the great boar's head, eaten
with mustard, held the first place; then came the peacock
in his plumes, and geese, capons, "pheasants drenched with
ambergrease," and pies of carps' tongues.

Of these savoury dishes many have disappeared from the
modern *menu*, whilst some are retained in the form of
survival, and amongst the latter is the boar's head, which, in
its ancient and natural form, is no longer seen amongst us
except at the Queen's table, and perhaps on that of some
other princes and potentates, but the ancient dish is still
imitated by our cooks in forcemeat, and at almost every
supper at Christmastide holds a conspicuous place, brown
and glazed, with long, curved, white tusks of some composition, lemon in mouth, and buttered adornments, altogether
a travesty of that great cruel beast, the pursuit of which has
in all ages been deemed such noble sport, which formed

the standing dish of Scandinavian heroes, in the Valhalla to which they aspired, and of which the ancient Romans were so fond, that it is related of Anthony that eight wild boars were usually roasted for his supper, not that they were all served and consumed at once, but they were held in various stages of preparation, that one might be ready whenever called for. The mode of dressing this boar appears to have have been to roast it stuffed with game and poultry. Horace writes of—

' A Lucanian boar of tender kind,
Caught, says our host, in a soft southern wind;
Around him lay whatever could excite,
With pungent force, the jaded appetite;
Rapes, lettuce, radishes, anchovy brine,
With skerrets, and the lees of coan wine.'

The modern Romans still love the flesh of the wild boar, and I have eaten it in Italy served up with a sauce, the chief ingredients of which were raisins and the kernels of pine cones, but the flesh of the Roman wild boar is lean and hard, and can scarcely rival that of the domestic porker, well fatted, and served with apple sauce in the old English style. But in various parts of Europe the wild boar still affords excellent sport, and heads from these sometimes find their way to England. It was probably to one of these that the anecdote of Solomon Hart, the Jewish R.A., related in ' Frith's Reminiscences,' applies—' On the occasion of a visit of a party of artists to Preston Hall, the pleasant seat of Mr. Betts, they were entertained, as always, in baronial fashion. At one of the splendid banquets for which hospitable Mr. Betts was famous, a huge boar's head, with the usual garniture, was placed upon the table. Hart was

said to have looked longingly at it, when he exclaimed,
" Almost thou persuadest me to be a Christian." '

It would appear from ' The Book of Days ' that in olden
times the boar's head garnished with bay and rosemary, and
heralded by trumpets, was borne to the king's table on a
dish of gold or silver by the server, followed by a long procession of nobles, knights, and ladies. The same book
gives the origin of the custom of serving this ancient dish
at Queen's College, Oxford, to a variation of the old carol.
This arose from the presence of mind of a student of the
college, who, when studying Aristotle in Shotover Forest,
encountered a wild boar, which rushed at him open-
mouthed, whereupon the scholar thrust the book down the
creature's throat, thus ' choking the savage with the sage.'
The carol used in serving the boar's head ran—

> ' " *Caput apri defero*
>   *Reddens laudes Domino.*"
> The boar's head in hand bring I
> With garlands gay and rosemary;
> I pray you all sing merrily
>   *Qui estis in convivio.*

> ' The boar's head, I understand,
> Is the chief service in this land;
> Look wherever it be found,
>   *Servite cum cantico.*

> ' Be glad, both more and less,
> For this hath ordained our steward,
> To cheer you all this Christmas—
> The boar's head and mustard !
>   " *Caput apri defero*
>   *Reddens laudes Domino.*" '

CHAPTER VI

SUNDRY MEATS

WE will begin this chapter by treating of that which, by universal consent, is allowed to be the best and most wholesome of animal food—that is, mutton.

In the colonies mutton ranks with daily bread as a prime necessity of life—mutton chops for breakfast, mutton roasted or boiled for dinner, and cold mutton for supper, till people say they are ashamed to look a sheep in the face; but it speaks well for the wholesomeness and toothsomeness of the meat, that it can thus be eaten daily from year's end to year's end without producing disease or satiety. Perhaps of no other meat could the same be said.

The sheep was probably the earliest of domesticated animals, for Abel was a keeper of sheep; but in many countries in which it now abounds it was unknown before the advent of Europeans. The many millions of sheep now pastured in Australia, Tasmania, and New Zealand owe their origin to those taken over from Europe, for there was no indigenous species in those countries; but there are many wild varieties of this useful animal in Europe, Asia, and Africa, and from these our domesticated varieties have sprung. All these are traced by some naturalists to that remarkable animal the mouflon, which is still found wild in Sardinia and Corsica, and certainly has the most singular resemblance to the sheep, the goat, and the deer combined.

There is a very curious wild sheep in the Rocky Mountains, much larger than any of our domestic breeds; it has close hair, rather than wool, whilst the wild goat of the same region has a very long fleece. The rams have such enormous horns that they are said to be unable to feed on level ground.

Our European sheep seem to belong to two principal divisions—the horned and the hornless—but of each of these there are innumerable varieties; and one very singular kind, common in Asia and Africa, is not known in Europe. This is the fat-tailed sheep.

When ancient writers spoke of sheep having hair instead of wool, and tails so long and so large that they were obliged to have little waggons to carry them on, the wise men of Europe laughed, and hinted at 'long-bows' and 'travellers' tales;' nevertheless, our friends in South Africa know these broad-tailed sheep well, and have even told us of small boughs being fastened under the precious caudal appendage, to prevent its being bruised and torn by dragging over rough ground, for the tail is a delicacy, and, being almost all firm fat, is often cured, and takes the place of bacon. It is also used for many culinary purposes, being superior to suet and equal to marrow; but as the sheep has no wool, and the flesh is coarse and poor, it seems wasteful in these utilitarian days to rear it for the sake of the tail, and in consequence the breed will probably soon die out—it is, in fact, seldom met with now in South Africa, except when kept as a curiosity, but the skin is valuable, having twice the strength and thickness of that of an ordinary sheep.

There are several varieties of this broad-tailed sheep in Asia, which are supposed to have been derived from Barbary, Egypt, and the Levant. Two very curious varieties of this sheep are found in Tibet: in one, known as the fat-rumped sheep, the tail is short and thin, and the rump extremely fat, whilst in the other the tail is very broad, and the head is adorned with four, five, or even six horns. The wool of the first is good, but that of the latter very coarse. Then there is the Angora sheep, found in Asiatic Turkey, long-legged, lop-eared, and with very long tails, but not particularly fat.

In almost all these varieties the wool is poor and hairy and the flesh coarse, but, in the present day, the sheep is bred entirely for its fleece and the quality of the meat, and, therefore, the hairy fat-tailed species is retained only in countries where farming is not carried out scientifically, or where the finer long-woolled varieties will not thrive.

The merino sheep seems to be the prime favourite among colonists, and certainly it would appear to possess many excellent qualities, both as regards flesh and wool. In England the Southdown mutton is esteemed the finest, and the little Welsh mutton, fed upon the short heathery mountain grasses, is a delicacy, although the housekeeper is frequently imposed upon by inferior kinds falsely denominated Welsh.

Mutton is not particularly good on the Continent, the sheep producing it being generally of the long-legged lop-eared variety, and not all the condiments with which it is served can conceal the coarse quality and woolly

F

flavour of the meat. Our own sheep possess naturally long thin tails, but it is found advisable, if not necessary, to amputate them at an early age to prevent injury to the fleece and to the animal itself. Lamb-tail pie is a 'dainty dish to set before a king,' but we have heard an anecdote regarding it which is worth repeating.

A lady sat at the table of a wealthy colonist, enjoying a delicious lamb-tail pie. 'But,' said she, addressing the host, 'is it not very extravagant to kill so many dear little lambs just for the sake of their tails?'

'Kill the lambs! my dear madam; why, bless my soul, no! That would never do! The lambs are all alive and well, and you shall see them skipping about and enjoying themselves to-morrow.'

'What?' exclaimed the lady, horrified, 'and have we been eating the tails of live lambs? How very dreadful!' and she put down her knife and fork in disgust.

The occupation of the shepherd has perhaps given rise to more poetic descriptions and to more artistic effects than any other known to man. The biblical similes relating to sheep and shepherds are innumerable, and no pastoral picture, no descriptive poem, would be complete without them. From the great god Pan, with his horns and goat's legs, who piped to his flocks in Arcady, to the dainty little Watteau shepherdesses in lovely costumes not at all suited to their vocation, artists have found exquisite subjects for their pencils, although not compatible with real life. Nevertheless, the shepherd of the Campagna, seated on a broken monument, with his pipe and shaggy goatskin breeches, is a picturesque object not so very unlike the Pan of ancient days. The Watteau shepherdess is only met with at fancy dress balls, but the Swiss and Tyrolean *senneren* are perhaps quite as picturesque. Nor must we omit the shepherd's faithful companion, friend, and helper—the dog—for without him no rural landscape would be complete. We all know Landseer's touching picture 'The Shepherd's Chief Mourner,' and, indeed, among the Highlands and the mountains of Wales, the dog is indispensable, for sheep have a peculiar faculty for going astray, and, like men, will follow their leader blindly into any boggle, so that whole flocks would frequently perish did not the sagacious dog come to the rescue. It is an interesting sight to see a well-trained dog watching his master's eye, and following his instructions far better than a two-legged servant could do, and the shepherd's dog will sometimes undertake voluntary duty. I witnessed a case of this kind some years ago in the Lake district.

A dog sat at the door of a cottage, watching the vain efforts of a man on the hills at some distance, to collect together a flock of sheep. Up and down he ran, and as fast as he got a dozen together they would start off again to join their comrades, scattering in all directions. The dog watched and watched, started up, lay down again, and fidgeted. At last he could stand it no longer: off he went as hard as he could go, and, without asking for instructions, collected the wandering flock in a very short time, drove them up to the shepherd, and then returned home and lay down quietly as before. I asked his owner if he knew the man he had been helping, but he said, ' Oh, no, it was just his nature;' and a very good nature, too, I thought.

We often wonder what would be the effect upon the very important industry of sheep farming should the fads of a few philosophers ever induce the bulk of mankind to become vegetarian in diet. Wool is so necessary in our manufactures that it must be had, so that sheep must be reared; but if the mutton is not to be eaten they could not be allowed to increase. There seems, however, little fear of that day arriving, for not one in a thousand can resist the savoury joint, or the chops and tomato sauce of the immortal Pickwick.

There are three meats tabooed by the doctors, but delighted in, nevertheless, by the cook and the gourmand, who know full well how exceedingly savoury they may be made. Lamb, veal, and pork, 'all sadly indigestible and unwholesome,' says the doctor with a shake of his wise head, 'and should never be eaten except by those who have the stomach of a horse or an ostrich.' Now, of course, the horse and the ostrich being graminivorous, could not digest these foods; but men, women, and children, with healthy stomachs, and good appetites not spoilt by physic, can certainly eat and digest all three, and derive both health and pleasure from their consumption. The crusade against lamb and veal as unwholesome because young and immature, to be carried to its legitimate conclusion should be extended to game and poultry, and a tough old hen, or a hare which has for years defied the sportsman, should be extolled before the tender chicken and the leveret.

The Jews, restricted in their diet by strict laws, rejected all pork as unclean; but veal and lamb, with kid, seem to have formed the staple of their feasts. The paschal lamb, roasted whole and eaten with bitter herbs, is familiar to every reader of the Bible; and lambs, as we know, formed a large proportion of the sacrifices offered daily, and, of course eaten, with the singular exception that all the fat should be burnt, for the fat as well as the blood of sacrifices seems to have been forbidden to be eaten; and, it may be remembered as one of the sins of the sons of Eli, that they sent their servant and demanded raw flesh with the fat, before it was burned according to the sacred law of sacrifices. The breast and the right shoulder of these sacrifices were allotted to the priests, and thus it came to pass that when Saul was sent to Samuel, the shoulder was set before him as the royal and priestly joint. As to the calf, that was not only offered in sacrifice, like the lamb, but it seems to have been set aside especially for family feasts. The fatted calf, killed to do honour to the returning prodigal, has passed into a proverb, and to 'kill the fatted calf' is now synonymous with making a feast of joy. But the calf was˙from the earliest times looked upon as a delicacy to set before an honoured guest; hence we are told that when, in the days of Abraham, the three angels came to him as he sat in his tent-door on the plains of Mamre, in the heat of the day, he ' ran unto the herd and fetched a calf, tender and good, and gave it to a young man, and he hasted to dress it. And he took butter and milk, and the calf which he had dressed, and set it before them; and he stood by them under the tree, and they did eat.'

What a vivid picture we have here of the hospitality of the patriarch, of his mode of life, and of the food he thought meet to place before his guests—the calf tender and good, eaten as at the present day, with butter and milk, the cake kneaded and baked upon the hearth by Sarah, to be eaten with it. It was no mean feast for hungry men in the wide plain, but the celerity with which it is prepared strikes one.

To kill a calf and skin it would take an English butcher a considerable time, and the cooking would not be attempted until the carcase was cold, but in hot climates this kind of rapid slaughtering and cooking is frequent and necessary. 'Sudden death,' as it is called, overtakes poultry very often, even in England, and if cooked without being allowed to get cold, the meat is tender and well-flavoured, and probably the same holds good with regard to larger animals.

In England the killing of calves was formerly attended with much cruelty, the poor animals being bled two or three times before they were killed, in order to make the meat white, which probably also made it hard and indigestible; but this is happily now done away with, as is the mode in which they were conveyed to market—packed in a cart with their legs tied, and lying one over another, with their heads hanging down over the tail-board, and making the most piteous cries.

Although veal is still eschewed by many in England as indigestible, we cannot imagine what our cooks would do without this savoury meat, which, above all others, is invaluable in the *menu*. What could supply the place of the delicate sweetbread, the ragoût, the calf's head with its accompaniments, the hash, the stew, the mince, the veal olives and cutlets, and the roast fillet, with its stuffing and lemon-juice, beloved of Oliver Cromwell? All over the Continent of Europe the value of veal is recognised, and a *côtelette de veau* is the one thing which may be safely ordered by the traveller.

. As for pork, what shall we say? A whole treatise would not suffice to recount all the virtues and uses of ' honest piggy'—the poor man's genuine friend—every portion of which is good for food. The Jewish law which condemned the pig as unclean, certainly deprived the Israelites of a savoury food, but it does not appear to have prevented them from keeping the unclean creature, and probably making it a profitable article of commerce with the Gentiles, respecting which, and the destruction of the herd of many swine, as reported in the New Testament, a lively controversy was lately carried on between two of our greatest men of light and leading.

The parable of the Prodigal Son marks the depth of his degradation by making him a swineherd. But our English chroniclers give a story, in which a herd of swine running into the water, caused the foundation of one of the best known and most beautiful cities of England. As the story is not generally known we will give it shortly. A British prince, named Bladud, became leprous, and was driven from his home, and, being forced to become a swineherd, he communicated his disease to his four-footed companions, and they wandered about, shunned by all. One day Bladud's pigs took a strange freak. Being on a steep hill in the forest, they all ran hastily down, and plunged into a marsh at the foot of the hill, and there they lay wallowing, and resisting all Bladud's efforts to draw them away. Day after day they returned to their mud bath, till Bladud saw with pleasure and surprise that they were all cured of the leprosy. Being a wise prince, he was not above learning— even of a pig—and, following their example, he too was soon cured, and enabled to return to his father, and eventually to become king in his place. He built a city on the spot where he was cured, with baths for lepers, and this was the origin of the far-famed baths of Bath—which certainly were held in repute even before the coming of the Romans. Should any of our readers visit that fairest of cities, they may see an ancient statue of Prince Bladud, with an assigned date of centuries B.C., still presiding over the hot bath, which is supposed to have been the scene of his cure, and will find in the city many allusions to the tradition.

The pig is, as we know, all in all to the Irish peasantry— 'the gintleman that pays the rint,' when allowed to do so— and the bacon exported from Ireland is not to be surpassed; but most of that consumed in London comes from the celebrated manufactory of Harris, of Calne, Wiltshire, where thousands of pigs are killed and cured somewhat after the Chicago fashion—going in at one end live pig, and coming out at the other, bacon or sausages. I cannot say I quite like this rapid curing process, which is not always perfect, and, as a housekeeper, I often long for the old-fashioned home-cured bacon and hams of my youth; but a taste has arisen for what is known in the market as mild-cured bacon, which to my mind means only half-cured; caterers for the public, however, find it profitable to supply mild-cured meat, which requires rapid consumption, so that it is difficult now to find really well-salted meat or fish of any kind.

We all know Lamb's amusing story of the origin of sucking pig, but few of us realise the vast importance of pork and bacon as human food. Pigs have been introduced into every country to which commerce has extended, and now exist in great numbers all over the South Sea Islands, which, when first discovered, had no quadrupeds fit for food; the inhabitants consequently feasted upon human victims. The vast quantities of bacon and hams which come to us yearly from America and Canada, show how important the pig has become commercially, but from the very earliest times the wild pig seems to have occupied a foremost place as an article of diet, for the bones of the wild boar are found in almost all kitchen-middens of pre-historic times, and the animal plays an important *rôle* in Scandinavian legends.

All our early poets have drawn inspiration from the noble sport of stag hunting, and certainly in all the *menus* of ancient times, venison figured prominently; but who can now compound such a venison pasty as that upon which the bold Friar Tuck regaled the Black Knight in Sherwood Forest?

Nothing gave such offence to our ancestors as the turning of waste lands into deer forests by some of the early Norman kings for the sake of sport ; and the preservation of the deer in these forests, required constant watchfulness on the part of the keepers, for the forests were haunted by poachers, some of whom, like Robin Hood and his merry men, were not of the lower orders, but outlawed noblemen, for it seems to be pretty well established that Robin Hood was really the Earl of Huntingdon, who had been banished by Richard I. for misdemeanours.

Everyone knows the story of the New Forest, in Hampshire, created by William the Conqueror, and the tragic death in it of his son William Rufus. But the New Forest, although the largest, was far from being the only deer forest in England; indeed, even as late as last century, there were no fewer than 68, besides 18 chases and 780 parks. In all, or in most of these, fallow-deer were allowed to roam freely, and the tenants of forest lands were forbidden to plough the land, and were obliged to preserve pasturage for the deer. The number of deer thus kept must have been enormous. In Cranbourne Chase alone we are told 12,000 were pastured, but the constant conflicts between the poachers and keepers, which often ended in loss of life, caused most of the forests to be disafforested, so that now the deer in England are reduced to a comparatively small number, and are mostly kept in gentlemen's parks, to the beauty of which they largely contribute.

As a sport, deer-stalking is now quite unknown in England, although carried on in Scotland, where the wild mountains and forests still shelter some of the noble red-deer, which is much fiercer than the beautiful dappled fallow deer of our parks, in some of which a few red deer are also kept.

There is a sport *called* stag-hunting still carried on in England, but which would be looked upon as a farce by those accustomed to the chase of wild animals. The Queen keeps a pack of stag-hounds and some trained stags, and when a stag hunt is announced, one of the trained stags is conveyed in a cart to a certain spot and there let loose. After a few minutes grace the hounds are sent in pursuit, followed by the whole field of hunters, till after a run of some miles the stag gets tired, and deliberately waits till the huntsman comes up and captures him, when he is again put into the cart and taken back to his snug quarters. Oh, shade of Robin Hood! with what utter contempt must thou regard this poor remnant of ancient British sport!

The death of the beautiful fallow-deer has always caused a certain feeling of remorseful pity, even in the breast of the successful hunter, and poets have drawn many beautiful similes from the chase and its accompaniments.

' As pants the hart for cooling streams,
  When heated in the chase,'

will occur to the mind at once, and Shakespeare
describes the melancholy Jaques moralising on the same
event :—

' As he lay along
Under an oak, whose antique root peeps out
Upon the brook that brawls along this wood ;
To the which place a poor sequester'd stag,
That from the hunter's aim had ta'en a hurt,
Did come to languish ; and, indeed, my lord,
The wretched animal heav'd forth such groans,
That their discharge did stretch his leathern coat
Almost to bursting ; and the big round tears
Cours'd one another down his innocent nose
In piteous chase : and thus the hairy fool,
Much marked of the melancholy Jaques,
Stood on the extremest verge of the swift brook,
Augmenting it with tears. . . .
"Poor deer," quoth he, "thou mak'st a testament
As worldlings do, giving thy sum of more
To that which had too much."'

Pity, however, does not weigh much in the scale when
savoury meat is the result of a day's hunting, and from time
immemorial venison has been regarded as a delicacy fit for
a king's table. Solomon in his magnificence had his venison
of stag and roebuck daily, and Cyrus of Persia would not
dine without it. But long before Cyrus and Solomon our
rude forefathers had found uses, not only for the flesh, but
also for the horns and sinews of various kinds of deer ; for
among the earliest known relics of man, the horns of the
deer are found forming handles for stone implements, picks
for digging flints, etc., whilst the sinews were used as thread

for sewing the skins together for clothing, and for making strings for bows, fishing lines, and other purposes.

One of the earliest known drawings found in the caves of France represents a group of reindeer, for the reindeer at that remote period lived in France and Great Britain, as it now does in Lapland, and appears to have been domesticated, and was probably as useful to the old cave-dwellers as it is now to the Lapps.

When we come to inquire how these old-world people cooked their venison, the answer is not easy: they probably broiled it over hot coals, or boiled it with hot stones after the method mentioned elsewhere; but in the old patriarchal days they must have cooked with considerable skill, otherwise Rebecca would not have been able so readily to convert the kid into savoury meat so nearly resembling venison as to be eaten for it by the blind old patriarch, who seems to have been fond of good living, and evidently appreciated venison as much as modern epicures.

Goat's flesh is so little appreciated among us at present, that it is not even named in modern English cookery books. Nevertheless, in the East and in southern Europe, even now, it is much eaten and esteemed, as it is also in South Africa where large flocks are kept for the hair, and for food. The many allusions to the goat in Scripture shows that it formed one of the staple articles of food among the Jews, as it did doubtless among the Greeks and Romans; and the goat is one of the most familiar objects in ancient sculpture, as it is in modern paintings of Italian landscape.

The Roman god Pan and his satyrs are depicted with goat's legs, and the modern herdsman of the Campagna, in his hairy goatskin breeches as he sits on a ruined tomb piping to his herd, with the graceful little kids playing around him, is a good representative of the ancient sylvan deity and his attendants.

In Italy at the present day, not only is the goat in great request for its flesh and its skin, but the milk is largely used, and a sort of cream cheese made of goat's milk is sold in the streets and highly appreciated, being, in truth, very sweet and palatable. A halfpenny spent on this *ricotta*, to be eaten with the sour Italian bread, makes an excellent meal for the frugal Roman, who cannot afford many table luxuries.

We used often to wonder that the useful goat, so easily reared and fed, was not more commonly kept by cottagers in England; but we have since found out that his constant activity, and the consequent difficulty of keeping him within due bounds, is a great drawback to his usefulness in a small and over-populated country like Great Britain. Among the mountains of Wales he still thrives, being, as is well known, an emblem of the country. The beautiful Angora goat, now naturalised at the Cape, is a native of Syria, and is not hardy enough for the cold, rough mountains of Europe, but its flesh, I am told, is more palatable, as its coat is more beautiful, than that of the common goat. A solitary goat is often kept in stables or among a herd of cows in England, being supposed to ward off disease; and in South Africa one is often trained to act as leader to a flock of sheep—a part it enacts with great sagacity.

CHAPTER VII

THERE may perhaps have been vegetarians in all ages, but they are certainly rare among the lower races of the present day, and have probably always been so of necessity rather than by choice, for doubtless man is by nature a hunter, and has ever been engaged in trapping and slaying for food the wild animals by which he has been surrounded.

The very earliest men of whom we have any record—whose weapons were of rough stone, and whose dwellings were in caves and rock shelters, who probably built no houses, and, as far as we know, wore no clothes except the skins of the animals they had slain and devoured—were hunters. Noble game, too, they hunted in those days in Europe, such as can now only be found in the wilds of Africa, and some not even there, for they have perished utterly. There were the cave lion and the cave bear, the great sabre-toothed tiger, the woolly-haired rhinoceros, and the great mammoth, with its long, curved tusks and shaggy coat, known to us only by its skeleton, and by its likeness—drawn by these savage hunters on a piece of its own tusk—until some years ago a great thaw in Siberia revealed the animal in its flesh, where it had lain packed in ice by the hand of nature for many centuries, yet still remaining fresh enough to be devoured by dogs, a fact which might have suggested the use of the refrigerating process to the wise men of that day; but they were so slow in following where nature led, that it has taken half a century to bring frozen meat into the European market. Then there was the reindeer, useful then as now, and abounding at that time in the south of France, instead of in the Arctic regions; but in those remote ages the south of France was itself Arctic in climate.

The wild cave men of those days have also left us portraits of the reindeer, and of a little shaggy pony, which they ate also, as well as fish and fowl, for people then were not particular as to the choice of food, and ate whatever they could catch, literally by hook or by crook, for, as they had no guns and no weapons of metal, they had to trust to their own skill and cunning rather than to their weapons for their game, and it seems astonishing that with such imperfect implements they should have succeeded in slaughtering such a huge beast as the mammoth; nevertheless, some even now can trap and destroy the elephant and other big game, using for the purpose poisoned arrows and having ingenious methods, whereby the flow of blood from the wound is increased, and, in some cases, the head of the arrow is made to detach itself and the shaft to drag along the ground, entangling itself in the long grass so as to hinder the flight of the wounded animal. Mr. Stanley has described the skill of the little African pigmies in destroying big game with their tiny but beautifully made weapons, and by traps.

European game has now dwindled down to small proportions. The mammoth, and other great beasts its contemporaries, are quite extinct; the reindeer has retreated to the Arctic circles; the horse and the ox, the goat and the pig, are no longer game, but domestic animals. There are still a few bears, wolves, and wild boars to be found, and several kinds of deer. The fox—at least in England —can hardly be looked upon as a wild animal, being carefully preserved; and even of birds, few are now found in the wild state, partridges and pheasants being reared by thousands in poultry yards and turned out to be shot. But in the north, grouse of several kind, blackcock, and capercailzies are still to be found, and wild duck, woodcock, and snipe may fall to the sportsman's gun in the lowlands.

There is, however, little excitement in the pursuit of that which is harmless, and so our genuine sportsmen go further afield for their game, and delight, like Nimrod of old, in hunting the tiger and the wild boar in India, or the lion, the elephant, the rhinoceros, the panther, and various species of deer and antelope in Africa. The latter continent still maintains the pre-eminence which caused it to be named 'the hunter's paradise,' and those who saw the great trophy of heads and horns displayed in the Cape Court at the Colonial and Indian Exhibition must have been struck with the vast variety of game there represented; and more especially they must have wondered at the number of species of antelopes, from the great eland * to the tiny little steinbok. The pursuit of these requires great skill and cunning, for they are all extremely agile, and easily scared, and frequent for the most part mountainous regions, very difficult of access.

* It has been proposed to make an attempt to acclimatise this giant antelope in England and to use it for food, which might, perhaps, be possible.

One antelope only remains in a wild state in Europe—namely, the chamois; and the hunting of this active little animal—which most nearly resembles the *klip-springer* of the Cape—is attended with a considerable amount of danger.

Those who would realise the pleasures and dangers of chamois hunting, must visit their haunts among the wild peaks of the Tyrolean Alps, and read the tales written by the Baroness Tautphœus—'The Initials' and 'Quits'—old now, but wonderfully true in their descriptions of the country and the people, and of that wild chamois hunter and his habits who has been thus described:—'The true chamois hunter is a man apart. Gaunt and bony, with " brown and sinewy knees, scarred and scratched, hair shaggy, dark piercing eyes, marked eyebrows, a bent eagle nose, and high, fleshless cheek-bones, with a hungry expression on his face," to borrow the words of a famous Alpine hunter, the " Gamsjäger" is of a build not to be acquired among the dwellers of cities.'

Once only have I tasted chamois flesh, and can testify to its extreme delicacy and excellence, but it rarely falls to the lot of modern tourists to taste the real article; the Swiss serve up goat flesh cunningly prepared to resemble chamois, but which is no more to be compared with it than is mutton to venison.

Time was when the only specimen of foreign game which appeared on English tables was the French partridge, which has long been naturalised among us, and of which a poet writes—

'As I was standing by a wood one day,
A little partridge came my way.

G

His slender legs were dainty red,
And in a foreign way he said,
      " Ne tirez pas, ne tirez pas !
      Je suis Français.
      Mon Dieu ! ne tirez pas !"

' Another hand (not mine) then fired ; he fell,
And, quivering, lay upon the ground.
But, ere the fluttering life had sped,
With little sob he bravely said,
      " N'y pensez plus, n'y pens'z plus.
      Allons ! Voyons !
      Je meurs Français.
      Adieu !"'

Now, however, the freezing system has allowed game, as
well as beef and mutton, to be sent from over the seas, and
thus we get the prairie hen from America, and are surprised
that we do not also get various other birds, even from greater
distances.   We are told that we receive many tons of rabbits
from Australia and New Zealand, both tinned and frozen,
and we certainly get shiploads of ptarmigan, capercailzie,
blackcock, and white hares from Norway and the north of
Scotland, which, coming as they do during the close season
for our native game, and when poultry also is scarce and
dear, are exceedingly acceptable to English housekeepers.
Why do we not also get the bush-turkey and other game-
birds from Australia, New Zealand, and the Cape ?   It also
seems a pity the Australians do not send us kangaroo meat ;
but then there is a prejudice to be overcome, for English
people don't like any outlandish meats, and even the
French, although they do enjoy frogs' legs and snails, and
were accustomed during the siege of Paris to all sorts of
strange viands, from rats to elephants, do not prefer these
delicacies in times of peace and plenty.   We believe

kangaroo tails may be purchased here, but the majority of people will doubtless continue to give preference to the bovine caudal appendage in making soup.*

Use is second nature, and it takes a long time to get used to strange dishes. The late Frank Buckland tried the flavour of everything he *could* try in the Zoo, from the snake to the hippopotamus, but he didn't get many to enjoy his savoury meats. However, game, whether bird or beast, is much more readily accepted than other strange meats, and we fancy if South Africa and Australia would send us game during their early autumn (not at pairing time) in a frozen state, it would be a most acceptable addition to the somewhat scanty *menu* of our backward spring, and, perhaps, delay for a time the threatened total extermination of our birds and hares, now apparently sold in season and out of season indiscriminately.

There is nothing which tickles the palate of the epicure more than a savoury dish of game of any kind, from the lordly stag to the humble lark, the long strings of which charming little songster hanging in the poulterers' shops often cause a pang of regret to the lover of birds, although, as a matter of fact it is no more cruel to kill and eat a lark than a woodcock, only in the former case the slaughter seems so wholesale, that the fear of total extermination arises; but when we look back to the days of the Roman emperors, and read that the table of Elagabalus was regularly supplied with ragoûts of the livers and brains of small birds, the heads

---

* The Australian aborigines insist that all animals must be cooked in their skins, and their method of cooking the kangaroo is to cut it open, take out the entrails and replace them by four hot stones ; the animal is then roasted on hot ashes.

of parrots and pheasants, and the tongues of peacocks and nightingales, and that Æsop, the tragic actor, entertained his guests with a dish of birds, each of which had been taught either to sing or to speak, we wonder that any singing birds should remain to be killed and eaten, especially when we remember that from the days of the Roman emperors to this present, an indiscriminate slaughter of all birds has been going on in Italy.

Even now the traveller is regaled with all sorts of birds daintily dressed and served under the name of ortolans or becaficos, but the poulterers' shops reveal a mass of strange birds of every kind from the owl to the kingfisher and the wren, all awaiting the same fate at the hands of the Italian cook, who does not disdain even the blood of his victims, which is sold in the form of little cakes, whilst the livers, mixed with poultry trimmings, help in the manufacture of the most savoury and delicious of pies; whereas our extravagant cooks throw everything away excepting, perhaps, the liver and gizzard of domestic poultry, although they will sometimes condescend to use the necks and pinions for making gravy.

Our domestic poultry now consists of fowls, ducks, geese, turkeys, and guinea-fowls, but formerly at all feasts the place of honour was assigned to the peacock, which, dressed in its full plumage, was carried to the dining-hall by the chief lady of the company, to the sound of music, the rest of the ladies following in due order, and was set down by the bearer before the master of the house or his most honoured guest. The 'Book of Days' says, 'to prepare Argus for the table was a task entailing no little trouble. The skin was first carefully stripped off, with the plumage adhering; the bird was then roasted; when done and partially cooled, it was sewed up again in its feathers, its beak gilt, and so sent to table. Sometimes the whole body was covered with leaf-gold, and a piece of cotton saturated with spirits placed in its beak and lighted before the carver commenced operations. - This "food for lovers and meat for lords" was stuffed with spices and sweet herbs, basted with yolk of eggs, and served with plenty of gravy; on great occasions as many as three fat wethers being braised to make enough for a single peacock.' The same book tells us that the bird when served up after a tournament, was usually placed in a pie, the head appearing at one end and the tail unfolded in all its glory at the other, and in this form was placed before the victorious knight. Over this peacock-pie the knights-errant swore, as Justice Shallow has it, 'by cock and pie,' to do all manner of chivalrous deeds.

The peacock is seldom if ever sent to table at the present day in its gorgeous plumes, the latest recorded instance of its appearance being at a dinner given to William IV. when Duke of Clarence, by the governor of Grenada; but our cooks still adorn the supper table with game pies embellished with the stuffed heads and displayed tails of pheasants; and young pea-fowls are still eaten with relish on the rare occasions when they are obtainable, as are also cygnets, the swan, like the peacock, having passed away from the ordinary cook's domain, but the great swannery at Abbotsbury still sends some yearly to the Queen's table, and we sometimes, though very rarely, see swans hanging in poulterers' shops.

The place of both these former favourites has been taken by the turkey, which, ever since its first introduction, has been growing in favour until it has now become so much a necessity, that there is scarcely a household in the three kingdoms of any social standing, which does not place a turkey on the table at Christmas, and one wonders in contemplating the tons upon tons displayed in shops and stores during the winter, where they can have come from. Norfolk turkeys take the first place in the market, and magnificent specimens they are, with sufficient white dainty meat on the breast to serve a family party, whilst all the masculine members of the household may breakfast on the well-devilled legs.

There has been much discussion as to whether the birds known to the ancients as meleagrides were the same as our turkeys, but the opinion is now generally held that the former birds were guinea-fowls, and that the turkey was unknown before the days of Columbus, being a native of America, where it is still found wild, and having been introduced to Europe by Jesuit missionaries, but it was certainly known in England in the reign of Henry VIII., and, according to Beckmann, began to appear as a Christmas dish about 1585.

The Talegalla or brush-turkey, which builds curious mounds in which to lay its eggs, allowing them to be hatched by the heat generated by the fermentation of the heaped-up material, is much sought by the Australian savages as an article of food, and, like all wild birds, is eaten with gusto by the sportsman, but it is not at all like the common turkey. The guinea-fowl, supposed to have been the bird known to the ancients as turkey, has long been domesticated in England, and is a most useful stop-gap, coming into season just when game and poultry are scarce : when young it is almost equal to pheasant. It is a very shy bird, and although you may pet the pretty little chicks, they are sure to fly away as soon as they can, and will seldom roost with common fowls, but will prefer the highest tree they can find, and lay their eggs in the most inaccessible places, by preference in a bed of stinging nettles.

The chief rival of the turkey is the goose, which is, indeed, so highly esteemed by the 'masses,' that goose clubs have long been established, to which the mechanic subscribes for many weeks before Christmas, in order to receive a fine fat goose for the delectation of himself and family at the winter festival. The savoury bird is not despised by more aristocratic palates, although from the sage and onion accompaniment which is indispensable, it may not appear on state occasions.

Cæsar tells us that the ancient Britons did not consider it lawful to eat the hare and the cock and the goose, probably because these animals were sacred among them, as they were—or at least the cock and the goose—among many other peoples. It seems probable that the geese which saved the Capitol were sacred birds kept for sacrifice, and the goose was certainly among the sacred animals of Egypt, but that did not prevent their being eaten; and since the day when Queen El'zabeth commanded the goose to be served on Michaelmas Day to commemorate the destruction of the Spanish Armada, the slaughter of the goose family has gone on in a yearly increasing ratio, and of late a foreign trade has sprung up in this favourite food, and we see in the market numberless frozen geese from Russia. Now that feather beds have gone so much out of fashion, the goose is seldom robbed of her down before death; but the process was never a very cruel one, as the housewife only took what the bird would have plucked off herself to line her nest. The greygoose quill has also been largely superseded by the steel pen, yet probably hundreds of thousands of goose quills are still used annually. The goose is not a favourite with the farmer, who declares that nothing will feed upon the pasture where geese are kept, as they make the grass rank and sour; nevertheless, large flocks are kept on commons, and share the pasture with horses, cows, and sheep. The liver of the goose was as highly esteemed by the ancient Romans as by lovers of *pâté de foie gras* nowadays, and means had even then been found to enlarge it artificially. Horace wrote—

> ' The slaves behind in mighty charger bore
> A crane in pieces torn, and powder'd o'er
> With salt and flour; and a white gander's l ver,
> Stuff'd fat with figs, bespoke the curious giv r.'
>
> Francis's Hor., B. ii., s. 8.

The duck does not seem to have been so highly esteemed among the ancients; nevertheless, in wisdom it beats the domestic fowl hollow. Naturalists have lately been maligning the tame duck, declaring that its brain is not so large as that of its wild brother—in fact, that it has lost in intelligence from associating with human beings instead of shunning them. It may probably have lost some of its native cunning, nevertheless, the tame duck is certainly not lacking in sense, and we have often been interested by the 'cuteness of this well-known bird. The way in which it will escape from danger in a crowded thoroughfare, notwithstanding its awkward gait, is quite curious, of which a very singular instance was related by an omnibus-driver, who saw a duck with five or six young ones cross safely from Hyde Park to Green Park in the middle of the day, when Hyde Park Corner was thronged with vehicles of all kinds. We remember an amusing episode relating to these birds which will interest our readers.

Whilst on a visit in the country some years ago we watched the polite behaviour of some neighbours' ducks with much amusement. Two ducks belonging to a cottage, desirous of mixing with their fellows, used to creep under a gate and cross the road in the early morning to a farmyard where many others of their kind disported themselves, and, after a day's grubbing, the drake from the farm used to conduct the visitors to their own quarters at sunset in a most ludicrous manner. After leading them to the gate of their domain, he stood by to watch them creep under, but never attempted to follow them : then a great deal of bowing and quacking would take place between the ducks on one side of the gate and the drake on the other—evidently a vote of thanks for polite attentions was duly conveyed and graciously accepted. Then the two ducks would waddle off across a small field to their bedchamber, whilst the drake remained outside the gate watching till they had entered their abode, when, after a few quacks from the ducks to announce their safe arrival, and a good-night in reply from the drake, he would turn away and waddle off to his own harem, to repeat the same polite performance the next night.

Everyone will allow that ducks are good eating, notwithstanding the assertion that they are foul feeders. Undoubtedly they will, like the pig, swallow any garbage, but their preference is for slugs and snails, and, if allowed to search for themselves in the early morning and late in the evening, they will soon fatten upon these gardeners' enemies, and require very little feeding except in dry, hot, and frosty weather; and, but that their waddling feet tread down the earth too much, they are excellent assistants to the gardener.

Seeing the enormous yearly consumption of the domestic fowl, it is matter of surprise that eggs and poultry are not more cultivated in England. There seems no reason why English farmers should not find it as profitable an industry as the French and Irish do; but there exists a general opinion that they cannot be made to pay, and consequently the egg and poultry trade is largely given over to foreigners, and of late an immense number of frozen fowls have found their way into the London market—little, short-necked, ill-favoured things, said to come from Russia, but, appearing at a time when English fowls are scarce and dear, they are a very acceptable addition to the *menu*, although not to be compared in quality with the home-grown fowls from Surrey, Norfolk, and the west of England. Fowls seem to have been domesticated from time immemorial. In Egypt they were even hatched by incubators many centuries B.C. In Greece and Rome the cock was frequently offered in sacrifice, and the regularity of the hour of crowing made it everywhere useful as a timekeeper before the days of clocks, so that we find cock-crowing referred to in Scripture as the time preceding the morning.

Cocks were largely used in divination in Greece and Rome, for not only were auguries derived from an inspection of the entrails, but they were supposed to divine by pecking grain from certain cards placed before them; but, as there are tricks in all trades, it was discovered that the priests had found the way to compel fate, by placing wax imitations of grain on those cards they did not wish to have chosen, and the bird was wise enough to prefer the real to the imitation grain.

Among the many breeds of fowls some are preferred for flavour, others for size, or for the superiority of their eggs. The Dorking and the game fowl are, perhaps, the prime favourites in England for cooking purposes, the Spanish for laying properties, and the Cochin China for the size and flavour of the eggs; but the breeds cultivated by poultry fanciers are too numerous to mention—for profit, probably the common barn-door fowl of mixed breed is the best.

CHAPTER VIII

EGGS

OF all articles of diet, eggs are perhaps the most generally accepted; they are relished alike by sage and savage, and form a nutritious meal for prince or peasant. Nor is the taste for this universal food confined to mankind, for the hens themselves, the providers of the feast, often develop cannibalistic tendencies, and will peck and devour the very egg they have just deposited with so much care and cackling; whilst snakes will lie in wait for the delicate morsel, and will either swallow it whole, or tap it with their teeth and suck out the contents; and rats are credited with making wheelbarrows of themselves, allowing themselves to be pulled along by the ears by their comrades, in order to secure the prize held safely in their paws. Dogs also often develop a taste for eggs, which they will steal from the nest without compunction, the only cure for the propensity being to hold a hot egg in the mouth of the delinquent. Monkeys, and particularly baboons, will also diligently seek for and greedily devour all the eggs they can lay their hands on, and are consequently much dreaded by small birds. But, probably, rapacious birds are the greatest devourers of the eggs of other species. It seems a well authenticated fact, that the grey crow in Africa, will carry stones up to a considerable height and drop them into an ostrich nest, in order to crack the hard shell which would otherwise be prohibitive of the coveted feast; whilst travellers assert that wild ostriches always place several eggs round the nest to serve as food for the young when first hatched.

Happily for mankind, the eggs of noxious reptiles and insects are relished as well as hen's eggs, and thus the excessive increase of deadly reptiles is prevented. The ichneumon greedily devours the eggs of snakes and crocodiles, and white ants' eggs are considered delicacies, even by men. In our own country the magpie and the jay are notorious thieves of the eggs of smaller birds; whilst turkeys, pheasants, and guinea-fowls, will swallow millions of ant eggs in a day, if they can get them.

The problem which puzzled the learned, centuries ago, as to which was first created, the egg or the hen, has never yet been unravelled. Theologians would probably say, the hen, certainly; but Darwin would be in favour of the egg, as being of the nature of that protoplasm from which all life originates. The ancients were certainly of Darwin's opinion, and looked upon the earth itself as developed from an egg by the power of various divinities, hence the egg became a sacred symbol in many countries, was hung up in Egyptian temples, and represented in paintings and sculptures as encircled in the folds of the good Agatho-dæmon, the serpent worshipped in so many lands, and which was doubtless connected with that other famous egg of antiquity, the serpent's egg of the Druids.

If we visit the British Museum we shall see eggs and egg-stands of various shapes and sizes, which have been

found in tombs in Egypt, Greece, and Etruria; among the
Etruscan relics are several ostrich eggs beautifully painted.
These sepulchral eggs were, doubtless, symbolical of a
future life, but were also probably designed as food for
the dead, for it was well-nigh a universal practice to provide
food for the departed spirit, a practice still in use among
savages.

The eggs which are given at Easter time are supposed
to symbolise the Resurrection, but it is certain that the
custom originated in pre-Christian times. Eggs wrapped
in various-coloured ribbons, and boiled—thus receiving the
dye from the ribbon used—were formerly sent as Easter
gifts. These are still sometimes seen in little shops, but
the Easter eggs now sent as presents by those who can
afford them do not owe their origin to any feathered fowl,
but are artificially made of various substances, and filled
with gifts of differing value, from chocolate creams to
diamond rings or costly shawls. It is both curious and
interesting to note that in almost all countries this custom
of giving and receiving brightly coloured eggs at a spring
festival, has prevailed from time immemorial; hence,
probably, we see in the painted ostrich eggs from Etruscan
tombs, which are at least two thousand years old, the
spring gift of friends to the beloved dead. A writer in the
Standard some years ago, in a very interesting article traced
this custom to China; he says:—'Gustave Schlegel,
during his official residence in China as representative of
the Netherlands, in his interesting and erudite researches
through a mass of Chinese literature discovered that the
"painted eggs," as they are called in China, were used
in the great Spring Festival of Tsing-ming, and are noticed

in the records of the ancient State of King-ts-oo under the
date B.C. 722. The giving gifts to one another of brightly
coloured hard-boiled eggs at this season he also found
occurring in the annals of the old State of Ye, between
the dates B.C. 481—B.C. 255. Schlegel tells us the custom
is met with in the records of the Tang Dynasty, A.D. 618—
A.D. 907. It seems the custom originated in China in this
wise. Annually, at the mid-spring time of year, which
answers to our Easter, Chinese functionaries were sent out
through the towns, villages, and country parts, each armed
with a wooden bell, their duty being to make proclamation
that all fires must be put out, and must remain out for the
space of three days, after which, by the friction of two pieces
of wood, new fire was obtained, and from this the household
hearths were rekindled. The three days specified seems to
have been intended to ensure that no smouldering ember
should by any possibility linger anywhere in the Celestial
Empire. For as the old Chinese writer has it—" All fire
under the expanse of Heaven ought to be extinguished
before the new fire is lighted." During those three days
" sacred to the revival of spring and the sun's heat," when in
honour of the sun there must be no fire, of course no
cooking was possible. It is highly probable a large number
of the less devout among the millions of John Chinaman's
compatriots were ill-pleased to have to submit to the
cheerless, unpalatable diet imposed upon them while the
fast from fire lasted. At any rate, the Chinese feast of
Tsing-ming came to be popularly called the " Cold Meat
Festival." Hard-boiled eggs would, of course, be an
acceptable addition to the prepared viands to be used
during the fireless three days. Whether they were so used

before I know not, but it is attributed to a certain "powerful chieftain of antiquity" who lived in the before-named ancient State of King-ts-oo to have been the first person who laid in stores of "painted eggs," and set the fashion of dispensing them as gifts to friends and acquaintances at that same time of year when we celebrate Easter.'

The Chinese spring festival always occurs in April when the sun enters the fifteenth degree of Aries, and as the cock is sacred to the sun, the egg may have come in this way to symbolise the new spring birth of nature through the vivifying influence of the sun. At all events the gift of brightly coloured eggs at the early spring festival can be traced not only in China but also in Persia, where we find them in connection with a festival, the origin of which is ascribed to the Persian mythical monarch Jemsheed, sixth in descent from Moses, who is said to have reigned 700 years. The writer above quoted says :—'The greatest of Jemsheed's festivals was the Nowroose, or Feast of the beginning of the Religious or Solar Year. It commenced at the time of the "natural reproduction of all that conduces to the sustenance of man." With a slight variation from the Chinese calculation, the Persian Festival is held to begin the moment the sun enters Aries, or towards the end of March. The Nowroose Festival is, of course, much older than Mahometanism. Some writers call it the "Feast of the Waters," and consider it a memorial of the Deluge ; while others suppose it to have been instituted to commemorate the Creation. A prominent feature that all travellers record as taking place at the time is the handing about of eggs dyed of various colours and gilt, given as gifts to each other, and even to strangers, in honour of the great Spring fast.

Whether the Nowroose was originally intended to commemorate the Deluge or the Creation may be questioned,
but the fact remains that here as elsewhere we find "painted
eggs" as gifts heralding the return of the sun in Spring at
the annual resurrection of Nature.'

The derivation of our Easter eggs from these ancient
sources is evident; it is not the only Pagan custom adapted
to Christianity by the early Church, and to quote once more
from the very interesting article referred to :—

'When Pope Paul V. drew up a ritual to be used in
England, Ireland, and Scotland, among many other prayers
of Benediction for Eastertide was the following :—" Bless,
Lord, we beseech Thee, this Thy creature of Eggs, that it
may become a wholesome sustenance to Thy faithful
servants, eating it in thankfulness to Thee on account of
the Resurrection of our Lord." Countless thousands of
eggs were thus annually blessed by the priests at Easter,
both before and after they were coloured. Having obtained
the blessing, the eggs became holy gifts, the bestowal of
which conferred much benefit on both givers and receivers.
It became a custom on Good Friday to "offer eggs and
bacon to the Lord Christ," and thus special favours were
secured to the donors. Some of our early Reformation
records bring strange matters before those who care to dip
into them; not the least strange referring to the mode of
making "presentations of eggs to the Cross." It is a
custom still in vogue in some parts of the Continent for
each member of a parish to present the priest with an egg
on Easter morning.'

In process of time Easter eggs, which were originally given
and received as symbols of the Resurrection, degenerated

into mere objects of sport, and were used as balls, or
for the performance of dances, which often took place in
churches; thus we are told that 'eggs always rose in price
at Easter, they were boiled very hard in water coloured with
red, blue, or violet dyes, with inscriptions or landscapes
traced upon them; these were offered as presents among
the valentines of the year, but more frequently played with
by the boys as balls, for ball-playing on Easter Monday
was universal in every rank. Even the clergy could not
forego its delights, and made this game a part of their
service. Bishops and deans took the ball into the church,
and at the commencement of the autiphone began to dance,
throwing the ball to the choristers, who handed it to each
other during the time of the dancing and autiphone. All
then retired for refreshment; a gammon of bacon, eaten in
abhorrence of the Jews, was a standard dish; with a tansy
pudding, symbolical of the bitter herbs commanded at the
paschal feast.' *

When we consider the lavish use of eggs in former days,
we are constrained to believe that our forefathers certainly
paid more attention to the keeping and rearing of poultry
than English farmers do at the present day, for eggs must
have been more plentiful and cheaper than they are now,
even with our abundant foreign supplies, or they could
never have been used as balls, and employed by the dozen
in cookery, as old receipts show us they were.

We are now supplied with eggs from Ireland, Germany,
Belgium, Italy, and France, and it is computed that from
the last named country alone one million come daily to the
London market. The number consumed in England yearly

* Chambers's 'Book of Days,' vol. i., p. 429.

must be incalculable; but new-laid English eggs are always difficult to procure, and during the winter are often sold at threepence apiece, whereas our grandmothers would probably have considered a shilling a score very dear. It has been calculated that we pay six millions of pounds per annum for eggs; and French cooks say they may be dressed in more than five hundred different ways. They are, however, used not only in cookery. In one photographic establishment, we are told, two millions are used every year; and they are also employed largely in calico printing, leather dressing, and bookbinding; and it is calculated that in France the number used in wine clarifying amounts to more than eighty millions a year. It may be well here to give a few of the uses of eggs in medicine, for they are valuable in many ways as household remedies.

'The white is the most efficacious of remedies for burns, and the oil extractable from the yolk is regarded by the Russians as an almost miraculous salve for cuts, bruises, and scratches. A raw egg, if swallowed in time, will effectually detach a fish-bone in the throat, and the white of two eggs will render the deadly corrosive sublimate as harmless as a dose of calomel. They strengthen the consumptive, invigorate the feeble, and render the most susceptible all but proof against jaundice in its more malignant phase.' The old saw had it—

> ' An egg, an apple, and a nut,
> You may eat after any slut.'

That, however, is not quite true as regards eggs, for the shell being porous readily absorbs anything malodorous which is placed near it, so that it is not uncommon to meet with eggs tasting of onions; and I remember once having had served to me three mornings running eggs highly flavoured with paraffin through a careless servant having thrown the cloth with which she cleaned the lamps over the egg basket.*   It is also believed that eggs are affected by the food consumed by the hens; and it is certain that portions of foreign bodies such as insects, seeds, small stones, etc., have been found in eggs, especially in ostrich eggs, the stones found in which have been polished and used as buttons or studs.

The ostrich egg is the largest egg at present known, but that of the giant dinornis of New Zealand exceeded it in size as much as the turkey's egg exceeds that of the hen. One of these gigantic eggs was exhibited, with the skeleton of the extinct bird, at the Colonial and Indian Exhibition, and a cast of one may be seen at the Natural History Museum, with an ostrich egg near it by way of comparison; but the dinornis egg is unique and unattainable, as well as uneatable, and we must be content with that of the ostrich as the largest now used for eating, one of which makes a tolerable meal for five or six people, being considered equal to twenty-four hens' eggs.   It is, however, rather strong in flavour, but makes excellent sponge-cakes, pancakes, or omelets, and a find of ostrich eggs in the desert is matter of great rejoicing to the wandering bushman ór the hungry traveller.

Besides the dinornis, there is another extinct bird, the great auk, which has left behind it two or three eggs, which are so much coveted as to fetch an extraordinary price; one of these famous eggs was sold a year or two ago for

---

* Eggs placed standing upright in salt may be kept good for weeks, and in China, salted goose eggs are highly esteemed as food for invalids.

£225. Rumour had it that it was stolen from one of the Paris museums during the troubles of 1848, but it is certain that it was sold a few years afterwards by a dealer in Paris to an English gentleman, in whose family it has remained until now. At this gentleman's death it fell into the hands of a married daughter, who resided near Reigate, but afterwards removed to near Brighton, taking the egg with her. It was lost trace of by ornithologists owing to this change of residence, and had quite recently once more been traced. The lady who owned it was induced to offer it for sale owing to what was thought the extraordinary price paid for another egg of the same bird, sold previously for £168.

We are not likely to find eggs of dinornis or great auk; but it is reported that eggs larger than that of the ostrich have occasionally been found in the deserts of Africa, and any traveller coming across such may find it a profitable investment, although not as an article of food, for as the bird which laid these eggs is unknown, and perhaps extinct, the eggs would probably be partially petrified, although it is possible that they may be found to be those of the gigantic ostrich recently discovered in the interior, a specimen of which has lately been forwarded as a present to the Queen.

Of eggs good for food we may mention, in addition to those of the hen, duck, turkey, goose, guinea-fowl, and plover, those of the penguin, which are much relished by sailors, and dwellers on the sea-coasts where these birds abound, as also the eggs of other sea-birds, although they are apt to have a somewhat rank and fishy flavour. The eggs of the turtle are eagerly sought by the epicure, and it is related that one gentleman, having found what he supposed to be a nest of them, took some home and cooked them, leaving the rest in the sand, but returning in a day or two for the remainder, found instead a number of lively young crocodiles, which would go far to prove that there is very little to choose between turtles' eggs and those of the crocodile, and probably those of snakes and lizards would be equally palatable if prejudice did not interfere with their consumption.

The Chinese are credited with a fondness for eggs half-rotten, but that is hardly to be believed when we remember the evil odour attached to them in this condition; they may, however, enjoy them with the chick in, even as many people will eat the young bees in the honey-comb, for it is possible to imagine that a half-hatched chicken may be palatable, but rotten eggs are certainly an abomination, which no gastronomic peculiarities could render endurable to a civilised taste, although they may not be worse than some other half-rotten comestibles which commend themselves to some palates. The Australians, when they find the eggs of the brush-turkey or the jungle-hen, make a hole in them lengthways, and lay them in hot ashes, and when they boil, eat the contents by means of a brush made of cane, with the end chewed. Should there be chicks in the eggs, as is often the case, they take them out, broil them on the ashes, and eat them after the other contents.

A bird, perhaps of the same species as the brush-turkey, and known in China as the Tabon, lays a very large egg in the sand of the sea-shore, leaving it to be hatched by the heat of the sun. These eggs are carefully sought, and are said to be best when stale, or with young birds in them.

CHAPTER IX

How shall we estimate the debt we owe to the man or woman who first thought of domesticating the useful cow for the sake of her milk? How early in the world's history that domestication took place it is impossible to say, but we know that the Egyptians appreciated the bovine race so highly that they worshipped the bull Apis, and it would not be hard to trace a similar worship through many other ancient nations, to the Hindoos of the present day.

The Egyptians probably made butter and cheese, as we do : certainly the Hebrews did, for the references to butter and cheese in the various books of the Old Testament are numerous. 'Hast thou not poured me out as milk, and curdled me like cheese?' says Job; and in another place he speaks of 'brooks of honey and butter.' Butter was one of the delicacies which Jael set before Sisera, and ten cheeses of milk was the present which Jesse sent by the hand of his son David to the captain of that thousand of Saul's army in which his brethren were serving. It is of course possible that this butter and these cheeses were made of the milk of sheep or goats, but in enumerating the presents sent to David by Barzillai, cheese of *kine* is especially mentioned, and from the proverb which says,

'Surely the churning of milk bringeth forth butter,' we may conclude that both butter and cheese were known to the ancients in much the same form as we have them now.

The most ancient butter of which we have any real knowledge is that known as bog butter, which is dug up from time to time in Irish peat-bogs. Two or three *crocks* of this butter may be seen in the Museum of the Royal Irish Academy, Dublin; it looks like a large lump of chalk, but still retains its fatty nature, and burns like oil. From the hairs which are found in it, the colour of the cows from which it was derived has been ascertained, but at what period it was buried, and for what reason, is not known. It may, perhaps, have been hidden in troublous times, or it is just possible it may have been buried as cream, in order that it might be converted into butter, this process having been resorted to with success at the Cape, after an accidental discovery that cream buried in the earth will turn into butter without churning, only the butter thus produced is not so good as that made in the ordinary way by churning. Even at the present day, in some parts of Ireland butter is made in a very primitive fashion, by churning unseparated milk, the temperature being raised by the addition of hot water. This, of course, leaves a very large proportion of buttermilk, which is eagerly sought by the peasantry to serve as sauce to their potatoes, or to make cakes, instead of yeast, for which purposes it is admirably adapted. Buttermaking in England, unfortunately, is by no means so much thought of as in the old times, when every farmer's wife and daughter looked upon that and cheese-making as a portion of their education, as well as their own especial daily task, and were not ashamed themselves to convey their produce to market. Things are altered now: the farmer sends milk instead of butter and cheese to market, and London is largely supplied with foreign butter and cheese, not only from Holland, which was formerly the chief source of import, but from Brittany, Sweden, America, and Canada, the imports of cheese from the latter country having increased so enormously of late years that it is almost impossible to obtain English cheese at an ordinary cheese factor's.

Then, too, the methods of butter and cheese-making have been greatly modified by the introduction of machinery. It is now no longer necessary to wait many hours for the cream to rise in order to skim it off—machinery separates the cream at once from the new milk, and at the great agricultural show at Windsor in 1887, a machine was exhibited which was a combination of churn and separator, making cream or butter from new milk as desired, by merely moving a lever, and turning out a pound of butter a minute.

In our childhood, to watch the process of cheese-making was a never-ending source of amusement. Great was the delight of being allowed to stand on a stool beside the big tub, deep enough to drown us, whilst the dairymaid first cut into the vast mass of curds and whey, sometimes good-naturedly giving us a basin of the delicious compound to eat, whilst she strained off the whey, cutting the curd with a large double-bladed knife, piling it up in huge flocculent masses, and dipping out the whey with a brass or tin dish; then, breaking up the curd with her hands, heaping it into vats lined with clean cloths, and putting the embryo cheeses into a press to squeeze away all the remaining whey, taking them out to pare them and turn them daily, till they had acquired solidity. We all remember the great cheese made in this way at Cheddar, in Somersetshire, for presentation to the Queen : it was formed from one meal's milk of all the cows in the parish, all the farmer's daughters assisting as dairymaids ; but the huge cheese was not, we believe, quite the success it deserved to be, its enormous size requiring too long a time to ripen properly. Cheddar, however, is even now at the head of British cheese-making, and turns out immense cheeses of excellent quality, still distancing all competitors, although Canadian Cheddar is very good, and is very frequently passed off as the genuine English article.

The prince of English cheeses is the Stilton, made of cream added to new milk, but this also is now frequently imitated, so that you can seldom be sure of getting the real Leicestershire product. A Stilton cheese is, and has always been, a famous Christmas dish, and when rich and fully ripe is not to be surpassed. Formerly, the whole cheese, with a napkin pinned round it, was set on the table, and scooped out until the rind only remained, the ripening process being hastened by a bottle of good port wine being poured into it. But these are degenerate days : people now seldom make their luncheon of bread and cheese, and even the Dorsetshire peasant is no longer content with a great crust of bread and that *mouldy cheesen* which proverbially required a hatchet to cut it, but which could be purchased at about threepence a pound, and was so appetising that it was commonly said it might be eaten till you were hungry again.

This was the poorer sort of Dorset cheese, made of milk

skimmed once, and sometimes twice; but the richer kind of *mouldy cheesen*, into which a portion of cream entered, was almost equal to Stilton, holding a place midway between that and the fashionable foreign makes known as Roquefort and Gorgonzola, but it is little made nowadays, and may be deemed extinct, as are also those thin cheeses which used to be made in Wiltshire and Gloucestershire, and known as single Gloucester, or toasting-cheese. The double Gloucester still enters the market, and is a good cheese, although not to be compared to Cheddar, or to that other well-known variety from Cheshire, which latter is also scarce in the London market, although you may purchase it in Rome. The little round Dutch cheeses are still much sold, but it is hard to see why they are chosen in preference to others of far superior quality and very little higher in price.

The ripening process for cheese is a somewhat lengthy affair, especially when the size is large, as in Cheddar. Most English dairy farms have a loft, or sometimes several, where the new cheeses are stored on racks, and frequently turned and scraped till they become fit for the market. The old way of sending cheese to table whole, scooping out the centre and leaving the rind to be dealt with by the cook, although perhaps extravagant, was commendable, for not only did the cheese retain its flavour better, but the necessity of eating close to the rind was avoided, and certainly the rind does not commend itself to many palates. We all know the story of the prudent young lover who, being desirous of choosing one of three sisters, selected as his bride the one who *scraped* her cheese. The one who cut off the rind was deemed extravagant, the one who ate it was a slut, whilst the third was supposed to be thrifty and cleanly. If put to the same test nowadays, there would be few chosen on account of that economy, for the bits of cheese sent to table are mostly free from rind when presented to the consumer.

There are some foreign cheeses which are deservedly esteemed, the chief objection to them being the strong odour which requires their being sent to table under cover. Of these we need only mention, in addition to the Roquefort and Gorgonzola, which are now to be found in every cheesemonger's shop, the Gruyère, always served on the Continent at dinner, and generally with the dessert. It is not, indeed, unusual in Italy, if you order fruit, to find a piece of this cheese sent up on the same dish, and it certainly does not eat badly, especially with dried fruits, which reminds us that in some parts of England it is customary to eat cheese with jam and marmalade, or with apple pie, and in other parts, thin slices of cheese are cut and floated on cups of tea.

Gruyère is made partly, if not entirely, of ewe's milk, and the famous Parmesan cheese is, I believe, also composed partly of ewe's milk. This cheese, used almost always in the form of powder, is a constant accompaniment of soups, macaroni, and other Italian dishes, and is sold in the grated form by the *sack* in all grocers' shops in Italy, and is invariably sent to table in the same way as pepper and salt in other places, to be used as a condiment. Even the Lazzaroni find a small coin wherewith to purchase this much-esteemed relish, which among ourselves is coming more and more into use, and may be bought in bottles ready grated, although it is best bought in a piece and grated at home, in order to ensure its genuineness.

There are many other foreign cheeses to be met with,

but they are not in general use. There are, however, several kinds of cream cheeses, and what are known as *soft cheeses*, much esteemed, such as Bath cheeses, Bon-dons, Camembert, etc.

The true cream cheese is made simply by putting cream in a cloth, and allowing all the moisture to run away from it, and then moulding it into shape, pressing and turning it daily till ripe; but soft cheeses are made in various ways, one of which is given in verse attributed to the celebrated Dr. Jenner, of vaccination fame, as follows :—

' Would you make a soft cheese? Then I'll tell you how :
Take a gallon of milk, quite fresh from the cow ;
Ere the rennet is added, the dairyman's daughter
Must throw in a quart of the clearest spring water.
When perfectly curdled, so white and so nice,
You must take it all out of the dish with a slice,
And put it 'thout breaking with care in the vat
With a cheese-cloth at bottom—be sure to mind that.
This delicate matter take care not to squeeze,
But fill as the whey passes off by degrees.
Next day you may turn it, and do not be loth
To wipe it quite dry with a fine linen cloth ;
That this must be done you cannot well doubt,
As long as you see the whey oozing out.
The cheese is now finished, and nice it will be,
If enveloped in leaves from the green ashen tree ;
Or, what will do better—at least, full as well—
In nettles just plucked from the bank of the dell.'

There is a kind of cream cheese made from goats' milk, which, under the name of *ricotta*, is much eaten in Italy; it is very sweet and palatable, and has evidently been in use from very ancient times. The vendors carry it through the streets on their heads, like the muffin sellers here, and retail it by the centime to poor purchasers.

A product of the dairy now seldom, if ever, seen, is the *syllabub*, for that which is sold as syllabub has very little affinity with the genuine article, as formerly set before guests on grand occasions in country houses, and which was made as follows :—

'Put into a large china punch-bowl a bottle of sherry, half a bottle of brandy, some loaf sugar, the juice of a lemon, and a nutmeg grated. Give the bowl thus charged to a careful dairymaid, and let her milk into it till nearly full, from a cow yielding good rich milk ; then set aside, covering the bowl with a cloth, and, after it has stood about half an hour or more, place it on the table, and fill the glasses with a silver punch-ladle. This is a capital recipe, and sufficient for a large party.'

Devonshire is celebrated not only for its butter and cream, but for that which is known as Devonshire Junket, and which is now largely made and sold by the various dairy companies in London. It is, in fact, the old-fashioned curds and whey with a little brandy and sugar added, and with a surface dressing of Devonshire cream, which makes it a very tempting dish, especially in the summer. It is very easily made.—

'Place in a glass dish a quart of new milk made *lukewarm*, add to it sugar to taste, a tablespoonful of brandy, a little sherry, and three teaspoonfuls of rennet. Let it stand till cold, then cover with Devonshire cream, and grate a little nutmeg over. The rennet can be bought at the chemist's in small bottles.'

Devonshire cream, which is so highly esteemed, and can now be purchased in jars, is made thus :

'The new milk from the cow is strained into large flat

pans or tins, and let stand for twenty-four hours (or twelve only in very hot weather) to allow the cream to rise. It is then placed, still in the same pan, upon a hot dresser or gas stove (not too hot), and let warm gently till *just on the point of boiling;* then removed and set aside till cold, when the cream may be taken off and used as cream, or it may be turned into butter with the hand or by gentle churning. Devonshire cream is always sold by the pint, equal to a pound, at the same price as butter.'

Cream of this kind is also made and largely consumed in Cornwall, and the Cornish hostess is quite insulted if you ask for *Devonshire* cream. One way of eating it in Cornwall I have not met with elsewhere, it is spread thickly on bread, and then a little treacle is allowed to flow over it, this is called Cornish thunder and lightning.

One very general use of cream and butter in former times was in the manufacture of melted butter, which at present too often consists of a sort of water-gruel made of flour-and-water, with a little bit of butter added, a sauce to be scrupulously avoided, but which, when made as follows, is a delicious adjunct to vegetables and poultry :

' Take a good lump of fresh butter and roll it in flour, place it in a lined saucepan with half a pint of good rich cream, stir it gently over a slow fire, *always the same way*, till it begins to simmer. Milk may be substituted for the cream, but the sauce will not be so good.'

One of the most delicious of the many dishes manu-factured from eggs and cream is the custard, which, either boiled or baked, is a dainty generally irresistible. The custards of our grandmothers, however, little resembled those set before us at the present day; they were composed

solely of the yolks of many eggs, pure rich cream, a little
sugar, and a flavouring of ratafia, or bay leaves and brandy,
and were not indebted to custard powders, corn-flour, or
other artificial thickening matter. They were used freely
as a covering to tipsy-cakes and trifles which were
genuinely tipsy with wine and spirits, and not merely
soaked with milk and water, for our ancestors were by no
means teetotallers, and could stand an amount of wine, as
their receipts show, which would prostrate their 'degenerate'
descendants.

At present the chief use of cream in cookery is for
making creams and ice-creams, which latter do not appear
in old recipes, as probably the artificial method of freezing
was then unknown, and hot dishes seem to have been
preferred to cold.

There is a very curious old custom described by Tennant
in his 'Tour in Scotland,' in which a kind of custard was
used as a propitiatory offering to animal gods or totems.
'A number of herdsmen at a certain season would form a
square trench, leaving the turf in the middle. They next
lighted a fire and cooked a dish composed of eggs, butter,
oatmeal, and milk. They had also oatmeal cakes on
which they raised nine square knobs. The ceremonies
then began by spilling, as a libation, some of the dish
prepared with eggs and milk. Each of the knobs on the
cakes was dedicated to some particular being, the supposed
protector of their flocks and herds, or to some particular
animal, the real destroyer of them. Each person, turning
his face to the fire, broke off a knob from his cake, and
flinging.it over his shoulder, said, "This I give to thee,
preserve thou my horses;" "This I give to thee, preserve

thou my sheep," and so on.　After this they used the same ceremony to the noxious animals, saying, " This I give to thee, O fox, spare thou my lambs;" " This I give to thee, O hooded crow ; " " This to thee, O eagle," etc., etc.' *

A similar custom existed also in the Isle of Man, and probably in many other parts, for these old superstitions prevailed everywhere among dwellers in the country, having come down from very ancient pre-historic times when animals were looked upon as supernatural beings or ancestors, and were assumed as totems, having power to protect those who thus placed themselves under their care.

* *Archæological Review*, June 1888.

CHAPTER X

FISH

FISH, which is at once the most common of food and the most difficult to procure, has been esteemed by almost all peoples in all ages. Nevertheless, some tribes, even at the present day, reject fish altogether, whilst the Jews, in accordance with the law of Moses, abhor all fish destitute of fins or scales.

There are few sights more charming than that of a fleet of fishing-boats putting off to sea, or returning after a successful cruise, and in watching them we are apt to forget the perils which these 'Toilers of the Sea' must encounter in search of our table luxuries. No wonder that in boisterous weather, as the old Scotch song has it, 'Wives and mithers, 'maist despairin', ca' them lives of men.' Yet along our coasts thousands of men, women, and children get their daily bread by various industries connected with the extensive fisheries, always a most important branch of commerce among seafaring peoples. There is first the making and repairing of nets, the work mostly of women and children, although fishermen are also adepts in the mysteries of netting—an art handed down to us from the remotest ages, and practised by the most ignorant of savages, although requiring considerable skill. Nets, however, are now largely made by machinery. Then there is the manufacture of fish hooks of various kinds—from the harpoon for the gigantic whale to the delicate hook, with artificial fly attached, for the capture of the wary trout. The making of these artificial flies is an art requiring great skill, and the kinds made are innumerable, and many of them extremely natural and beautiful; but the South Sea islanders take almost as much pains with their fish-hooks, which are attached to a piece of highly-polished shell, to attract and dazzle the fish.

Angling has always been a fascinating sport to most men, although the spectator is rather inclined to agree with the cynic, who defined it as a rod with a worm at one end and a fool at the other; but it doubtless exercises the patience and skill as well as the strength of the fisherman, especially where the lordly salmon is the prey, for the landing of such fish as we sometimes see on the fishmonger's slab, must be a feat of considerable strength and agility, as well as patience.

The enthusiasm inspired by the sport was rather amusingly illustrated by a newspaper correspondent some time since, who wrote :—' On one occasion in Ireland, our train was brought almost to a standstill by a river, "just to see if the gentleman would land his salmon," and not a single remonstrance was heard from the passengers, who entered into the matter as warmly as the driver and guard, and cheered enthusiastically when a fine fish was brought safely to the bank.'

To enumerate the various fishes good for food would be impossible. In a certain sense, the proverb, 'All's fish that comes to net' is literally true, for there is hardly a monster of the deep—from the great whale to the porpoise

and the seal—that is not deemed good for food by some ;
whilst the tiniest of sea-creatures, such as whitebait and
shrimps, and the ugliest, such as sea-slugs and anglers, are
all esteemed delicacies by others.   It will be remembered
that the unfortunate Greely and his companions, during
their terrible sufferings in the Arctic regions, had to sustain
life for weeks on small shrimps, or sea-fleas ; and many a
shipwrecked mariner has been glad to gather limpets and
mussels to appease his hunger.

Along the shores of Great Britain and Ireland the herring,
'Bonnie fish and halesome farin',' holds the first place
among the fisheries, and many hundreds of boats are
employed in this industry on the east and north coasts
of Great Britain, Ireland, and the Isle of Man.   In the
latter interesting little island the herring is, or was, the
staple food of the people, and the chosen emblem of
justice, the *deemsters* or judges taking the singular oath
that they will administer justice as evenly ' as the backbone
of the herring lieth in the middle of the fish.' *

In Cornwall, the herring gives place to its first cousin,
the pilchard, a smaller and fatter fish, from which a large
quantity of oil is extracted.   These pilchards, when cured
as herrings, are known as 'fair maids,' and are largely
exported to Italy and the south of France, where they
are eaten by the peasantry during Lent.   The pilgrims
who visit Rome during Holy Week, and whose feet are
washed by the noble ladies and gentlemen of the Eternal
City, are all feasted (?) upon a dish of salad, with one of

* The vast consumption of herrings in olden times may be judged
from the fact that the tax levied upon almost all seaports, in the reigns
of the early kings, consisted of from 50,000 to 100,000 herrings annually.

these pilchards on the top, and a roll of bread, not very substantial fare after a long and toilsome pilgrimage.

It is very interesting to see the process of curing the pilchards. As soon as the laden boats arrive, the fish are carried in baskets up the steep streets of the Cornish fishing-towns, where cellars exist devoted to this especial use; in these cellars semicircles are drawn on the floor, in accordance with the quantity of fish brought in; within these the fish are piled, all the heads outwards, making a heap as high as the fish belonging to each boat will allow, some heaps being three, or four, or even ten times as large as others; then gentle pressure is applied to the mass in order to express the oil, which runs, by means of grooves in the stone floor, into barrels placed to receive it. After this the fish are taken up and salted into barrels for export, the oil also being a valuable product.

Herrings are salted at once into barrels in Ireland, and Dublin Bay herrings are highly esteemed; but at Yarmouth and in Scotland they are rather differently cured, some being converted into the famous bloaters, whilst others are split open and put into a ham pickle, and sold as kippers, and others more heavily salted, smoked, and dried, become the palatable red herrings, or Digby chicks. Unfortunately, of late years many badly-cured herrings have been placed on the London Market under the name of Yarmouth bloaters; these consist of fish cured in London, being those fresh herrings remaining unsold, and already a little tainted before being salted, so that it has become almost impossible to obtain bloaters in perfection except in Norfolk and Suffolk.

Next to herrings, probably whiting and mackerel are

the most numerous fish met with on our coasts; but large quantities of mackerel are now brought from Norway, as well as cod and salmon. Cod has an immense consumption, and during Lent many tons of salted cod may be seen in the fishmongers' shops. This, when not *too* salt, and served with plenty of egg sauce and parsnips, is not to be despised, and is still eaten by the orthodox on Ash Wednesday and Good Friday, as it used to be by our forefathers, although there is great laxity in our day, and we often find fresh cod or even salmon, substituted for the ancient Lenten dish. We do not often see now the dry salt cod, which used to be sold so cheaply tied up in bundles. It is probably still consumed by sailors and fishermen, and can be purchased at Billingsgate and other fish markets, but it has been quite superseded by the wet fish in the fishmongers' shops.

The red mullet, so greatly esteemed by the Romans, who gratified their æsthetic taste by having it brought alive to table that they might watch the lovely changing colours produced during the death struggle, and did not object to give from £15 to £60 apiece for them, according to size, is still considered a delicacy, and is too scarce ever to become food for the million. The same may be said of almost all flat fish, although plaice, brill, and flounders are usually tolerably cheap; but soles and turbot, which may be regarded as the kings of sea fish, remain scarce and dear. It is related that the Emperor Domitian called the Senate together to decide how a turbot of extraordinary size should be cooked, and the grave senators decided that it should be boiled, which our modern taste also approves as the best way of cooking it.

Aquariums have given us an opportunity of studying the graceful movements of fish, and especially of flat fish, which, from their burrowing propensities, are rarely seen in their natural state. It is most interesting to watch them in an aquarium rising to the surface with that beautiful undulatory motion, which reminds one of the flight of a bird, and then sinking to bury themselves in the sand, or to rest on the surface, when their colouring so exactly resembles the sand and pebbles upon which they lie that it is difficult to distinguish them. Once at the aquarium at Southport I was highly interested and amused by the curiosity exhibited by the soles. It was evening, and the electric light was exhibited for the first time, whereupon the soles sat up on their tails one behind the other, reminding one of Indian pictures of the cobra, evidently astonished at the light and the moving multitude. Their attitude was ludicrous, but it showed an amount of intelligence for which we are slow to give fish credit. Flat fish, from their burrowing habits, are rather difficult to procure, a trawl net being required for their capture; and the use of this trawl net is much resented by orthodox fishermen, for not only does it gather all sorts and sizes of fish, but it cuts through the herring and mackerel nets, and drives the shoals of herrings away.

We must not omit to mention the useful haddock, St. Peter's fish, still retaining, it is said, the marks of the apostle's thumb, when he opened its mouth to take therefrom the piece of tribute money. 'Finnon haddies' are prime breakfast fish, but the majority of those sold in London are only surplus fresh haddocks, slightly salted and smoked, and do not possess the flavour of the Scotch-cured 'haddies.' Another very good breakfast fish is the gurnet, or gurnard, which, cut open and broiled, with a little pepper, salt, and butter added, makes a capital dish. The ugly John Dory, which shares with the haddock the honour of being St. Peter's fish, is seldom seen now, but is excellent eating. The imperial sturgeon, formerly reserved for royal personages, is sometimes seen in the modern fish-market, but it is not generally esteemed, the flesh resembling veal with a fishy flavour; nevertheless, the ancient Romans thought it such a delicacy, that the servants bringing it to table were crowned with wreaths of flowers. The Russian dainty, *caviare*, is prepared from the roe of the sturgeon.

The salmon, the king of fish, is caught in the chief rivers of Scotland and Ireland, and in some of those in England, that of the Severn being particularly delicate; but great quantities now come from Norway, where it is so plentiful that tourists get tired of seeing it brought to table at every meal. It seems formerly to have been equally abundant in England, as many of the indentures of apprentices contained a clause to the effect that they were not to be obliged to eat salmon more than three days a week: now they would be only too glad to be allowed it once a week. Next to the salmon the trout is the most delicate of river fish, but there is a species of trout called the char, found only in certain lakes in Westmoreland, which is considered by many superior to both salmon and trout; the flesh is of a lovely pink colour, and the flavour delicious. Tradition asserts that this fish was introduced into Britain by the Romans. It is, however, very scarce, and, being too delicate for transport, is only eaten in perfection near the lakes in which it is found, although it is sometimes to be

bought potted. Let me advise all who may visit Winder-
mere to taste this very delicious fish. There is a species
of trout much esteemed, and which probably resembles the
char, found in the lakes of the Tyrol. Travelling in this
region, *en route* to Ober-Ammergau, and arriving at a little
village inn about the time of *mittag's essen* (*i.e.*, dinner at
12.30 P.M.), we ordered a dish of these trout (*forellen*),
which we saw others eating, and a dish of cutlets; but it
happened to be a fast-day, and mine host was a good
Catholic, so, although there was a dispensation for travellers
to Ober-Ammergau, we were told we might have either
fish *or* flesh, but not *both*, a difficulty which was overcome
by ordering fish for half our party and cutlets for the others,
and then dividing the spoils. One of the most picturesque
sights I remember to have seen was that of a Tyrolese
peasant spearing fish on a very lonely lake among the
Dolomite Mountains. He stood in a very small boat,
holding aloft a trident, which he darted into the fish, and,
drawing it out of the water still writhing on the trident,
offered it to us for a small coin.

Some of my readers who have, like myself, long passed
the season of youth, will remember how, in our juvenile
days, the more sophisticated of our fellows used to try to
puzzle our infantine intellect by a jangling rhyme having
the semblance of Latin, which ran thus :—

> Infirtaris inoaknonis,
> Inmudeelsare inclaynoneis ;

and in this way we learnt two very useful scraps of knowledge, viz., that tar was obtained from fir trees and not from
oaks, and that eels might be found in mud, but not in clay.
But there are eels and eels, and the great conger, the head

of the clan, instead of hiding himself timidly in a mud bank, swims boldly about in the ocean, and lays him down to rest fearlessly on a rocky shelf, in sight of other fishes, most of which are too weak to attack him and drive him from his chosen resting-place. It is only of late years that the conger has found a place among edible fishes in England, although credited with forming the chief ingredient in turtle soup; but on the Continent it has long been valued, especially for imparting richness to soups and gravies. There is, however, a *soupçon* of danger in the delicacy, for our medical works recognise a special poison appertaining to the conger, which sometimes produces a disease resembling cholera, although it may usually be eaten with impunity. This applies also to other fish, and may probably be referred to unwholesome food on the part of the fish, which is certainly the case with oysters living near the mouths of rivers, the waters of which are contaminated with lead or other minerals.

But in South Africa the eating of a dried fish known as snoek produces a curious effect, causing the face to swell as though there existed an epidemic of mumps. This, it is believed, is due to the fish having been hung up to dry in the moonlight. Men of science are slow to believe in lunar influence, but in this case it appears to be a well-known fact which seems deserving of investigation.

There are a great number of kinds of eels beside the conger sold in the market, most of which come from Holland, and it is calculated that each vessel will bring over from 15,000 to 20,000 lbs. of live eels; but eels are also found in most of the English rivers, and during the cold months they bury themselves in the mud of the river banks. People in Somersetshire find out their hiding-places by observing that the hoar frost is absent in certain spots, and, digging there, find them in great numbers. In America they are taken by spears thrust into the mud. Eels are generally believed to migrate to the sea in the autumn, and to return to the rivers in the spring, but, from their being so frequently found hibernating in mud banks during the winter, it is evident they do not all go out to sea.

A gentleman kept some eels in a walled garden near Montrose for several years, and noticed that they always became very restless about August, trying to get out of the pond whenever it overflowed, and were always found travelling in the direction of the sea. The eels lay torpid during the winter, but became voracious in the spring, one swallowing as many as twenty-seven large worms at a meal. The eel would seem a singular kind of pet, yet we read in Ellis's book on the South Seas that a chief of Otaheite had a pet eel, which would come to the surface when he whistled for it, and feed out of his hand.

The lamprey strongly resembles the eel, but belongs to a different class. It is not often seen in the market now, but was formerly considered a great delicacy; and it will be remembered that King Henry I. died from the effects of eating too many of them. The Severn is famous for lampreys, and Pennant says that it is an ancient custom in the city of Gloucester to present the Sovereign annually with a lamprey pie, covered with a large raised crust.* The Thames formerly supplied a million or more lampreys to Dutch fishermen for bait.

* In 1341, £12, 5s. 8d. was paid to the Sheriff of Gloucester for forty-four lampreys for the king.

The most remarkable of the eel tribe is the *gymnotus*, or electric eel, a native of tropical America, which has the faculty of imparting a very powerful electric shock to anyone touching it.   Humboldt wrote that this creature was caught by driving horses into the water to receive the shock, after which they are for a time powerless, but his account has not been verified.   One of these electric eels was kept for many years in a tank in the old Polytechnic Institution.   Some of the species may still sometimes be seen in aquariums.

Turning from these wriggling semi-serpents to edible crustacea, we find a large number of shell-fish to a certain extent resembling each other, but varying in size from the great crab, lobster, and crayfish—weighing several pounds, to the tiny shrimp—all excellent eating, although condemned by physicians as unwholesome.

The aquarium has revealed to us a great deal with regard to these as well as to other denizens of the 'vasty deep,' and it is a most amusing and interesting sight to watch two lobsters stalking, with measured strides, on their toes across the sand of their tank, and sitting down opposite to each other in a threatening attitude, each apparently waiting for the other to commence hostilities, and both being too lazy to begin; whilst the frisky little shrimps go darting through the water at full speed as though bound on an errand of life or death.   The fishermen at Gordon Haven say, according to Mr. Peach, that they have often seen the old lobsters with their young ones playing around them, and that when they have found themselves watched, the mother lobster would give a danger-signal by rattling her claws, whereupon they would all rush to shelter under the rocks.

Almost all these crustacea change colour in boiling—a fact now known to everybody, but we have probably all heard the story of the great artist who, in painting the miraculous draught of fishes, took his models from the fishmonger's shop, and, all unconsciously, painted his lobsters red. Upon his error being pointed out to him he coolly exclaimed, 'That makes it all the greater miracle.'

It is also well known that all these crustacea cast their shells, and just before and after this performance they are soft and watery, and so unfit to eat; but the hermit crab never possessed a shell on the hinder part of the body, so he requisitions disused shells of various species of molluscs, and uses them as his habitation, changing from time to time as need or inclination dictates.

Among molluscs we find many dainty morsels, the prime favourite being the oyster. Nothing can exceed the delicate flavour of a 'Whitstable native,' but, unfortunately, notwithstanding the laudable efforts of the late Frank Buckland to preserve and cultivate this oyster, it continues scarce and dear, 'natives' which come from beds at Whitstable, Rochester, Melton, Colchester, Burnham, and a few other places, being seldom, if ever, to be had under half-a-crown a dozen. There are, however, other kinds, such as the Anglo-Dutch, which are brought from abroad and laid down in English waters, which are cheaper, and fairly good; and, of late, deep sea oysters, in great, rough, heavy shells, but of good flavour, have been sold as low as sixpence a dozen. We get also great numbers of cheap American oysters— blue points—relished by some people, but the flavour of which does not commend itself to palates used to English 'natives.' There are such vast beds of oysters on the shores of some of our Colonies—notably at the Cape—that we cannot help thinking a great industry might be developed in exporting them to Europe.   Even in days when travelling was so slow that it probably took longer for vessels to come from Italy to Britain than it now does from the Cape, the Romans contrived to transport the highly-prized British oyster to gratify the palate of Roman epicures; and Juvenal speaks of the taste of one who—

> ' At the first bite each oyster's birthplace knew,
> Whether a Lucrine or Circæan he'd bitten,
> Or one from Rutupinian deeps in Britain.' *

The fact is the ancients were not only greater epicures than the moderns, but took much more trouble than we do to gratify their tastes.   In many respects this was a decided gain to the community, for it led to the acclimatisation of various animals and plants; and in the case of fish, not only were they transported long distances, but they were much more carefully preserved in ponds and lakes than at present. It is even said that Lucullus had a canal cut through a mountain in the neighbourhood of Naples, that fish might more easily be transported to his villa, whilst many noble Romans seem to have kept fish as pets.   It is related that the daughter of Drusus adorned one of her finny pets with rings of gold ; whilst Hortensius, the orator, wept at the death of a turbot which he had fed with his own hand.

Coming down to mediæval times, we find fishponds

---

* It is to the Romans we are indebted for the discovery of our native oyster, for antiquaries are agreed that it formed no part of the dietary of the Britons prior to the Roman occupation, so that whenever oyster shells are found in the excavation of tombs or habitations, the remains discovered are relegated to Roman or post-Roman times.

attached to every monastery. The pilgrim adorned his hat with the scallop-shell, the reason for which practice is rather obscure : it seems probable that it was taken in the first place as a useful article, a substitute for a plate or spoon, in which doles of various kinds might be received, and that it afterwards became the badge of pilgrimage, especially to the shrine of St. James of Compostella ; and it is a curious fact that even at the present day, oyster eating commences in London on St. James' Day, when the children collect the shells to form a grotto or shrine, in which they burn a candle in honour of the saint, and solicit alms from the passers-by, the contribution being received in an oyster shell. The scallop is not so delicate in flavour as the oyster, but is more substantial, and, fried in egg and bread crumbs, is not to be despised ; neither are those plebeian delicacies—periwinkles, cockles, and whelks—sold so largely on barrows in the London streets, so many of the latter piled on shells, with vinegar and pepper *ad libitum* for a penny.

It would seem that in the fourteenth century, whale, porpoise, and grampus were sold as fish, large prices being paid for slices of these creatures during Lent, and one of the Harleian manuscripts contains a recipe for making ' puddynge of porpoise.'

CHAPTER XI

'NECESSITY knows no law,' says the proverb, and starvation will cause people to eat anything, but nothing short of that would induce the average English man or woman, to partake of some of the dishes which foreigners relish. There are, however, some who are ready to experiment upon anything and everything presented to them in the shape of food. The late Dr. Buckland made soup of the bones of extinct animals, and his son, Mr. Frank Buckland, tasted every animal he could get at from the Zoo, and induced some of the members of the Zoological Society to join him in his 'feast of reason,' although it is doubtful whether the 'flow of soul' was quite up to that which would have followed a feast of turtle, oysters, etc., followed by mutton, beef, and game. And yet there seems no reason why turtle should occupy the proud position it enjoys, whilst we reject the land tortoise its near relation, and why oysters should be prized and snails rejected.

In eating and drinking there is a great deal of fashion and prejudice. We know that during the siege of Paris the Parisians were reduced to the necessity of eating all the animals in the Jardin des Plantes, as well as 'rats and mice and such small deer,' and since then they have retained a fondness for horseflesh, to which we have never yet attained, although, as we know, it has been eaten from time imme-morial by the Tartars; whilst hunters in Africa, as well as natives, highly appreciate the meat of the zebra or quagga, and that of the donkey is said to be superior to both; but, if placed upon the London market, in all probability all three of these kindred meats would be allowed to rot unpurchased. In like manner the porcupine is esteemed a delicacy in South Africa, but its next-of-kin here, the hedgehog, is only eaten by gipsies. The eel, and even the great conger, is eaten with relish; but the snake, which is said to be good and wholesome, is regarded with horror and loathing by men rendered squeamish by civilisation.

The lordly elephant is made to contribute his quota of food to his pursuers, the foot being the tit-bit; but the lion and tiger, being carnivorous, are not appreciated by civilised man any more than the shark, the eagle, the vulture, and many other birds of the air, beasts of the earth, and fishes of the great sea, which are greedily devoured by savages. Even the hyæna is eaten by the Bushmen, although it is so hated by them that every one passing the carcase gives it a blow with a whip or stick.*

The whale and the seal are highly appreciated by the Greenlanders and Eskimos, although hunger alone would cause them to be relished by ourselves. Yet a whale or a good fat seal would have saved the lives of many an Arctic voyager, and the eagerness with which Greely and his

* Miss Gordon Cumming tells us that the Veddahs 'never eat elephant, buffalo, or bear, though squirrels, mongooses and tortoises, kites and crows, owls, rats, and bats are highly esteemed; while a roast monkey, or a huge, hideous iguana-lizard, is an ideal dainty.' —'Two Happy Years in Ceylon,' vol. ii., p. 91.

K

starving followers hunted foxes and the great Polar bears, shows how hunger will whet the appetite; and certainly, if the choice lay between old boots, skins, and candle ends, and a seal steak, or piece of whale, there is no doubt which would be taken.. We are told 'the seal, when young, is excellent, and as a material for soup is quite equal to the hare; while the skin of any of the *Cetacea*, especially that of the whalebone whale, if boiled down to a jelly, is a dish fit "to set before a king." It is often sent in hermetically-closed tins from Greenland to Christian IX., of Denmark, and therefore has in reality that destination.'

When, however, we turn to countries where food is plentiful, we are surprised at the singularities of taste in the choice of viands. Take, for instance, China, with its fatted dogs, its bird-nest soup, and trepang, all of which seem to us disgusting, yet doubtless had we been bred in China we should have esteemed them delicacies, as the Chinese do. There is no reason why dogs should not be good eating when well and carefully fed; but we from time immemorial have made of them such pets and companions that to eat them would seem like cannibalism. As to the birds' nests, they are of a peculiar kind, made of a gelatinous substance, and might probably be esteemed a delicacy by ourselves, were they not too scarce for export. Rats and mice are also relished by the Celestials, and in the account of the astonishing escape from death of some entombed miners in America, we read that they managed to preserve life by catching and eating the rats which came to prey upon them. This was, of course, a case of dire necessity; but an African traveller tells of a little Bushman, who picked up the mice which had been caught, and after putting them in the hot ashes for a few moments, devoured them greedily half-raw, entrails and all.

There is no one in England so poor as to eat these rodents willingly, but we remember hearing a French gentleman relate how, during the siege of Paris, he and his companions were attracted by a savoury smell in a restaurant, and determined *coûte qui coûte* to satisfy their hunger with the appetising delicacy. Upon paying a good round sum they secured the dish, and learnt with surprise that they had partaken of a ragôut of rats. This was, of course, an exceptional dish; but the French habitually indulge in some viands which we despise, as, for instance, frogs. Of these, the hind legs only are taken, skinned, and the claws twisted together. In this form they resemble delicate little lamb cutlets, and are, as we can testify, extremely palatable. Then, all along the sea coasts of France and Italy may be seen the octopus occupying a place in the fishermen's baskets, and often boiled in cauldrons of oil in the streets, and taken out to be offered for sale to the passer-by, always with the recommendation, 'It is *good, very good;*' and, indeed, it smells good, and is said to enter largely into the savoury soups at the hotels.

Again, in the south of France and Italy you see people eating with relish the sea urchin, brought to table, like oysters, in the shell, and scooped out with a spoon. Having purchased some of these to bring home as curiosities, I could not induce the natives to believe I did not want to eat them, so they invariably cut and trimmed them for table, thus spoiling them as specimens. The *trepang* of the Chinese, consisting of the sea cucumber dried, most probably strongly resembles these sea urchins in flavour.

We have left to the last a favourite French and Italian
dish, namely *snails*—in French *escargots*—which several
writers have lately been advocating both as food and
medicine. It would seem from these articles, that snails
and slugs are still sought and eaten in some parts of
Wiltshire, being in season only when dormant during the
winter, when they are taken, soaked in salt and water, and
grilled on the bars of the grate. Probably they are quite as
good as the periwinkle, so greedily devoured by those who
would look upon the snail with disgust, and who would
reject a dish of spring cabbage, because a careless cook had
allowed a slug to remain ensconced in the leaf upon which
it had been feeding when consigned to the pot.

Snails and slugs—especially the latter—are supposed to
be particularly efficacious as a remedy in consumption,
being not only eaten, but also crushed and rubbed on
the chest and back, and we have known this snail juice
extolled as superior to cod-liver oil. In France the
escargots are dried and prepared as a lozenge for coughs.
It would appear, according to the writer of a very interesting article on the subject in the *Standard*, that ' in several
parts of England snails are regularly eaten ; not, it is true,
as an ordinary article of diet, but at stated feasts, and
considerable quantities are collected round London and
exported to France.' But the same writer adds :—'The
Latin people are its principal friends, whilst it is rejected
by all Scandinavian and Teutonic peoples. The Romans
were its especial patrons. Not content with eating it
stewed in every form, they fattened it in "*cochlearia*,'
or styes, meal boiled in wine being regarded as the food
best fitted for producing large and juicy specimens. How

successful they were, may be inferred from the fact—if fact it be—that some of the shells of these domesticated snails would hold a pint of wine. But the trade in them is perhaps better than ever it was during the palmy days of Roman luxury. In the neighbourhood of Dijon, a small farmer has been known to clear £300 per annum from snails, the vine growers keeping them in dry cellars, or in trenches under coverings of leaves and earth; and from certain *escargotières* near Ulm, in Würtemburg, no fewer than ten millions of the vineyard snails are sent every year to other gardens to be fattened before they are dispatched for the use of the Austrian convents during Lent. From Troyes it has been calculated that snails to the value of £20,000—the wholesale price being 4s. per hundred —are forwarded to the Paris markets. Packed in casks, they are also exported in a small way to the United States.'

Would it not pay Cape Colonists to institute ' *cochlearia* ' of the great Tiger snail for the French or Portuguese markets? Anyone who has passed through the Lisbon fruit market in autumn, must have noticed the huge baskets of snails for sale, and in Madrid and other wealthy Spanish cities as many as fifteen different kinds may sometimes be counted on the slabs of the dealers. In Italy they are equally popular, but no sooner are the Alps passed than the snail begins to disappear from the *menus*, until, by the time Denmark and Sweden are reached, it is never seen on the table.*

* Friends report that, having at Barcelona been served with a very tempting dish, ornamented with large snail shells, they partook of it and enjoyed it greatly, believing the snails to be still in the shells, but after having eaten the savoury morsels, they discovered they had been eating the snails, the shells being empty and used only as garnishing.

Our French neighbours have of late years suffered considerably from a scarcity of *escargots*, for it was found that the sulphate of iron used to destroy the phylloxera, also poisoned the snails, and rendered them wholly unfit for food, so that it became necessary to have snail farms, in order to guarantee them on the market as free from the sulphate, and consequently wholesome. '*Escargots à la mode de Burgogne*' are not to be despised as a food. Stewed in butter, with eggs and savoury herbs, they might well tempt even a prejudiced English palate, but then you must not whisper *snails* to the eater, although snail feasts are still known to the glass-workers of Newcastle. Perhaps in these feasts the snails are conspicuous by their absence ; but in Greece, snails dressed with garlic are still a favourite dish.

Much has been written of late in recommendation of insect food, including caterpillars, cockchafers, ants, and even spiders and wire-worms.* Locusts are certainly much relished in those countries which are subject to their depredations, and we have seen boys in Germany greedily devour the cockchafer alive, first depriving it of its legs and wings, and declaring it was just like a nut. Fried white ants are also highly esteemed in some countries, and the grubs of bees are relished even by Englishmen, but we think some considerable time must elapse before we adopt of free will the articles of diet of which we have been writing. Siege and famine might reconcile us to some of them, but as long

* Kirby and Spence tell us that spiders are eaten by Bushmen and the inhabitants of New Caledonia ; and Reaumur relates that a young lady cracked and ate every spider she came across. Anna Maria Schurman ate them like nuts. Lalande, the astronomer, was equally fond of them ; and a German, immortalised by Rosel, used to spread them on his bread like butter.

as we can get beef, mutton, and pork, eggs, poultry, and game, economists may write and reason as long as they please—they will not induce a score of English men and women to sit down to a dish of snails and caterpillars, frogs or mice; and even horseflesh, which is, we are told, beginning to find its way into the English market, will continue to be regarded by the vast majority as food fit only for dogs and cats.

Nevertheless, our forefathers were certainly less squeamish than we are; they eat the queerest conglomerations, and seasoned their dishes with ambergris and other strange sauces, nor has the taste for odd combinations quite died out from among us, as witness the Scotch haggis and the Cornish pasties, for which a writer in the *Western Antiquary*, after quoting the Cornish saying that 'The devil will not venture into Cornwall for fear of being put in a pie,' gives the following recipes. 'The composition of the Squab-pie, deemed luxurious beyond all others, has been given by an unknown writer in verse, as follows :—

> " Of wheaten walls erect your paste ;
> Let the round mass expand its breast,
> Next slice your apples cull'd so fresh :
> Let the fat sheep supply its flesh :
> Then add an onion's stinging juice—
> A sprinkling—be not too profuse.
> Well mix't these nice ingredients, sure,
> Might gratify an epicure ! "

'The Herby-pie is another peculiar dish, composed of nettles, pepper-cress, parsley, mustard, and spinach, together with thin slices of pork ! Leeks and pilchards form a third sort, and a fourth is filled with goose feet, gizzard, and blood, with raisins, sugar, and apples; a fifth of leeks and bacon, cooled, before eaten, by Cornish cream ; a sixth of mackerel, parsley, and cream. All these, how piquant to the palate of Cornish people especially.'

The same writer gives the following impromptu. 'In a season of scarcity, the attorneys at Quarter Sessions resolved to abstain from eating pasties, and the following epigram was extemporaneously delivered on the occasion :—

> " If the proverb be true that the fame of our pies
> Prevents us from falling to Satan a prey,
> It is clear that his *friends* the attorneys are wise
> In moving such obstacles out of the way." '

The Spanish *olla podrida* seems nearly related to these Cornish pasties. Carli, whose travels are given in Pinkerton's collection, speaks thus of this famous dish :—

' Being come to Cordova, I went to our monastery, where I was forced to be satisfied with the Spanish dish they call Olla Podrida, signifying rotten pot; which name is not improper, for it is an extravagant medley of several things, as onions, garlic, pumkin, cucumber, white beets, a bit of pork, and two of mutton, which, being boiled with the rest, are almost lost. The fathers asked me whether I liked it. I told them it was very fit to kill me, being as I was almost sick, and so weak that I had need of some better restorative than that Podrida, to which I was not used. They put so much saffron in it that, had I not been yellow enough already with my distemper, that alone might have been enough to dye my skin of that colour. It is a great dainty for Spaniards, but a scurvy mess for those that are not used to it.'

All these things are, however, as nothing to some of the dainties enjoyed by the old Romans, who not only feasted upon snails, and the maggots found in old timber, but thought

'A lamb's fat paunch was a delicious treat,'

and revelled upon water rats and stewed sow's teats, which Martial says were prepared by a certain cook with so much art as to appear still full of milk, and upon sucking puppies, which Pliny declared were worthy of being served at a supper for the gods.

Then there were dormouse sausages, of which a quaint writer remarks:—'Petronius delivers us an odd receipt for dressing 'em and serving 'em up with Poppies and Honey, which must be a very Soporiferous Dainty, and as good as Owl Pye to such as want a Nap after Dinner.'*

After such an account of the dainties indulged in by the highly civilised masters of the world, we need not feel any disgust at the taste of the Chinese and Red Indians for dog's flesh, or of the poor Australian savages, who regale themselves upon the larvæ of beetles found in decaying timber, that from the acacia tree being, says Lumholtz, of excellent flavour, in size the thickness of a finger, and glittering white, the taste resembling nuts. The natives roast these larvæ, and also the beetles and wood-lice, but will sometimes eat the larvæ alive.†

It would seem that nothing in the way of food comes amiss to savages; but they do not, as a rule, eat their meat raw. The iguana and its eggs are considered delicacies by the Australians, and so are snakes, which they will hunt fearlessly. Some tribes eat even the poisonous kinds,

* 'The Art of Cookery,' by the author of 'A Journey to London.'
† The aurelias of the silk-worm, as well as the white earth-grub and the larva of the sphynx-moth, are esteemed delicacies in China.

but others content themselves with the non-poisonous, of which the python, being often twenty feet long, makes a splendid meal. The mode of cooking this dainty we have given elsewhere. Lumholtz says of snakes that the meat is white, but dry and almost tasteless, but that the liver is excellent, resembling ptarmigan in flavour.

The natives first eat the fat, which is considered the best part, then the heart, liver, and lungs, and finally the body is divided, after which the backbone is crushed between stones and eaten, every morsel being consumed, and every drop of grease licked up, which reminds one of many European and Asiatic folk-lore stories, in which serpents are cooked and eaten for the purpose of acquiring the language of animals, which in many cases is imparted accidentally to the cook, in the act of sucking a finger which has been burnt by touching the roasted snake, or dipped in the broth in which it has been boiled.

Most savages revel in grease, which they use both externally and internally. We can understand this taste in cold regions, so that the fondness of the Eskimo for whale's blubber and train oil seems justified by the necessity for nitrogenous food; but it seems strange that dwellers in hot climates should also relish oily compounds. Yet, as we have seen, the Australians revel in the fat of snakes, and imagine that when a man is ill, it is because some enemy has stolen his kidney fat; and of the Bushmen in South Africa we are told :—' Occasionally we had an opportunity of presenting our Bushmen friends with an ample supply of grease, and then would follow a scene. The elder personages first helped themselves, smearing their bodies to their heart's content; the children were next treated, until all had changed their rough, weather-beaten exteriors for a glorious shining appearance. Often not contented with this external embalming, they would drink cups of melted fat, and when asked for a reason, the reply was, "Oh, sir, it is so very comfortable (or nice) to smear both in and outside."'* The Bushmen also enjoy locusts greatly, and the writer quoted above gives the following as the method of preparing them :—' Fire being applied to the brushwood, the legs and wings of the locusts were consumed, the bodies dropped in heaps to the ground, and were collected next morning, and having been exposed to dry in the sun on skins, when sufficiently desiccated they were pounded to powder, to be cooked with a little fat, milk, or water. This paste formed a material part of the food of this poor race of human beings.'

In Soyer's 'History of Food' we are given the *menu* of a Roman supper which is worth transcribing: 'First course —Sea hedgehogs, raw oysters, all sorts of shell fish and asparagus. Second course—A fatted pullet, a fresh dish of oysters and other shell fish, different kinds of dates, univalve shell fish, as whelks, conchs, etc., more oysters of different kinds, sea nettles, beccaficos, chines of roebuck and wild boar, fowls covered with a perfumed paste, a second dish of shell fish and purples (a very costly crustacean). Third course—A wild boar's head, fish, a second set of *hors d'œuvres*, chicks, potted river-fish, leverets, roast fowls, and cakes from the marshes of Ancona.'

Here we see several curious combinations, many of the favourite dishes of modern times mixed with others which would now be relished only by Chinese, such as sea hedge-

* 'Memoir of Petrus Borchardus Borcherds, Esq.'

hogs (which, however, are still eaten in Italy), sea nettles, whelks, conchs, and fowls covered with perfumed paste, reminding one of the ambergris and rose water so much used in the last century. After all, we are constrained to see that the tastes of civilised man do not vary much from those of the savage, and that the unappreciated trifles of to-day were highly esteemed by those who, in former ages, were regarded as the most fastidious of epicures.

The feast of Tetuan, described by Hall Caine in the 'Scapegoat,' deserves to be recorded here as showing the strange mixtures still eaten, and the ceremonies observed in Mohammedan countries. First, steaming dishes of meat, in which each plunged his fingers, then a dish of dates, followed by fish in garlic; keskoos covered with powdered sugar and cinnamon; meat on skewers; browned fowls and fowls with olives; flake pastry and sponge fritters; and, in conclusion, three cups of green tea as thick and sweet as syrup. After which a washing of hands, and fumigating of garments with scented wood burnt in a brass censer.

CHAPTER XII

THE proverb that 'hunger is the best sauce' is, like many other proverbs, trite, and true to a certain extent, for a starving man would not ask for pepper and mustard to make his meat relish, although he probably would look for a little salt, that being Nature's own condiment, lavishly provided, and grateful alike to the palate of man and beast. Nevertheless, there are tribes of savages in various parts of the world who did not use salt until it was introduced among them by Europeans, and never felt the want of it; although many semi-civilised tribes have adopted various condiments, the most common being the betel, which is a species of pepper, universally chewed by the Malays of all ages, and by the inhabitants of almost all the East Indian islands, where it is regarded as one of the necessaries of life. Slices of the Pinang or Areca nut are wrapped in a betel leaf, previously sprinked with *chunam*, or quicklime, and chewed, causing the gums and lips to assume a bright red hue, and the teeth to become black. The ingredients for this indulgence are carried about everywhere—the rich possessing boxes of silver and gold, whilst the poor man has the same articles in a brass box, or mat bag—and the betel box is invariably offered to a guest, as the snuff-box used to be among ourselves.

In South America the coça plant is substituted for the

betel, and is also chewed with lime, and carried about in curiously-carved boxes. In both hemispheres this custom is of immense antiquity.

Amongst ourselves the coça, in the form of cocaine, has recently come greatly into use in medicine, being of great value as a local anæsthetic; but it was first heard of in the form in which it is used in South America, the leaves being chewed for their sustaining properties. As to the betel, we seldom use it in England, its place being supplied by the pepper of commerce, which, in its three forms of pepper-corns, ground black pepper, and white pepper, has become a requisite, no dish of meat, and scarcely any of vegetables, being properly seasoned without it. Many people fancy that white pepper is quite different from black, but it is in reality the same, being prepared from the black pepper-corn deprived of its outer husk.

Cayenne pepper, so useful in highly-seasoned dishes, is made from the ground fruit or seed pods of different kinds of capsicums, some of which are yellow and others red, which accounts for the difference in the colour of the pepper. Next to the pungent peppers, all of foreign origin, comes the old English condiment, mustard, used for centuries as a seasoning for roast beef.*

'Good Master Mustard-seed,' says Bottom in the 'Midsummer Night's Dream,' 'I know your patience well: that same cowardly, giant-like ox-beef hath devoured many a gentleman of your house: I promise you, your kindred hath made my eyes water ere now.'

⁓ * Coriander seed was considered by the Romans to be like mustard, strengthening and digestive, and was used with vinegar to keep meat fresh.

This would seem to prove that mustard as a condiment for roast beef was in common use in Shakespeare's time; but it was probably used then coarsely pounded, for we are told that mustard in its present finely-powdered form, was introduced by a Mrs. Clements, of Durham, about the year 1729, and was hence known as Durham mustard. We sometimes think that a return to the old form—that is, the genuine seed coarsely pounded—would be preferable to the frequently adulterated article which now often appears at table. The French make their mustard with tarragon vinegar, which renders it more agreeable to some palates. Horse-radish is another English condiment largely consumed with the national roast beef, but accidents have from time to time occurred from the likeness of the root to the poisonous aconite or monk's-hood. The leaves of the two plants are, however, so very distinct, that they cannot be mistaken the one for the other when growing.

The adaptation of certain herbs and sauces as condiments to particular meats dates from very early times. The Paschal lamb was to be eaten with bitter herbs. What these herbs were is not definitely known, but mint, which is still the favourite condiment for lamb, was perhaps one, since we find it mentioned, with rue, and all manner of herbs, as being tithed by the Pharisees. Mint sauce and gooseberry sauce are the appropriate condiments for lamb. Red currant jelly and tomato sauce, and sometimes that very dirty-looking seaweed known as laver, are eaten with roast mutton, and caper sauce with boiled; whilst on veal we bestow a forcemeat composed of various herbs, such as thyme, parsley, marjoram, savory, basil, lemon peel, pepper, salt, a soupçon of onion and mace or nutmeg, suet, and bread crumbs—which same forcemeat we use for turkeys and other poultry. With game we serve bread sauce; whilst pork, ducks, and geese are considered properly dressed with a seasoning of sage and onions, and apple sauce.

These are the chief of old English condiments, used from time immemorial; and it is only of late years that these things have been supplemented by the highly-flavoured Indian curries and chutneys, and by a variety of piquant sauces with names sufficient to make our grand-mothers' hair stand on end. Our schools of cookery have made us familiar with aspic, béchamel, consommé, maitre d'hôtel sauce, mayonnaise, sauce piquante, and a variety of other names which glide smoothly from the tongue of the initiated, but are meaningless to those who have not studied in the modern schools.

Nevertheless, our forefathers were as highly appreciative of spices as we are, and those who could afford them, used them perhaps more than we do. We learn from Chambers's 'Book of Days' that the arrival of a ship laden with spices 'was an event of such importance, and perhaps rarity, that the King usually hastened to satisfy his wants before the cargo was landed. Thus, in the reign of Henry III., the bailiffs of Sandwich were commanded to detain, upon their coming into port, two great ships laden with spices and precious merchandise which were exported from Bayonne, and not to allow anything to be sold until the King had had his choice of their contents.' At that time vegetables were scarce, but pot-herbs, such as parsley, mint, purslane, fennel, smallage, thyme, and hyssop, are mentioned, and also lettuce, celery, beetroot, and small white onions; some of which were eaten raw, with olive oil and spices. Thus we find that salads were in use in the fifteenth century, but are somewhat surprised to find olive oil mentioned, as even to the present day it is very little used in England, except among those who have travelled much on the Continent.

The spices known in the reign of Henry III. were of course those of the East Indies—cinnamon, nutmeg (with its outer network, known as mace), cloves, pepper, and ginger; and to these must be added the most important of all condiments, which has come to be regarded, not as a luxury, but a necessity—that is, sugar, which Strabo tells us was found in the East Indies by Nearchus, Admiral of Alexander the Great, 325 B.C.

Pliny speaks of sugar as an article of merchandise brought from Arabia and India used only as medicine. He describes it as 'honey collected from canes, gum-like at first in appearance, but which becomes whitish and brittle when dry.' There is a passage in Isaiah which runs, 'Thou hast bought me no sweet cane with money,' which would seem to prove that the sugar-cane was an article of commerce in Judea also at an early date; the sweet cane is likewise mentioned by Jeremiah, who speaks of it as coming from a far country. Paulus Ægineta, writing in the seventh century, calls sugar the Indian salt, being in form and colour like common salt, but in taste and sweetness like honey, and recommends that a piece should be kept in the mouth to moisten it during fevers.

Eleven camels laden with sugar were captured by the Crusaders in 1110, and shortly after this time the cane was grown as a curiosity in Spain and Southern Italy.

The date of its introduction into England seems

L

uncertain, but in 1546 a manuscript letter to Lord Cobham speaks of 'twenty-five sugar loaves at six shillings a loaf, which is eightpence a pound,' the penny at that time being worth much more than at present; and the diary of a lady of Herefordshire at the time of the Civil War, October 29, 1640, has the following entry—'For a pound of shugger to send Mrs. Eaton when her son Fitz-Wm. lay on his death-bed, 20*d*.'

If we compare this with the importation of sugar at the present day, and the price per pound, we shall realise the enormous growth in the consumption of this condiment since its cultivation in the West Indies.

In 1887 the importation of sugar to the United Kingdom reached the enormous total of 1,080,590 tons, and this was rather under the quantity consumed in the two previous years. With these figures before us it seems hard to realise that there was a time when sugar was unknown, its place being supplied by honey, which has now sunk into a subordinate position; but we see also how extremely important must have been the keeping of bees among the ancients, since almost all the sweetness required in cookery was dependent upon the productive industry of these little insects. The Egyptians sent boats laden with bees up the Nile to enable the industrious insects to fill their combs from the flowers near its banks. The Greeks celebrated the honey of Mount Hymettus, and even to the present day this honey is highly prized, and the modern Greeks use it, as probably their ancestors and the ancient Egyptians used it, mixed with flour and oil in the manufacture of pastry.

Honey, says Soyer, was the basis of the seasoning of

Apicius, and Pythagoras, who ate only bread and honey, lived to be ninety; and we are told 'whoever wishes to preserve his health should eat, every morning before breakfast, young onions with honey.' Honey, indeed, seems to have entered into every sauce among the Romans, and mixed with mustard was served as a condiment with brawn, but it was also freely used formerly in British cookery.

The anonymous author of 'The Art of Cookery' says—

> ' Our fathers most admired their Sauces sweet,
> And often ask'd for Sugar with their meat;
> They butter'd Currants on fat Veal bestowed,
> And rumps of Beef with virgin Honey strew'd.' *

Olive oil was almost as important as honey in ancient cookery, but it was not the only oil used, for Horace gives the recipes for two sauces of the Romans as follows :—

> ' Two sorts of sauce are worthy to be known,
> Simple the first and of sweet oil alone;
> The other, mix'd with rich and generous wine,
> And the true pickle of Byzantian brine,
> Let it, with shredded herbs and saffron boil,
> And when it cools pour in Venafran oil.'

Brine was water in which bay salt had been dissolved, but we read also of herring and anchovy brine, and of that remarkable compound garum, made of the semi-putrid intestines of fish, put into a vessel with much salt, and exposed to the sun till fermentation began, after which wine was sometimes added, and it was filtered through willow baskets, and kept for use. The best and most expensive garum was made of the liver of the red mullet.

The sauce of Apicius was thus compounded :—' Mix

---

* Nor must it be forgotten that among the ancients honey was frequently used in embalming the dead, and coffins full of honey are still sometimes found.

with honey ½ oz. pepper, 3 scruples eschalots, 6 scruples cardamum, 1 scruple spikenard, and 6 scruples mint, add vinegar, and pour in some garum.' And the same *chef* gives us a stomachic condiment in which garum figures : 'Mix carefully some pine nuts, pepper, benzoin, mint, dried raisins and dates, with fresh unsalted cheese, vinegar, oil, honey, and wine, reduced by boiling to one half; add garum.'

Vinegar appears to have been used as a beverage in ancient Rome, and to have been commonly served at banquets, probably mixed with water. The extravagance of Cleopatra, in dissolving her splendid pearl earring in vinegar and drinking it, is frequently quoted, but this is not a solitary instance of wasteful lavishness at Roman banquets; the same story is told of Caligula, and of the son of Æsop the actor, of whom Horace writes :—

> ' An actor's son dissolved a wealthy pearl
> (The precious earring of his favourite girl)
> In vinegar, and thus luxurious quaff'd
> A thousand solid talents at a draught.'

And since our vinegar would certainly not be powerful enough to dissolve pearls, we must suppose that used in Egypt and Rome to have been much more powerful, so that to drink it, even much diluted, must have been anything but agreeable.

One of the English condiments greatly in favour formerly seems to have fallen into disuse except in certain counties, this is saffron, which at one time was used in many sauces and cakes, and appears very frequently in old recipes, but is now seldom used except in Cornwall, where it still forms the flavouring and colouring matter of almost all the cakes.

In modern Greece, mastich is used in the same way to give a pleasant flavour to bread; and in Germany, carraways, aniseed, and pimento are freely used for the same purpose, whilst almost all sweet sauces are flavoured with rum, which is rejected among ourselves in favour of brandy or ratafia. A more recent flavouring, vanilla, the product of a Mexican orchid, has become the prime favourite among French and English cooks.

There are two or three important condiments which come to us from the West Indies. One of these is molasses or treacle, beloved of children, and another, the pimento or allspice; but there is another which is very little known, but which is supposed to form the basis of most modern sauces. This is *casareep*, a dark fluid prepared from bitter *cassava*, which gives both colour and piquancy to the sauce to which it is added. Tamarinds, too, are much used by modern cooks in curries and sauces, and the very hot West Indian pickles are highly esteemed.

Curry-powder, mulligatawny, chutney, and various pickles and preserves from India are now so common, that it is unnecessary to do more than name them, but the following South African condiments may, perhaps, be new to most of our readers.

For *blachang*—to eat with fish or meat—one table-spoonful of powdered chili, one teaspoonful coriander seed pounded, twenty pounded almonds, one baked onion, two cloves of garlic, enough vinegar for proper consistency, and a little salt. For *samball*—peel a cucumber and cut it into pieces two inches long, slice each piece round and round till you get to the seedy part, which throw away. Roll the sliced part into a small roll, and then slice it

again very fine into cold water with a little salt. Let it
stand two hours. Pour boiling water over two onions
sliced as thin as possible ; which also let stand two hours,
then strain off the water from both and squeeze as dry as
possible. Take a teaspoonful of vinegar, a dessertspoonful
of anchovy sauce, cayenne pepper, and a little mustard, mix
together and pour over the onion and cucumber.

To these we may add an old English recipe for making
walnut soy :—Take 120 green walnuts, cut them into slices ;
shalots skinned and sliced, one pound ; salt, a quarter of a
pound. Pound all together in a stone mortar, then put the
mixture into an earthen pan with a pint of vinegar. Cover
it over for a week or ten days, and stir it three or four times
a day. Strain the liquor through a thick flannel bag. By
means of a press, pass it a second time through the bag ;
then put it into a stewpan with a quarter of a pound of the
best anchovies, half an ounce of whole pepper, and a little
sliced ginger. Boil the whole as long as any scum arises,
which must be carefully taken off : then bottle it, and add
of cloves, mace, and nutmeg, each a quarter of an ounce.
Cork, and keep it in a cool, dry place, till fit for use, which
will be in about six months.

Mayonnaise, which is now so much used for salads, fish,
etc., is rather a difficult sauce to manipulate, so that the
following may be useful to amateur cooks :—Beat the yolks
of six eggs with six tablespoonfuls of broth, six tablespoonfuls of best salad oil, one tablespoonful and a half of vinegar,
and a good pinch of salt, in a narrow bowl, until all is well
mixed and smooth. Place the bowl into a pan with boiling
water over a slow fire, beating the mixture briskly with an
egg whisk until it becomes stiffened, so that it can be easily

spread over the salad, taking care that it does not get hard, and that no water boils into it. If more acidity is desired, add some lemon juice.

It would be impossible even to name the innumerable sauces and condiments deemed necessary in the kitchens of the present day to add flavour and piquancy to modern dishes. Instead of the pints of wine and brandy, the ambergris, saffron, and rose water of the last century, we get delicate sauces compounded of a soupçon of a score of different ingredients carefully mixed. There are, however, certain old sauces which have never been superseded, such as mushroom and walnut catsups; and it may be safely asserted that a good housewife, anxious to tickle the palate of her lord and master, and her guests, both male and female, will see that her store-closet is well supplied not only with such universal condiments as salt, pepper whole and ground, vinegar, and mustard, but also with cayenne, ginger, cloves, allspice, cinnamon, garlic, shalots, a large variety of potherbs, especially mint, thyme, sage, marjoram, celery seed and celery salt, chili and tarragon vinegar, curry-powder, chutneys, anchovies and anchovy sauce, tomato, mushroom, and walnut catsups, Worcester sauce, soy, Harvey sauce, almonds, pistachio nuts, and various essences and flavourings such as lemon, ratafia, and vanilla, as well as all kinds of pickles, preserves, and jellies. A tolerably long list, but far from exhaustive; whilst the gardener must be called upon to supply fresh vegetables and salads, and the fishmonger to provide lobsters, shrimps, and oysters for sauces, as, although all three may be kept stored in tins, they are infinitely better fresh.

PART III

VEGETABLES

' Onions will make e'en Heirs or Widows weep.
The tender Lettice brings on softer sleep.
Cornwal Squab=Pye and Devon White=pot brings,
And Leister Beans and Bacon Food of Kings.'

CHAPTER XIII

OF all the fruits of the earth, perhaps nuts are the most important and the most highly appreciated, for every part of the world has one or more, forming a great portion of the food of the people.

Of course, in civilised countries nuts do not hold so important a position as in uncivilised, for with the growth of civilisation comes luxury, and with luxury a variety of food brought from all parts. But in early times nuts were in especial request, as may be seen by referring to almost all archæological discoveries; for wherever pre-historic human remains are discovered in Europe, there the hazel-nut is almost always found. The hazel tree was largely used in divination, and is still employed by those who profess to discover water by means of the divining-rod.

Among the relics of the Swiss lake-dwellers, the beech-nut and the water-chestnut are found, as well as the hazel-nut, all three having been used as food; but the hazel-nuts found among pre-historic relics have probably been used in some sort of religious or superstitious rites, a remnant of which is found in the Hallowe'en festival (October 31), at which time, even now, in many parts of England, Scotland, Ireland, and the Isle of Man (but more particularly in the two latter), when a young girl wishes to know whether her lovers are faithful, she takes three nuts and places them on the bars of the grate, naming two after her lovers and the middle one for herself. If a nut pops and jumps, the lover represented by that nut is unfaithful, but if the nuts named after the girl and her favoured lover burn together, they will be married. Burns's poem on ' Halloween ' describes this country custom so well, that we will quote a couple of verses :—

> ' The auld guidwife's weel-hoordit nits
>   Are round and round divided,
> And mony lads' and lasses' fates
>   Are there that night decided :
> Some kindle couthie, side by side,
>   And burn thegither trimly ;
> Some start awa' wi' saucy pride,
>   And jump out owre the chimlie
>   Fu' high that night.
>
> Jean slips in twa wi' tentie e'e ;
>   Wha 'twas she wudna tell ;
> But this is Jock, and this is me,
>   She says in to hersel :
> He bleezed owre her, and she owre him,
>   As they wad never mair part ;
> Till, fuff ! he started up the lum,
>   And Jean had e'en a sair heart
>   To see 't that night.'

The hazel-nut grows abundantly in woods throughout the British Isles, and it is one of the delights of autumn to form nutting parties, with hooked sticks, to pull down the branches, and bags, to carry home the ripe fruit to store for winter use. The squirrel has taught us that nuts stored underground retain their freshness for a long time, but we may also assure our readers, from observation, that nuts put in an empty jar which has held spirit, and corked tightly, will keep beautifully fresh for months, in a cool place.

The *filbert* is a cultivated variety of the hazel-nut, and so also is the cob-nut, which is extensively grown in Kent, and is the largest kind. But it is not equal in flavour to the filbert, which name is a corruption of the old English name *full-beard*, from the long fringed husk.

Next to the hazel-nut and its varieties—which include the Constantinople nut, the American nut, and those brought over kiln-dried from Spain—the chestnut probably ranks second in importance in Europe as food for man. In Italy and Spain the chestnut groves yield food much appreciated by the lower orders, who not only eat it in its natural state, but also make it into meal; and a pudding made of this meal, under the name of *polenda dolce*, is sold in the streets of Italy, and forms a staple food of the Italian peasants. The sweet chestnut, although it will grow in England, and even in Scotland, and produce eatable fruit, is not largely cultivated at present, although it appears to have been one of the trees introduced by the Romans, for it is found among the relics unearthed at Rushmore by General Pitt-Rivers. The ornamental horse-chestnut, red and white, is one of the best known trees of our parks, and we often wonder that some use has not been found for the abundant nuts it produces, which are too acrid even for the taste of children, who delight in them as playthings. These nuts were formerly used in washing instead of soap, and have lately been made into soap, which is especially useful for coloured garments; and we are told that a portion of the flour of these nuts added to common flour improves its quality.

The walnut, which is very valuable as a timber tree, is also useful in many other ways, the green fruit being used for pickling, and the green outer skin for dyeing, for which purpose the gipsies employed it largely, centuries ago. It is now sometimes used as a hair dye, but the fruit is the product most highly and generally esteemed. It is too well known to need description, but there is one way in which it is prepared on the Continent which might be easily carried out wherever walnuts are abundant. In Italy, they take and peel the fresh walnut, dividing it into quarters, which are stuck on small white sticks and dipped into melted barley sugar. The Venetians treat other fruits, such as the almond and orange, in the same manner, but none equal the walnut in flavour.

The hickory nut, so much talked of in American books, is a species of walnut, but not equal in flavour to the European.

In the early spring the almond forms the chief ornament of our gardens, with its bright pink blossoms on a leafless stem, respecting which Moore writes :—

> ' The hope, in dreams, of a happier hour,
>   That alights on misery's brow
>   Springs out of the silvery almond flower
>   That blooms on a leafless bough.'

The almond does not come to perfection in our cold climate. It is a native of the East, and was considered one of the most important of the products of Palestine. In Rome it was known as the Greek nut. The almond is much used in cookery ; the oil of the bitter almond is a powerful poison, but in very small quantities it is useful for flavouring.

When we journey into tropical regions we find a great many very tough, but extremely valuable, nuts to crack, and first and foremost is the cocoanut, which is the principal food and wealth of the natives of the South Sea Islands, the tree itself (*Cocos nucifera*) serving all the multifarious uses of the household. It forms the timber of the huts, the leaves are used for thatch, the fibre for mats and ropes, the nuts for eating, the shells for drinking and cooking utensils ; the milky juice in the nut forms a pleasant drink, and in the East Indies, toddy and arrack are extracted from the tree.

Latterly the cocoanut has become a favourite ingredient for cakes, puddings, and biscuits, but it always appears indigestible, probably because not used when quite fresh. The oil extracted from the nut has also many uses, but it quickly becomes rancid. Each cocoa palm yields about a hundred nuts, and it may be readily understood that a grove of these trees would be of extreme value in the tropical countries which produce them. Two of these graceful cocoa palms may be seen growing in the gardens of the Duc de Rochefoucault, at Cannes, but, like the other palms, they do not thrive and bear fruit in Europe.

The Brazil nut, although well known as a fruit, is not so much used in this country as the other nuts we have mentioned, and few people are aware that these triangular nuts are the contents of a large outer shell of extreme hardness, which forms a nut as large as a child's head, within which the Brazil nuts of commerce are tightly packed, sometimes to the number of fifteen to twenty or more. Humboldt described this nut as one of the most extraordinary fruits of South America. It grows on a tree 120 feet high, and at the time of ripening the natives dare not enter the woods where they grow without a wooden buckler over the head, lest they should be killed by the falling nuts. The monkeys are said to unite to break the shell with stones, and the Indians hold a feast at the ingathering, which they say is the feast of animals as well as of men. The fall of the ripe nut from so great a height is, it may be supposed, generally sufficient to break it, otherwise it must be a very hard nut to crack even for men ; but, besides the reputed breaking by the Capuchin apes, the *Cavia aguti* is said to be able to gnaw through the shell and eat the nuts.

Another very hard-shelled nut, the butter nut of the West Indies, known locally as the Souari nut, was brought over among the products of. Guiana at the Colonial and Indian Exhibition, and when fresh is a most delicious nut, eating like rich cream, but I suspect that it very frequently becomes rancid when old, otherwise it would seem a fruit well suited for exportation.

The cashew nut, also a product of the West Indies, strongly resembles the walnut, and is much used in flavouring various dishes. In India and the Philippine Islands it is roasted in the husk and eaten with salt, and the husk itself produces an indelible stain used in the manufacture of marking ink, and also for burning warts and ulcers.

The pistachio nut, now so much used, comes to us from Persia and from Western Africa, which is rich in nuts of various kinds, and these nuts, with the oil extracted from them, form a very important branch of commerce. The chief of these are palm nuts and ground nuts, the oil from the latter being often sold as olive oil.

The nut of the poisonous palm, *Cycas media*, is eaten by

the Australian natives, after the kernel has been subjected to much pounding and soaking in water, a process which I have pointed out in Chapter III. as that adopted by many savages in the case of poisonous plants, such as the manioc. The porridge made from these roasted and pounded nuts, which is called *Kadjera*, forms the chief food of the Australian natives from October to December, when other fruits come in.

The acorn, which was formerly eaten in Britain, had to be prepared in the same manner before it could be made palatable, but we are told that acorns were esteemed delicacies among the Arcadians and Spaniards, and Pliny says the latter eat them as dessert, roasted in wood ashes. Acorns, like beech-nuts and horse-chestnuts, are now consigned to pigs, goats, deer, sheep, and poultry.

Next to nuts, we may perhaps place apples as the fruit of greatest value, at all events in temperate climates. In the extreme north the apple is unknown, and in the tropics it is supplanted by more luscious fruits. 'An apple a day keeps the doctor away,' says the proverb, and there can be no doubt that in temperate climes the apple, from its excellent hygienic and keeping qualities, ranks first in usefulness. It has a very extensive range, for it is found apparently wild in Persia and Syria, in Africa, and through-out the continent of Europe. In Great Britain the crab or wild apple is very frequently referred to by old writers, and roasted crabs were always the accompaniment to the Christmas wassail bowl; but when the art of grafting became known the crab was soon supplanted by a great variety of excellent apples brought, probably, in the first place from

M

France, as their names testify, aηd cultivated largely by the monks. It is greatly to. be regretted that these famous old sorts, such as the nonpareil, the rennet, and the codlin, have been allowed to die out or to degenerate, for they are scarcely equalled in flavour by the innumerable varieties of modern times, and it is also matter of regret that English apples should have been supplanted of late years in the London market by foreign consignments, chiefly American, and yet those who have visited the late exhibitions and congresses of fruit-growers would hardly suppose that the cultivation of this favourite old English fruit was on the wane; the innumerable varieties exhibited at the Mansion House in 1890, and at the Horticultural Exhibition this year, and the crowds assembled to gaze upon and admire with longing eyes and watering mouths the juicy fruit displayed, seemed to show a great revival of interest in British apples and pears, but as I overheard a grower remark of some of the splendid fruit exhibited, 'This is all very well for exhibition, but it would not pay to grow, for a tree could not carry a bushel of such fruit;' added to which our uncertain climate always renders fruit of any kind a precarious crop, and a good apple season seldom comes oftener than once in three years, so that we are obliged to resort to America and our colonies to supply the deficiency in years of scarcity, and this so lowers the market price as to render a good crop unprofitable to the English grower, although I believe most housekeepers are willing to pay more for English than for foreign apples, as being of better flavour and more juicy.

The common tradition that the apple was the forbidden

fruit, with which Eve was tempted, shows at all events the pre-eminence of the fruit in the esteem of ancient gastronomers, although the much lamented General Gordon was not only heterodox enough to locate the Garden of Eden in the Seychelle Islands, but also to recognise as the forbidden fruit the great double cocoa-nut, which certainly would have required some assistance, Satanic or other, to break it before eating.

There are several other fruits which bear the name of apple, but which are in no way related to the well-known orchard fruit. First of these comes the pine-apple, grown to perfection by careful cultivation in English hothouses. It is said to have been introduced into England in the reign of Charles II. It was certainly known earlier in Holland, and was probably first brought from America or the West Indies, of which it is supposed to be a native; but it is found also wild in Asia and both on the west and east coasts of Africa, where many varieties are found. Those sold commonly in the streets of London come mostly from the West Indies, but in tinned fruit that from Singapore is the best.

The custard apple which is now frequently met with in fruiterers' shops is a tropical fruit, found in Asia, Africa, and America. There are several species of custard apple; that best known looks somewhat like an artichoke, but when the rind is removed a soft pulp is found which resembles sweet cream with the scent of a rose; this is known as the sweet-sop, whilst another and coarser variety is called the sour-sop, and is said to resemble the black currant in flavour and scent. Two other species of custard apple are sometimes seen, one is the alligator apple, which is a strong narcotic, and the other the cherimoyer, much praised by Humboldt; it is an American fruit, and very little known in England.*

Then there is the mammee apple of the West Indies, which somewhat resembles a large russet apple, the pulp is very delicious and is compared to a fine ripe apricot, but the rind and seeds are bitter and resinous.

The star apple, which is also a West Indian fruit, resembles a large apple externally, but the interior is divided into ten cells, each containing a black seed set in a gelatinous pulp.

The quince, which is regarded by some antiquaries as the golden apple of the Hesperides, resembles a pear in shape, but the common sort grown in our gardens is not eatable raw, although it makes a delicious marmalade, and, in fact, is the origin of the name, as the Portuguese name for quince is *marmelo*. The quince is eaten raw in South Africa and perhaps in China and other eastern countries, but the fruit must be a different variety from that grown in England. The tree is extensively used in France as a stock for grafting pears.

The pear, which botanically is nearly related to the apple, is one of the most delicious fruits grown, and the modern varieties are innumerable, yet in flavour none can excel the old varieties known as *beurries, jargonelles, chaumontelles*, etc., all of which show a French origin. Jersey is now famous for pears, and they are grown of immense size there, as also in many of our colonies, but none seem to attain the

---

* For many particulars relating to fruits and vegetables I am indebted to a little book entitled 'Vegetable Substances used for the Food of Man,' published in 1846.

weight of those seen by Marco Polo in China, which weighed ten pounds each, and were yet of excellent flavour. The Romans are said to have introduced this fruit into England, and it was certainly very anciently cultivated in Greece, for it is named by Homer.

Of apples and their kindred we need only mention further the Siberian crab, which used to be cultivated in its two varieties of yellow and red, chiefly for the beauty of the flowers and fruit, which latter is not of much value except as a preserve. The red variety with the stems attached, lightly boiled in a rich syrup, makes a very ornamental dessert dish, and is well flavoured; but the core is large in proportion to the pulp.

The medlar, like the quince, cannot be eaten as it comes from the tree; but when suffered to decay, the flavour is very fine, and an excellent jelly, resembling guava, may be made from it. The small fruit is much superior in flavour to the large variety, but it is one of those fruits which is less cultivated and esteemed than formerly, having been supplanted by others which now reach our shores from many distant lands.

Apples were formerly much used in old English sports and were always ducked for by the girls and boys on Halloween, causing great merriment and much dabbling in water, which would now be thought hurtful. But there was another sport indulged in, wherein a stick with an apple at one end and a lighted candle at the other being tied up to the ceiling, was jumped at, the lucky jumper catching the apple, whilst the awkward or unlucky, found himself burnt by the lighted candle. The apple also entered into another old superstitious ceremony of Halloween, for it was believed that if a young woman on that night ate an apple in front of a looking-glass, her future husband would appear and look over her shoulder, regarding which custom Burns makes an old grandmother thus reprove her grandchild :—

> ' Ye little skelpie-limmer's face !
> I daur you try sic sportin',
> As seek the foul thief ony place,
> For him to spae your fortune ;
> Nae doubt but ye may get a sight !
> Great cause ye hae to fear it ;
> For mony a ane has gotten a fright,
> And lived and died deleeret,
>   On sic a night.'

CHAPTER XIV

GRAPES, FIGS, AND ORANGES

How is it that we always think of the grape rather as a wine-producer than as a fruit? Perhaps because the earliest historical record of it is when Noah began to be a husband-man and planted a vineyard, and, instead of being content, as so good a man should have been, to eat the fruit of his vines in a rational way, or to press out the pure juice into his cup—as the temperance people, had they then been living, would have persuaded him was the only true wine—he set to work to make experiments, and, as people do under such circumstances, got bemuddled over them, until he did not know exactly what he was about, and hence the vine has been associated with wine, and the juice of the grape with drunkenness, ever since.

And yet the grape as a fruit is excellent, as we all know, and the great luscious bunches which hang in our green-houses are tempting in the extreme; but these are only produced at a cost which puts them beyond the reach of the *million*, and fits them only for a place on the table of the *millionaire*.

In countries where grapes grow with little care, the ripe clusters are gathered and eaten as required, and the rest are thrown into the wine vat, for it is a fruit which will not bear much handling and packing, although of late years it has been found possible to pack the ripe bunches in barrels, filling up the interstices with sawdust or with cork-dust, and thus the London market is supplied all the year round with a fruit always grateful to the palate, especially of invalids, at a ridiculously low price. The best qualities of these foreign grapes seldom exceed a shilling a pound, and they are sometimes to be had for fourpence. Most of these grapes come from Lisbon, but some were sent over from Australia during the Colonial and Indian Exhibition, and arrived in good condition.

It seems a pity that in lands so remote, the superabundant grapes should not be converted into raisins, and sent to us in that form, for grapes *au naturel* are of no use in the kitchen; but the dried grapes, both raisins and currants, are indispensable. Where would be our country's boast, sent all over the world now—the Christmas plum pudding —if we could not get raisins and currants? What dismay there would be amongst our cooks, if the markets of Malaga and Valencia were closed to us! And yet we have seen raisins from Cape Colony and Natal equal to any of these.* Why do they not send us more of them, and of dessert fruit, too,—muscatels dried on the stalk, which, with almonds, blanched or not, are the delight of all children, and not despised by those of more mature age, for we have seen grey-haired men discuss a dish of them with considerable relish, without thinking much of Tommy's disgust at finding the dish empty.

* Two Australian colonies, of which the chief is Mildura in Victoria, have lately been formed for the cultivation and drying of raisins, figs, apricots, peaches, etc., so that we may soon hope to have sun-dried fruit in the market, from the Antipodes.

Greatly as grapes are esteemed and valued, especially by invalids, it would seem possible to have too much of them sometimes, as those know who have been ordered to Meran in the Tyrol, to undergo that celebrated grape-cure, wherein the patient, beginning with a pound or two a day, has to increase the dose to nine or ten pounds, of course eating nothing else. It might be supposed that such a regimen would not only cure the patient of his disease, but would so disgust him with grapes that he would never eat another, but it is said people have been known to return again and again for the grape-cure.

Dried raisins bring us naturally to another favourite dessert fruit—dried Turkey figs, as they are called, although they certainly do not all now come from Turkey, whatever may have been the case originally, but the Smyrna brand is still regarded as the best.

The fig, quite unlike the grape, is grown only as a fruit, and a very delicious fruit it is, too, when ripened under a good hot sun; but in England, although the fig will thrive and bear fruit, it always appears to us wanting in flavour and in lusciousness. Singularly enough, the fig tree will flourish and grow to an immense size, even in the dirt and smoke of London. There is one house, close to the Foundling Hospital, which is covered to the very top with a fig tree of most luxuriant growth, but I have never seen any fruit upon it. The fig tree is said to have been first introduced into England by Cardinal Pole, but it was probably known here long before his day, for there are many historical fig trees, and one is spoken of as an old tree in the time of James I.; it grew in the Dean's garden, Winchester, and bore small red figs, and on the stone wall near was an inscription to the effect that in 1623 King James I. tasted of the fruit with great pleasure. We, however, certainly do not much relish the ripe fig in this country; it has, in fact, passed into a term of contempt— 'I don't care a fig for it.' But very different is the estimation in which it is held in the East, and in the south of Europe. The constant references to it in the Bible prove how important it was considered by the Israelites, the two or even three crops a-year produced by fig trees in the East, causing it to be looked upon as a staple food, the failure of which meant famine. The first of these crops comes to maturity about June, whilst the second is forming; it is the second which is dried for export, and then in some climates a third crop appears, which hangs and ripens on the tree after the leaves are shed.

The fig entered largely into the food of the Greeks, for, when Lycurgus ordained that the Spartans should dine in a common hall, almost everyone contributed wine, cheese, and figs to the fare. Those who have not studied the origin of words will be surprised to hear that our word sycophant comes from two Greek words signifying 'a fig' and 'to show,' and that in its original meaning it was applied to those who informed against the breakers of an edict made by the Athenians against the export of figs, and, even as used by our older writers, sycophant means a tale bearer. The French still use the word in the sense of liar and impostor, instead of flatterer only.

The present importation of dried figs into Great Britain must be enormous. Many years ago, from Turkey only, it amounted to nine hundred tons annually, besides those coming from France, Italy, and Spain.

The fig enters very little into recipes for cooking—it is too luscious and devoid of pungency; but I have tasted green figs from the Cape, preserved in bottles, which are excellent, although the peculiar, resinous flavour would perhaps not quite suit everybody's palate. There seems no good reason why this should not be added to our list of English preserves. Thousands of green figs are allowed to drop off the trees year after year, which might thus be utilised and rendered valuable, especially in seasons of scarcity of other fruits.

A writer in 1846 estimated that 272,000,000 oranges were imported annually into Great Britain, allowing about a dozen to every individual, and adds: 'This extraordinary consumption of a product which is brought here from very distant places, is a natural consequence of certain qualities which fit the orange in a remarkable degree for being the universal fruit of commerce. If we would have foreign figs and grapes, they must be dried, for the undried grapes which we bring even from the short distance of Portugal are flat and vapid; the tamarind is a liquid preserve; the guava must be made into a jelly; the mango destined for us requires to be pulled before it is ripe, and is pickled; the date must be dried, and the cocoa-nut becomes, when here, consolidated and indigestible. But the orange, man may have fresh in every region of the world, and at almost every season of the year. The aromatic oil and the rind, preserve it from the effects both of heat and cold, and the acridity of the former renders it proof against the attacks of insects. It is true that oranges rot like other fruits, but that does not happen for a long time if the rind is uninjured and they are kept from moisture, and so ventilated as not to ferment.' *

With the improved means of transport since the above was written the import of oranges must have increased enormously, so that now it would be almost impossible to estimate the number imported, although the tonnage might perhaps be found by reference to the Board of Trade returns.   It is, however, sufficient for our purpose to know that now, all the year round, oranges and lemons may be bought at a penny a-piece, and often at three or four a penny, whilst only a few years ago they could scarcely be eaten before Christmas, and were not to be had after June. Nevertheless, the facility with which they are now conveyed, even from Australia, does not tend to the perfection of the fruit, inferior sorts being thrown on the market, because of their abundance, to the partial exclusion of those which require greater care in cultivation and in packing.   The St. Michael—prince of oranges—is now seldom to be seen, whilst thick-skinned, coarse-grained, and bitterish-flavoured varieties are foisted upon the purchaser as equally good. Very few people are good judges of oranges in the fruiterers' shops: they look to size and darkness of skin, instead of weight, fineness and delicacy of skin, with medium size, which are the points of excellence in an orange.   The genuine St. Michael is flattish, pale in colour, and destitute of pips, whereas that sold for it, is full of pips, and pale only because unripe.

The orange requires abundance of heat and sun to bring it to perfection, and therefore cannot be cultivated success- fully in Northern Europe ; the trees may, indeed, be grown in tubs in greenhouses, and will produce fruit, but the fruit

* 'The Food of Man,' p. 79.

is not good. Even in 'the south of France and Northern Italy the orange is never met with in 'perfection, although the trees will grow luxuriantly in the open air, and bear abundant fruit; but it is cultivated there chiefly for the rind, from which the essential oil is extracted which is so much used in the manufacture of perfumes. The streets in the south of France are frequently festooned with orange peel to be dried for this purpose, whilst women and children sit at their doors peeling oranges as we should peel potatoes, the fruit divested of its peel being used for making citric acid, so useful both in the kitchen and the laboratory. The orange trees in the south of France are cut and trimmed till they resemble nothing so much as the trees out of a child's Noah's ark, but in South Italy they are allowed more liberty, and the miles of orange groves about Sorrento are beautiful with loads of golden fruit, and fragrant at the same time with the lovely blossom. There, too, it is a pretty sight to see the peasant women and girls, in their bright costumes, tripping down to the coast with large trays on their heads laden with half-green oranges and lemons ready to be packed for exportation, for the fruit must be gathered before it is quite ripe, or it would not bear the carriage.

In Spain, Southern Italy, and Sicily the orange comes to perfection, but the far East is looked upon as its native habitat, and the Arabs are credited with the introduction of this valuable fruit to the West. According to Galessio, the Arabs penetrated farther into India than Alexander the Great, and found there various kinds of oranges growing, and they brought them thence by two routes—the sweet ones, known as China oranges, through Persia and Syria, and thence to Italy and the south of

France; and the bitter or Seville oranges by Arabia, Egypt, and the north of Africa to Spain. But it is thought that the sweet orange introduced by the Arabs was not the variety known as St. Michael's, but rather that still cultivated in Italy. The St. Michael orange was brought direct from China by the Portuguese, who sent it from Portugal to the Azores, whilst the Spaniards are credited with having introduced it to America. Humboldt found wild oranges growing in a forest in America, but they are not believed to be indigenous to that continent, although at present they are cultivated there with great success, the orange groves of Florida, California, and other Western States being very extensive.

Oranges grow and thrive wonderfully in South Africa, where they are supposed to have been introduced by the Portuguese, but the early Portuguese navigators speak of them as growing on the eastern coast; and it is a singular fact that the Chartered Company of British South Africa found miles of wild orange trees growing in Manicaland, with many other fruits not supposed to be indigenous. The orange found would seem, from the description given of it, to be quite an unknown species, and one which may prove of great value. One of the pioneers writes :—'Riding along we came to groves of wild orange trees, laden with ripe fruit of a yellow colour; the fruit is encased in a hardish shell; inside it has the appearance of an over-ripe sweet melon; the flavour is a combination of sweet melon, pine-apple, and orange, and is very nice eating.'

Oranges have been divided into eight species, known as sweet oranges, bitter oranges, bergamots, limes, pampelucos, sweet limes, lemons, and citrons, and of each of these there are numerous varieties. The variety known as the blood orange, which comes from Malta, is said to derive its colour from being grafted on the pomegranate.

The lemon is a more delicate tree than the orange, and requires more warmth ; it will not flourish in the south of France, except at Mentone, which has given rise to an interesting legend. They say when Eve was driven out of Paradise she managed to carry away with her two or three of her favourite fruits, and among them the lemon : with these she wandered over the earth till she came to Mentone, where, finding the climate and the soil so much resembled the lost Eden, she planted the lemon, which has grown and flourished ever since.

What the cook would now do without lemons we can hardly surmise : they seem an indispensable adjunct to so many savoury dishes, and are become so plentiful that it is no uncommon thing to hear them hawked about the streets of London at three or four a penny. The lime, on the contrary, is very seldom seen, although lime-juice cordial has long been used as a beverage, and the little island of Montserrat has become famous for the production of this useful fruit, the juice of which seems indispensable, where vegetables cannot be obtained, and the lack of which has so often caused the decimation by scurvy of the crews of vessels engaged in Arctic exploration.

The citron is chiefly known to us by the preserved peel, which forms such a delicious condiment for cakes, Christmas puddings, and mince pies.

The Shaddock, so called in honour of the ship captain who introduced it into the West Indies from China, is now little valued, although in China, its native habitat, it is known as the 'sweet ball.' We occasionally see it in the market, as well as its near relative the pomelo, but the bitterness of the rind prevents its becoming a popular fruit. On the contrary, the little Mandarin orange, called *nartje* at the Cape, the rind of which is so highly perfumed, has of late years been very freely imported—chiefly from Malta and Spain, from which latter country we also receive the bitter Seville, so valuable for many purposes, and especially for making that favourite adjunct to the breakfast table— orange marmalade—of which many tons must be consumed annually.

We have by no means exhausted the uses of the varieties of the orange family, which are as valuable medicinally as in a culinary sense, and seem to bear out the Mentone legend that they were brought originally from the Garden of Eden. Undoubtedly they are all natives of the far East, and the probability is that they were indigenous in India and China, and were introduced into Africa in very early times by traders, possibly Chinese, although Galessio believes them to have been brought originally from India by the Arabs; and it is pointed out that they were apparently unknown to Pliny and other early naturalists.

All the varieties now grow in perfection at the Cape, in the West Indies, Australia, and America—in fact, wherever there is abundance of warmth and sun; and with care they will live to the age of three hundred years, even in England, there being some at Hampton Court said to be of that age, but the fruit will not compare with that of foreign climates, for these golden apples of the Hesperides require the sun-dragon to guard them from frost and blight, and to bring them to perfection.

CHAPTER XV

PRUDENT folks are always impressing the fact upon juveniles that stone fruits are unwholesome, but what boy or girl can resist the cry of 'Cherry Ripe!' or avoid the luscious plum, and the still more luscious apricot, peach, or nectarine, when it falls in his or her way? Indeed, we do not believe that even the most prudent of mothers can always be proof against the temptation of these much-maligned delicacies.

As regards apricots, peaches, and nectarines, we in England are never likely to get a surfeit of either, for they cost too much to grow in this part of the world, ever to become a food for the million. In truth, there are millions who probably never taste a peach, or a nectarine; and although apricots are more plentiful, being imported, half ripe, in boxes from France, yet these are also too dear for poor people to buy, and when bought are not satisfactory, the flavour being poor compared with the ripe Moor Park apricot grown on a sunny wall in England. The envy of the British youth is great when he hears that in America, and in South Africa and Australia, pigs are fed upon peaches, and he wishes they would just send some of them over here; but, in truth, these fruits are too delicate for export, unless bottled or dried, although a consignment of peaches has recently arrived from South Africa in excellent condition, packed each in a separate compartment like eggs, and wrapped in cotton wool. Many of these fruits come to us in tins and bottles from America, but they seem to lose flavour in the process, and will never take the place of the highly-cultivated wall-fruits of England at the tables of the rich, although convenient as a substitute, when the superior article is deficient or out of season. The best mode of importing these fruits is in a dried form—especially in the case of apricots. The colonists of the Cape prepare apricots in various ways : one called 'meibos'—known also as 'matrimony,' from being sour and sweet—is very good. The fruit is, as it were, crystallised by being dipped in a strong ley, dried in the sun, and then laid in sugar ; but this is never seen in England, except when brought over by individuals as a present to friends. We have seen and tasted another preparation of this fruit, and of peaches, in the form of paste. The fruit is peeled, slightly boiled without water, mashed, and spread out very thin on buttered boards or sheets of paper, dried in the sun, and folded up like paper, forming a pleasant refreshment in travelling, or at any time when a little fruit is desired and not otherwise obtainable.

It need hardly be said that all these fruits, although brought to great perfection by careful cultivation in England, are natives of sunnier climes. The peach and nectarine, which are so closely allied as to be virtually the same fruit —although one has a smooth coat and the other a rough one—belong to the same botanical family as the almond, and are supposed to have been brought originally from

Persia by the Romans. The peach has been cultivated in England since the sixteenth century, and seems to have been introduced wherever civilised man has appeared. The natives of South Africa are indebted to the traveller Burchell for it, he having given a bag of peach stones as the best present he could think of, to the chief of the Bachapins, upon which he remarks, 'Nor did I fail to impress on his mind a just idea of their value and nature, by telling him that they would produce trees which would continue every year to yield, without further trouble, abundance of large fruit of a more agreeable flavour than any which grew in the country of the Bachapins.' Whether the natives appreciated the wisdom of the benevolent traveller in making this gift to them, and whether they continue to cultivate the fruit, is not known; but the colonists of South Africa generally do so largely, finding the tree very easily reared and the fruit excellent. It is not, however, indigenous to South Africa, although a small apricot is found growing wild there.

The country recently traversed by the pioneer force of the Chartered Company would seem at one time to have been quite a garden of fruits, as the following extract from a letter of one of the men shows:—'I called the country around these parts (Matabeleland, about one hundred and fifty miles from Mount Hampden) the land of fruits, for the whole place is like a great orchard of fruit trees growing wild. Although the winter season (July), many are loaded with fruit. Imagine riding for miles and miles under the shade of wild orange trees, branches weighed down with fruit, and more of others than I can name—wild grapes, guavas, limes, plums, apples, and pomegranates—a veritable garden of Eden, and this under a cloudless sky and delightful climate.'

The apricot belongs to the plum tribe (*Prunus Armeniaca*), a tribe very widely distributed, and including the cherry, the laurel, the sloe, and a vast number of cultivated species of plum, chief among which is the delicious greengage, the Reine Claude of the French. Some naturalists believe that the apricot has been developed from the wild African species; but it is generally supposed to be a native of the East, where it grows in great abundance, from China and Japan to the Caucasus. It is perhaps a greater favourite than the peach in cookery, making a most excellent jam, *apropos* of which I may say that the pulp, now imported in tins, is almost equal to the fresh fruit for this delicate preserve; but it requires its full weight of sugar and a few bitter almonds as a substitute for the kernels. Apricots crystallised and in syrup are also much esteemed, and in all these forms our colonies might supply the English market quite as well as the French do now.

There is also another mode of utilising these abundant gifts of Nature to sunny climes, which is in the making of noyau, or *ratafia*, from the kernels. Years ago we used to collect the kernels of all the apricots and peaches consumed in the house, putting them into a bottle filled up with brandy, and this home-made *ratafia* was the very best flavouring we could ever obtain for custards, puddings, etc. Surely, in countries where these fruits are so superabundant as in South Africa, and where brandy is also largely manufactured, something might be made both of the fruit and its kernels.

The most singular of the peach family is the flat peach of China, which somewhat resembles a Normandy pippin with a stone in the centre, of which the flavour is said to be excellent.

Of the plum there are more than three hundred varieties, so that we cannot attempt to enumerate them, but must mention two or three of the principal. Two wild plums grow in Britain, the bullace and the sloe—the one white or yellow, the other black. They are not eatable in the raw state, but the former is used for making tarts and puddings —very highly esteemed by many—and the sloe is, or was, used in making an excellent cordial known as sloe-gin. Of the cultivated sorts the palm is given to the greengage—so named after the first English cultivator. The Orleans, which came to us from France, is the best for puddings and pies, but for table fruit the many varieties of the egg plum are preferable, whilst that known as the London plum is capital for preserves. We do not know the species of plum which, under the name of prunes, or French plums, forms such a splendid addition to desserts at Christmas, but believe it to be the Imperial. It appears to be a very rich fruit, and one which might be cultivated and preserved in the same manner in our southern colonies. A very delicious variety, about the size of the bullace, known as the golden drop, seems to have ceased to be cultivated in this country. And now we must hark back to the cherry, which is perhaps the most interesting and highly-esteemed of all stone fruits, because the most easily obtained, for two hundred and fifty varieties are said to be cultivated in England, and the little black cherry grows wild even in Scotland.

The cherry orchards of Kent are famous, and in good seasons extremely profitable, realising as much as £30 to £35 the acre, the fruit being sold on the trees, the buyer taking all risk and the cost and trouble of picking and conveying them to market. One of the greatest risks is from the birds, which will strip a cherry tree in an hour or two in the early morning. But although cherries are grown in England in perfection, we yet receive vast quantities from France and Germany, in which latter country, miles of cherry trees line the roads, the fruit being used not only in cookery but for making the favourite liqueur known as Kirschwasser. It is also used for making Maraschino and ratafia, to say nothing of our old English favourite liqueur, cherry-brandy — particularly favoured during the winter season by sportsmen. For this the Morella cherry is best, which is generally gathered before it is ripe, and is therefore regarded as sour and unpalatable, but if allowed to hang on the tree till October it is a most delicious fruit. The cherry was formerly much used in games: that called cherry pit, which consisted of pitching the stones into a little hole, is often alluded to by old writers, as well as bob cherry, which is still played by children. The song of ' Cherry Ripe ' was written by the poet Herrick, in the time of Charles I. The French make a *tisane* of the cherry stalks for colds and coughs. Cherries, we believe, cannot be grown in hot countries, where they revert to the wild type.

Berries have from the remotest ages formed an important part of the food of man. Milton speaks of the banquet of Eve as formed of fruits and berries from all climes.

> ' Whatever earth, all-bearing mother, yields
> In India, East or West, or middle shore,
> In Pontus or the Punic coast, or where
> Aleinous reign'd, fruit of all kinds, in coat
> Rough, or smooth rind, or bearded husk, or shell.'

And, indeed, the fruits of the earth seem to be so widely distributed, and their cultivation dates back to such hoar antiquity, that it seems hardly possible to trace the primitive home of the commoner varieties. Thus, among the relics of the Lake-dwellers we find the strawberry, raspberry, blackberry, elderberry, bilberry, and whortleberry; and although all these grow wild in the woods, yet, when they are found stored with corn and other plants requiring cultivation, and with apples and plums, we may fairly suppose that they were, to a certain extent cultivated also, probably in gardens on the mainland, and they were perhaps boiled, or in some way preserved for use; otherwise the seeds would have germinated in the mud in which they have lain for so many centuries.

The gooseberry and currant do not appear among these fruits of the Lake-dwellers, probably because they belong naturally to our northern climes, and were unknown in early times in Southern Europe, for these are hardy fruits, which thrive better in Scotland than England, although they grow freely and abundantly all over the British Isles.

Currants—red, white, and black—are most valuable fruits to the British housewife, for, although even at the best they are too acrid to be much relished as dessert fruits, they are largely employed in puddings, pies, tarts, and preserves—indeed, some people add red currant juice to all preserves, which appears to me a great mistake, being calculated to destroy the flavour of the other fruits to which it is added. Used alone, the juice of the red currant forms the most delicious jelly in universal use as an accompaniment to game, venison, and roast mutton, and for making sauce for various puddings. The black currant, which is a different species, has excellent medicinal properties, and finds an honourable place in the Pharmacopœia; indeed, there is nothing better for sore throat, hoarseness, and cold on the chest, than black currant jam, or jelly, with boiling water. There is a belief that tons of black currants get exported to Oporto yearly, to supplement the juice of the grape in making that famous *vino d'Oporto* which for centuries has been the panacea of all physicians, and the source of many of the ills it is supposed to cure.

Turning to the gooseberry—also a native British fruit— we find it more used in the green than in the ripe state. Green gooseberry puddings and pies, green gooseberry jam, gooseberry-fool, and that famous beverage of our grand-mothers—green gooseberry wine—which, when well made, was a fair home substitute for champagne—such are a few of the uses of this much-esteemed fruit.

South African colonists compare this old British fruit with that which is called the Cape gooseberry, and are inclined to believe—like our American cousins with the Indian corn —that theirs is the genuine article and ours the counterfeit, forgetting that centuries before the Cape gooseberry was known, the British fruit was widely cultivated and highly esteemed. The Cape gooseberry is, in fact, no gooseberry, but a kind of winter cherry, which, although much relished by those who are accustomed to the flavour, is not quite to the taste of those who enjoy the British gooseberry; and although it makes a splendid jam—which might, we believe, be imported profitably—yet the resinous flavour requires an educated palate to be fully appreciated. This fruit is also cultivated in India, and a jam known as *teparee* is made from it, and sometimes imported.

Few colonists have the opportunity of tasting our British

fruits in perfection, and especially berries, such as gooseberries, which, when ripe, should be picked and eaten from
the bush, as they get flat and tasteless when sent to market.
We venture to think that could they wander through an
English garden when gooseberries—yellow, green, and red
—are ripe, they would find them worth running the risk of
a few scratches from the superabundant thorns, to obtain.
The same may be said of the raspberry, and that universal
favourite the strawberry, both of which, to be enjoyed in
perfection, should be picked and eaten where they grow.
Nevertheless, tons of strawberries find their way daily to
Covent Garden market from the provinces, and even from
Jersey and France, in the season, to be eaten and enjoyed
by those who, if they had to pick for themselves, would
never taste a berry. Yet they are still grown largely in the
immediate neighbourhood of London, and a feast of strawberries freshly picked may even now be eaten with cream
and sugar in many gardens in the suburbs; but to those
accustomed to the smoke and dirt of this great Metropolis
it seems impossible that strawberries could ever have been
grown in Holborn, yet Shakespeare repeats an historic fact
when he makes Glo'ster say to the Bishop of Ely—

> ' My Lord of Ely, when I was last in Holborn
> I saw good strawberries in your garden there.'

Ely Place, the site of the Bishop's palace and garden, may
now be searched in vain for any fruit, except such as is
brought there in baskets from Covent Garden.

There is now an endless variety both of strawberries and
raspberries cultivated, but whilst in the latter the flavour is
improved as the size is increased, in the strawberry the very
large berries are seldom equal in flavour to those of medium

size. Both these fruits are also much esteemed in their wild
state, and, strange to say, the wild raspberry becomes more
luscious and more highly flavoured, the farther north it is
found, forming the most delicious of fruits in Norway and
Sweden; whilst the wild strawberry is an indispensable adjunct to the dinner table in Alpine countries, as all travellers
know, for heaped-up dishes of strawberries appear daily at
every hotel and restaurant in Switzerland and Northern
Italy during the season, till one is constrained to wonder at
the abundance of the fruit, and the patient industry of the
gatherers, who must wander over miles of mountainous
country to supply innumerable voracious travellers daily with
this never-failing luxury. There are numerous other wild
berries, which have their use in due season, although not so
universally esteemed as the strawberry and the raspberry.
In mountainous districts the bilberry—a little black berry—
growing abundantly on low bushes, is excellent for pies and
puddings, whilst the cranberry—which is of the same family,
but red—is not only used when fresh and ripe, but is imported in barrels from Norway and Russia, and a larger kind,
though not so juicy, from America, to the extent of many
thousands of gallons annually. The blackberry, which is
the fruit of the bramble, comes into the market at a season
when fruit is scarce, otherwise it would hardly hold a high
place in public favour; but, mixed with apple, it makes
excellent puddings and pies, and blackberry jam and jelly
are highly esteemed by many. The fruit of one species of
bramble which grows in the extreme north is highly lauded
by Linnæus; and the cloudberry is also a great boon to
dwellers in the cold and barren regions of Northern
Scandinavia and Lapland, even to the North Cape.

The elderberry, once so highly esteemed as a wine producer, is now neglected. Fifty years ago a glass of hot spiced elder wine, with sippets of toast, formed a Christmas beverage handed nightly to honoured guests in country houses. Now, even our peasants must have port or sherry, and the flower and berry of the elder are left to 'waste their sweetness on the desert air.' Yet elder-flower wine was once thought equal to Frontignac, and there was a scramble between man and bird for the berries : the latter are now allowed to enjoy them unmolested, and they do not let them hang long upon the tree when ripe. The elder was also formerly much esteemed in medicine, and is still used in ointments and soaps, being an excellent emollient for the skin.

The barberry is also a fruit which has gone out of fashion. Once upon a time preserved barberries were used in tarts, and thought delicious ; now, however, you very seldom see them in the market, and, if used at all, it is only by way of garnishing, for which they are eminently suitable.

The mulberry, too, although when fully ripe it is the most delicious of berries, is so little esteemed in England that we have seen the ground red with the fruit which the owner has not thought worth gathering. This, however, was not the opinion of our ancestors, who prided themselves upon their mulberry trees, which they cultivated with care, and many of which survive and still bear abundance of fruit, although planted in the sixteenth century. The earliest recorded were planted at Sion House in 1548, and still bear fruit. The mulberry tree is considered the wisest of trees because it never puts forth its leaves until the frosts are over, for which reason it is employed in heraldry to signify wisdom. The white mulberry, which is cultivated abroad for the sake of its leaves, upon which the silk-worm thrives better than on the black variety, is not grown in England, probably because it is not so hardy as the other; but should silk ever become an industry in Ireland, as many philanthropists have proposed to make it, the cultivation of the white mulberry must also be attempted, and planted in hedges, as in the Tyrol, it would probably thrive.

The olive, so famous for its oil, which is indispensable in salads, will not thrive in Northern Europe, but is largely grown in Spain, Italy, and the south of France. At Cap St Martin, between Mentone and Monte Carlo, there are some fine trees, said to have been planted by the Romans, for the olive will live and bear fruit for a thousand years, and the great gnarled trunks, twisted and contorted into the most weird and fanciful shapes, give a truly venerable appearance to these valuable trees. There is one tree, not far from Mentone, which is said to have been planted by Julius Cæsar.

We in England do not make much use of the olive as an article of food, but it forms an excellent addition to stews and hashes, and is served at table as an appetiser. Spanish olives are imported in small barrels, but the French are usually sold in bottles, both being pickled in brine.

In Italy a single olive tree often forms a family patrimony, the sole source of income to several sons; but, as may be supposed, the living derived from it is scanty and precarious.

The olive grows wild at the Cape, and attempts have been made from time to time to cultivate it, but as yet with little success. The olive, as we know, was one of the famous trees of Palestine, and the oil was used in the sacrifices and for the making of cakes and pastry, as also in Egypt.

Among stone fruits,, we ought perhaps to name the tamarind, although it is hardly a fruit to be classed with peaches, plums, and cherries, being exceedingly acid; nevertheless, the acidity is its most valuable property, rendering it of special use in flavouring various dishes, especially curries. This pleasant acidity causes it also to be much valued when mixed with water as a cooling drink in fevers and other diseases. The tamarind tree is a native of the East and West Indies, and also of Arabia, and the fruit is a long pod, containing from three to six hard seeds enclosed in the acid pulp. Tamarinds are imported in the form of preserves, both from the East and West Indies. The latter are best for cooking purposes, and the East Indian for medicinal, as the latter are prepared without sugar.

The mango may also be called a stone fruit, of which, however, we do not know the true flavour, as it is known to us only in the form of chutney; but when eaten ripe from the tree it is said to be delicious.

Many other delicate Indian fruits might also be mentioned here, but as they seldom appear in our markets they may be omitted. The loquat or Japanese medlar comes to us sometimes in the natural state, but is much cultivated in the south of France, and forms a considerable item in that excellent preserve of various fruits made at Grasse, which is so commonly introduced at luncheons on the Riviera. The guava also is known to us chiefly in the form of that delicious jelly which has for more than a century formed one of the exports of India.

CHAPTER XVI

ON THE BORDERLAND 'TWIXT FRUIT AND VEGETABLE

In visiting national collections of pictures in this country and on the Continent we are almost sure to come across one of Murillo's charming Spanish boys, sitting, ragged and dirty, munching a huge slice of melon—the very picture of contented enjoyment.   In hot weather the mouth fairly waters at the luscious-looking morsel, deeply indented with the teeth of the ragged urchin, and we wonder why this delicious, cool fruit has so long been beyond the reach of the little dirty boys of London, when for centuries their representatives in sunny Spain and all over the south of Europe, as well as in the Eastern Bible lands of Asia, almost live upon it and its congeners—the water-melon, the cucumber, and the pumpkin; whilst, if perchance this watery diet should disagree, 'a hair of the same dog' may perhaps be administered in the shape of a dose of colocynth, or bitter cucumber.

The most remarkable point in the history of this family of fruits is their power of absorbing and retaining moisture. Growing abundantly in the hottest and most arid countries, they are eagerly sought as a means of assuaging thirst as well as hunger.   Humboldt says of the water-melon, that in the Peninsula of Araya, where rain does not fall sometimes for fifteen months, water-melons weighing from 15 to 70 lbs. are not uncommon. Many a traveller's life has been saved by finding a patch of these water-reservoirs in the thirsty desert. It is said to be a native of the south of Europe, the Levant, Egypt, and South America; but several species abound in South Africa, and of one of them Dr. Livingstone writes :—

'The most surprising plant of the Kalahari Desert is the water-melon—kengwe or kème. When more than the usual quantity of rain falls, vast tracts of the country are literally covered with these melons. Then animals of every sort and name, including man, rejoice in the rich supply. The elephant—true lord of the forest—and the different species of rhinoceros revel in the fruit, although naturally so diverse in their choice of pasture. The various kinds of antelopes feed on them with avidity, and lions, hyænas, jackals, and mice, all seem to appreciate the common blessing. These melons are not, however, all eatable, some being sweet and others bitter. The natives select them by striking them with a hatchet and applying the tongue to the gashes.'

In the East and in Egypt, melons serve also as food for man and beast. Niebuhr, speaking of Arabia, says :—'Of pumpkins and melons several sorts grow naturally in the woods, and serve for feeding camels, but the proper melons are planted in the fields, where a great variety of them is to be found, and in such abundance that the Arabians of all ranks use them for some part of the year as their principal article of food. They afford a very agreeable liquor. When the fruit is nearly ripe, a hole is pierced into the pulp; this hole is then stopped with wax, and the melon left upon the stalk. Within a few days the pulp is, in con-

sequence of this process, converted into a delicious liquor.'
We wonder whether this practice is still continued.   It
sounds so simple that people in those favoured lands where
melons grow so abundantly might try it advantageously.
Here, although melons have been grown successfully on
hot-beds for some centuries, they are still articles of luxury,
and the crop cannot be depended upon, for one day's
neglect will often cause the loss of a promising bed of
melons.   Nevertheless, at our flower shows may always be
seen numbers of varieties, reared with great care, and
brought to the highest perfection, from seed obtained from
all parts of the world.   The chief varieties are the red
fleshed and the green, each of which has its vehement
admirers.   They also vary considerably in size, some of the
very small kinds being greatly esteemed for their fineness
of flavour.

Pliny and Columella speak of the fondness of the Emperor
Tiberius for melons, and of the contrivances by which they
were provided for him at all seasons; whilst of another
Emperor, Frederick the Great, it is related that his physician,
finding him suffering greatly from indigestion during his last
illness, learned that he had eaten three or four melons
(small ones, we may suppose) daily for breakfast, and his
only reply to the physician's remonstrance was, that he
would send him some to taste, thinking the excellence of
the fruit would show the doctor the difficulty of abstaining
from so favourite a dish.

Many people besides Frederick of Prussia have found
melons indigestible in our colder climes.   In truth, they
are best suited to hot climates and hot weather, and will
be sure to disagree in cold seasons; and so well was this

understood formerly, that melons were never sent to table without an accompaniment of ground ginger. Nowadays people risk indigestion, and eat them with sugar only, or sometimes with pepper and salt. Melons of some kind have of late become almost as abundant in our streets as in those of the sunny South, for they are imported by thousands from Spain—great green-looking things *called* water-melons, but not really so, and of very good flavour when ripe—slices being now sold in the streets at a halfpenny, or even less, so that it is no longer an uncommon sight to see our ragged urchins munching their slice of melon, like Murillo's little Spanish boys.

It is not easy to say whether the cucumber should be classed as a fruit or a vegetable; it stands upon the borderland, and may be eaten as either, but whether fresh, stewed, or pickled, is a very delicious accompaniment to many savoury dishes, and especially salads; and what would those pleasant cooling summer beverages, claret and champagne cup, be, without a slice or two of cucumber floating on the top? Cucumbers, like melons, have become so much more plentiful of late, that they may be purchased all the year round for a few pence, being cultivated largely in greenhouses, and, in the summer, in the open air. 'A lodge in a garden of cucumbers' will come to the mind in writing of them. Here we have not to put up sheds to safeguard them from foxes and jackals, as in Syria, but the market gardener has to watch against human prowlers, ever on the alert to fill their own pockets at the expense of their neighbours; for a crop of cucumbers—the plants trained under glass in greenhouses like vines, the fruit hanging from them by hundreds, straight, and often half a yard in length—if

O

they can be brought forward early enough in the spring, is worth a very large sum, but they diminish rapidly in value as the season advances.

Pumpkins and vegetable marrows, which belong to the same tribe as the melon and the cucumber, are certainly vegetables, not being eaten in the raw state. As vegetables they are much more esteemed abroad than in England, although the vegetable marrow has grown greatly in favour of late years, but the pumpkin—so much used on the Continent, in America, and in our Colonies—is still utterly rejected by our peasantry, as fit only for pigs. In vain do philanthropists show how easily it is grown, and how it may be stored for winter use. Hodge will have none of it. Nevertheless, of late pumpkin in slices has been sold at the greengrocers for soups, etc., during the winter, and appears to meet with a ready sale, so that perhaps in time the prejudice may be overcome.

Singularly enough, it would seem that the pumpkin was very early introduced into England, and was then known as the *melon*, the melon itself being called *musk melon*. The cucumber, too, is said to have been commonly grown in England in the reign of Edward III., but was afterwards neglected and disused until the reign of Henry VIII., and not generally cultivated till the middle of the seventeenth century.

There is another plant standing on the borderland between fruit and vegetables which has lately come into great request. This is the tomato, long known as the love-apple. The tomato belongs to a poisonous tribe of plants, known botanically as *solanaceæ*, which includes the nightshades of deadly fame, and also the well-known and highly-prized potato. The potato and tomato are both natives of America. Both were introduced about the same time; but their history has been very different, for whilst the potato has found its way into every home, and has been the chief stay and solace of the poorest, the tomato has, until quite recently, been cultivated very sparingly, and more as a curiosity than an article of food. I remember seeing them grown against a wall as ornamental plants, in the days when potatoes flourished abundantly, before the deadly blight had fallen upon them. But although the *love-apple*, as it was called, was regarded as a curiosity, and admired for its beautiful colour, we should no more have thought of eating it than the seeds of the potato, which were reputed poisonous, and we believe a similar reputation was attached at that time to the tomato by the ignorant, although it was used for making sauce, and the fruit when green was sometimes pickled.

The name of the tomato, *Lycopersicum*, signifies 'wolf-peach,' says Macintosh's 'Book of the Garden,' 'and was given to it because of the deceptive value of the fruit.' But that was at a time when, as we said above, it was regarded as only a semi-poisonous curiosity. Nowadays the tomato is highly valued, as it deserves to be, for, as a vegetable, it has found its way at last into English kitchens, and is recognised by our cooks as an excellent adjunct to soups, stews, curries, etc., but the poor still despise and dislike it, and indeed its price would prevent its free use among them. On the Continent it has long been highly prized, as well as in America, and its medicinal properties in cases of liver complaint have been long recognised. Our market gardeners are beginning to cultivate it largely, and a splendid show of this fruit, or vegetable, of numerous varieties, all grown in the open, has been held at the Crystal Palace. We may, therefore, hope soon to have it abundant in English markets; meanwhile the tinned tomatoes from America and France answer fairly well for cooking purposes. The African egg plant belongs to the same family as the tomato, and is eaten boiled and stewed in some places, being highly valued in China and the West Indies.

There is another kind of semi-fruit largely consumed in tropical countries; this is the plantain, which, with its near relation the banana, forms the staple food of innumerable tribes in Asia, Africa, America, and the oceanic islands of the Atlantic and Pacific. The plantain and banana grow in immense clusters, often weighing from seventy to eighty pounds on a single plant, and they are so easily cultivated, that even the most savage races understand how to produce them. The banana is said to bear a crop every three months, so that a plantation of from thirty to forty roots will yield more than four thousand pounds of fruit. The banana is rather smaller than the plantain, but both varieties are now frequently seen in our fruiterers' shops. The taste resembles that of a mealy pear, with a little butter added; the banana is sometimes dried like the fig, and is then pounded and used as meal.*

Perhaps we may include among those plants which serve both as fruit and vegetable the date palm, which yields a farinaceous substance resembling sago (which is the product of another species of palm), as well as the invaluable date,

* A lady writing from South Africa says they found bananas growing wild with upwards of 100 pods in a bunch.

which, both in its green and dried state, forms the staple food of the people wherever it grows. The failure of the crop means famine, and to cut down the date trees is the first act of an enemy. The dates we buy here are dried in the sun, or pressed into baskets before they are quite ripe, as the ripe fruit would not bear transport. The centre or crown of the date palm is sometimes eaten as a cabbage, but as this destroys the tree, it is only cut from sterile trees, and after the removal of this cabbage the sap rises, and palm wine or toddy flows from the cavity at the rate of about a gallon a day, continuing for nearly six weeks in diminishing quantities. From this palm-wine, arrack is made by distillation, and a spirit is also obtained by soaking the dates in water, and afterwards distilling it, whilst the stalks are boiled and used as food for cattle. A few years ago a company was formed for the manufacture of date coffee, which was made from the date stones roasted and ground, but this spurious coffee has now been nearly, if not quite, abandoned.

That useful plant the rhubarb, may properly find a place in this chapter, for although chiefly used as a substitute for fruit, it is only the leaf stalk of a plant which came originally from the East, but which has apparently been cultivated in England since the latter part of the sixteenth century, and seems to grow yearly in popularity, as, when forced, it is attainable during the winter months when fruits are scarce, whilst the giant out-door leaf stalks are sold at a very cheap rate all through the summer and autumn, when it is largely used for puddings and tarts, and also for stewing, preserving, and wine-making.

The far-famed legendary lotos must also find a place here. It is variously described as a lily, and as a shrub bearing a fruit of a sweet taste resembling gingerbread. This last was probably the lotos of the Lotophagi, which is described by Polybius as a stiff, thorny shrub, with small green leaves. The fruit, when green, is said to resemble myrtle berries, but when ripe they are like round olives of a reddish colour, and, like olives, contain a hard nut. The fruit is gathered, crushed, and kept in close vessels, and resembles figs or dates in flavour; it is reckoned next to the date in value, and was said to have formed the chief food of man, being so delicious that whosoever tasted it ceased to desire any other food, and forgot everything in the pleasure of eating it. It grows in Egypt and Northern Africa. But although this was probably the lotos of the poets, it is certain that the Egyptians eat also the fruit and seeds of the lotos lily, as well as the root of the arum, which is eaten in many countries, either roasted or pounded, and precipitated as a starch, resembling manioc or tapioca.

CHAPTER XVII

ROOTS

It is hard to realise the fact that three hundred years ago the potato was unknown in Europe, and we wonder what our ancestors could have done without a vegetable which is now regarded as indispensable. Yet, at the date of its introduction, it was so little thought of, that it is still a disputed point as to whom belongs the honour of having brought it over, and whether it came from Chili or Peru, where it grows wild, or from Virginia. We used to believe that Sir Walter Raleigh was this benefactor, but Sir John Hawkins (1565), Sir Francis Drake (1586), and Thomas Herriott (1585) are also credited with its first introduction; at any rate, most people are agreed that Ireland was its first European home, and that the neighbourhood of Cork was the spot where the earliest potato crop was raised. Nevertheless, a century after its first planting, Houghton, the botanist, writing in 1681, says :—'The potato is a *bacciferous* herb with esculent roots, bearing winged leaves and a bell flower. . . . . This, I have been informed, was brought first out of Virginia by Sir Walter Raleigh, and he stopping at Ireland, some was planted there, where it thrived very well and to good purpose, for, in their succeeding wars, when all the corn above ground was destroyed, this supported them, for the soldiers, unless they had dug up all the ground where they grew and almost sifted it, could not extirpate them. From thence they were brought to Lancashire, where they are very numerous, and now they *begin to spread all the kingdom over.* They are a pleasant food, boiled or roasted, and eaten with butter and *sugar.*' Fancy eating *sugar* with potatoes! He then goes on to say, 'There is a sort brought from Spain that are of a longer form (*Convolvulus Batatas*), and are much more luscious than ours, for they are much set by, and sold for 6d. or 8d. a pound.' Sweet potatoes—which, by-the-by, are not potatoes at all—are now very little thought of in comparison with the commoner potato, and, although they are eaten and relished by the few, would certainly be rejected by the many, whilst the potato is cultivated everywhere, occupying 512,471 acres in Great Britain in 1877, and in the same year 7,964,840 cwt. were imported, valued at £2,348,749.

I well remember the terrible time of the first appearance of the potato blight in 1845, and the great change wrought by it in this favourite vegetable. Previously great fields of potatoes grew and flourished abundantly, producing their white or purple blossom, according to their kind, followed by green or purplish seed-pods, the haulm, when withered, being pulled up and burnt, or left to rot as manure, whilst the tubers were dug and pitted for winter use, the great aim being to preserve them from frost. The consternation which took possession of people when they saw the haulm getting black and dying away, long before it was time for the blossom, may be imagined, and when it was found that the tuber was rotting in the ground, a wail went up from one end of the country to the other—and no wonder, for it meant to many in England, and to all in Ireland, a grievous famine. At first the pigs were fed on the diseased roots, but they soon got too bad even for pigs to eat; then it was found out that, if taken in time, the roots might be grated, and starch made from them, and so, at every cottage door sat women and children grating the fast-rotting roots into pans of water; but little could be gained by that, although potato starch is still used, and called English arrowroot. People, however, could not live on that, and soon got tired of trying, and the potatoes were left to rot in the ground. Year after year this went on, and no one seemed to know how to remedy the evil; but at last the natural history of the disease came to be known, and now by careful cultivation of sorts less liable to be attacked by the fungus which causes the disease, the potato again begins to hold up its head, and may be seen blossoming and bearing seed as before. But many of the sorts most prized prior to 1845 have entirely disappeared, and among them one which was the delight of our childhood, known as the China orange, which came to table in its skin, just bursting, and showing a beautiful red under coat, covering a great floury ball of most delicious flavour. The Irish, who may be supposed to know the best mode of cooking their favourite vegetable, always boil them in their skins, and in so doing retain the full flavour, but they also like them slightly hard in the middle—'with the bones in,' as they say—which is not so much to English taste.

The latest method of preventing the potato blight is that recommended by Mr. Jensen, namely to disinfect the seed tubers by storing them for four or five days in a dry-air chamber, at a temperature of 100 to 105 degs. Fahrenheit; but others recommend syringing the leaves with a solution of sulphate of copper and quicklime, which is also said to increase the growth of the tubers.

Edible roots have always formed a large portion of man's food, from the most primitive times. Savages in all lands have their digging sticks, with which they turn up such things as experience has taught them will prove good to eat, and the most singular thing is that instinct appears to act with them as with the lower animals, preventing them from taking that which is poisonous; and where they find poisonous roots, as in many of the lily tribe, they have learnt to nullify the poison by roasting the root, or by scraping it and extracting the acrid juice by pressure or by soaking in water before cooking, as in the manioc, of which we wrote in a former chapter. But civilised man has not forsaken the habits of his remote ancestors, and still delves as Adam did for the produce of the soil, although he no longer depends upon the chance of finding a supply when needed, but plants and waters, weeds and watches, till he may dig the anticipated crop; and then he very commonly buries the roots again snugly beneath the soil, carefully covered up with straw and trenched round to keep the treasure from that which may corrupt, in order that he may have them sound and good during the frost and snows of winter, when most needed for the household, and for those domestic animals which form a large portion of his wealth, but which in early times had mainly to shift for themselves, and die of starvation when the grass of the field failed them.

Next to the potato, the most important root of modern times

is undoubtedly the turnip, which in its many varieties keeps thousands of cattle alive, and is not despised as a vegetable on the most lordly table; but we remember a time when it was not considered right to feed milch cows upon turnips, lest it should injure the flavour of the milk and butter. Yet we find that turnips were grown abundantly by the Romans as food for cattle, and they seem to have devoted themselves to the cultivation of this vegetable as we do now, for Pliny speaks of roots weighing 40 lbs., which far exceeds our greatest efforts. The beet, we are told, grew in the country of the Sabines, and was sold in Rome for a sum equal to 2d. each in our money.

The Romans doubtless introduced the cultivation of the turnip into our country, but it seems to have been neglected for many centuries, and was probably reintroduced by the Flemings; it seems however to have been only used as a vegetable, for in a book called the 'Haven of Health,' published in 1597, we are told, 'Although many men love to eat turnips, yet do swine abhor them.' By which we may learn that the taste even of pigs may be educated, for at present piggy will certainly eat his turnip with as much relish as his master. It would, however, appear that the turnip was not cultivated in fields until the end of the seventeenth century.

As food for man, it seems to be more highly esteemed in foreign countries than here. Linnæus tells us the Laplanders are so fond of this root that they will give a whole cheese in exchange for a single turnip; and from Clarke's 'Travels in Russia' we learn that in Russia, turnips are used as fruit, and in the houses of the nobility a raw turnip cut in slices is handed about on a silver salver

with brandy, to stimulate the appetite. The Maltese golden
turnip, which is of a beautiful orange colour and quite round,
is frequently eaten as fruit.

The Swedish turnip—commonly known as the swede—
is principally cultivated for cattle, but there is a small yellow
variety grown in Scotland, which is there much esteemed
as a vegetable, but is never seen in the London market,
although far superior in flavour to the turnip commonly
sold. It is recorded that in the years 1629 and 1630, when
there was a dearth in England, very good, white, lasting,
and wholesome bread was made of boiled turnips deprived
of their moisture by pressure, and then kneaded with an
equal quantity of wheaten flour into what was known as
turnip bread ; and the same substitute for wheat was used
again in Essex in 1693, when there was a scarcity of
corn. At present there is no temptation to adulterate
bread with turnips, but probably bread thus made would
be much more wholesome than that which now makes
its appearance artificially whitened with plaster of Paris
and alum.

Turnip tops are much esteemed as a vegetable, but few
people know that the long, white shoots of turnips or swedes
which have been pitted, may be cooked, and rival sea-kail in
flavour. We remember a use for the swede also not generally known, which is to cut a swede in slices like a loaf of
bread, sprinkle each slice with brown sugar, placing the
slices again in their order, and allowing them to stand for
some hours. The juice which runs from it is reckoned by
country people an excellent remedy for a cough.

Next to the turnip, the carrot probably ranks highest in
culinary estimation. Although, like the turnip, it seems

to have been only introduced into this country by the Flemings, in the reign of Elizabeth, it made its way into public favour much more quickly than the turnip, and in the reign of James the First, the foliage was used by the ladies to adorn their headdresses. The graceful leaf is still often seen in bouquets, and we are told this simple decoration may be obtained even in winter, by cutting off the thick end of the carrot and placing it in a shallow pan of water, when a crown of delicate leaves will soon appear. The carrot is not so extensively cultivated as food for cattle as the turnip, although eaten by them with much relish, the horse being extremely fond of it, and its use is said to be particularly beneficial in preserving and restoring the wind of horses. Pigs, also, are very fond of carrots, and fatten very quickly upon them; nevertheless, the turnip is more favoured by the agriculturist, perhaps because more pro-ductive, although we are told that 'at Parlington, in Yorkshire, the stock of a farm, consisting of twenty working horses, four bullocks, and six milch cows, were fed from the end of September to the beginning of May on the carrots produced from three acres of land, with a very small quantity of hay, and thirty hogs were fattened on the refuse left by the cattle.' If this account can be relied on, we wonder that farmers do not cultivate the carrot more largely, but they seem to prefer beet and mangold wurtzel —which latter is said to produce the largest roots and the most weighty crop in a given space of land, whilst beetroot is credited with improving the quantity and quality of milk in cows. The mangold is never sent to table, but beet is much esteemed, and is commonly added to salads, although it requires to be boiled carefully, and not cut or pricked, or it will lose all its colour. It is now usually sold ready boiled by the greengrocer.

The parsnip, although good and nutritious, is not a favourite vegetable, except in certain localities. In the north of Scotland, we are told, parsnips mixed with potatoes and butter are much esteemed, and to this mess salt fish is added in Catholic countries, and they certainly eat well either with salt fish or salt beef, but should always have a little dripping added to them in boiling. The Dutch cook them by pouring over them, after they are boiled, a little butter in which a small quantity of sugar has been dissolved, and then browning them in the oven.

A root in many respects similar to the parsnip is the skirret, formerly so highly esteemed by the Romans as to have been specially imported from the Rhine for the emperor's table, whilst it served as one of the ingredients used to garnish the famous Lucanian boar.

> ' Around him lay whatever could excite,
> With pungent force, the jaded appetite ;
> Rapes, lettuce, radishes, anchovy brine,
> With skirrets, and the lees of Coan wine.'

Skirrets have recently re-appeared in the market, and perhaps will once more become the fashion, although they appear to be too sweet to suit modern taste as a vegetable. Those, however, who enjoy parsnips and sweet potatoes may probably relish the skirret, as also the scorzonera, which at one time was highly esteemed, not only as a vegetable, but as a cure for snake bites. It is still sometimes sent to table in France and Spain.

The yam, that gigantic root extensively cultivated in Africa, Asia, America, and the West Indies, is never seen in our markets, but is eaten as bread, either roasted or boiled, by the natives of the countries in which it grows. The roots sometimes weigh as much as thirty pounds, but are not relished by Europeans.

The only other root we need notice here is the Jerusalem artichoke—a name corrupted from *girasole,* which is the Italian name for sunflower, of which it is a species. It is very easily grown, and not very readily exterminated when once introduced into a garden. It is a native of Brazil, and was brought over in 1667, being much esteemed before potatoes became so generally cultivated. It is not much relished now by the poor, but is frequently found on the tables of the wealthy, and, when well cooked, is excellent, especially when sent to table, as in France, with white sauce and a garnishing of Parmesan cheese lightly browned. It also makes a capital soup.

But of all vegetables known to us, perhaps the onion and its allies—notwithstanding the suspicion of vulgarity attaching to them—are the most universal and indispensable in the culinary art, for how insipid would soups, sauces, hashes, stews, gravies, salads, and seasonings of all kinds be without the *soupçon* of the onion, the shalot, or the stronger —and yet more vulgar—garlic. Whilst, as a vegetable, what can be found more grateful to the general palate, and more wholesome also, than the Spanish onion—roasted or stewed—or the leek, the national badge of Wales, and appreciated by epicures everywhere?

The pedigree of the onion family can be traced back to hoar antiquity—so hoary, indeed, that the first parent is unknown, although supposed to have sprung from Central Asia, whence it spread north, south, east, and west, branching off—as aristocratic families, and even plebeian, are apt to do—and assuming new forms under altered circumstances, until all our modern varieties have become developed through the survival of the fittest, and we can now call to our aid the onion proper, in many different sizes and varieties of flavour, from the little pickling onion to the great Spanish bulb weighing half a pound or more; garlic, with its root conveniently divided into cloves, that our cooks may not spoil the dish by too lavish use of that of which very little suffices; the eschalot—or, shortly, shalot—not quite so pungent in flavour, but equally useful; chives, usually eaten green to flavour omelettes, salads, etc.; the leek, so esteemed by the Emperor Nero that his subjects gave him the name of Porrophagus (the Latin name for the leek being *Allium porrum*), for he ate them, with oil only, for several days in every month to clear his voice, abstaining from bread on these leek-eating days; and, lastly, there is a curious tree-onion, which bears the bulbs on the top of the stem instead of seeds, as in the other species—this is supposed to be a variety of the common onion changed by transplantation to Canada, whence we derive it.

The Welsh, we are told, plant the bulbs of the tree onion as they drop off the parent stem, and they grow to a considerable size. The French call this *l'ognon d'Egypte*, although it is not supposed to have come originally from that country. The ancient Egyptians (2000 B.C.) venerated —some say worshipped—the common onion, and certainly possessed several of the varieties, for we are told that the Israelites in the desert pined for 'the leeks and the onions and the garlic' they had enjoyed so abundantly in Egypt; and, if we are to believe travellers, the onions of Egypt were, and still are, especially good, being larger, softer, and more delicate in flavour than ours.

We have seen how great was the devotion of the Emperor Nero to the leek, although according to Pliny they had not long been introduced in his day, having been brought from Egypt; but onions were largely used by the Romans much earlier, for they gave them to their labourers to strengthen them, and to their soldiers and gamecocks to excite their courage.

Alphonse Karr, in that charming book ' A Tour round my Garden,' thus speaks of the yellow garlic, the *moly* of Homer : ' The yellow garlic is more than it appears to be; the yellow garlic has the power of keeping us safe from enchantments, spells, and evil presages. A crow may fly by you on your left hand, but you need not entertain any fear, if you have only the yellow garlic in your garden. You meet with a spider in the morning, don't be afraid of it; you spill the salt, the mischance will not fall to you; a hare crosses your path in the morning, be not on that account apprehensive of the crosses of the world; the yellow garlic is cherished by you in your garden and watches over you; the yellow garlic will not allow any of these evil omens to affect you. . . .

' Pliny says that it is one of the most valuable plants to man. Homer relates that it was to the virtues of the yellow garlic that Ulysses owed his fortunate escape from being turned into a pig by Circe as well as his companions, whom he delivered from this disagreeable transformation.'

Although the Greeks cultivated several of the onion tribe for culinary purposes, they are said to have regarded onion-eaters in such abhorrence as to look upon them as profane persons. This we might readily infer from the straight classical nose of the race, to which fastidious organ the rank smell of raw onions would be peculiarly abhorrent. Even to ourselves, the smell of onions or garlic in a public conveyance or place of amusement, is intensely disagreeable, and the strongly-flavoured dishes of the Spaniards and Portuguese—the people of all Europe most given to the eating of garlic—are most unpleasant to the palate of Englishmen; and yet, if we attempted to give a list of English dishes into which the onion in some form enters, we should wellnigh exhaust the cookery book.

Formerly the onion and garlic played an important part in pharmacopœias, but at present the doctor has given them over to the cook; nevertheless, their medicinal value is known and acknowledged, and the old remedy for cold—onion broth—is still prepared in many households, whilst the garlic has recently regained somewhat of its former reputation as a remedy for bronchial coughs and shortness of breath.

M'Intosh's ' Book of the Garden ' tells us that ' Palladius, a Greek physician, recommends the onion to be sown with *savory*, in which curious opinion Pliny agrees, observing that onions prosper better when savory is sown with them.' ' It was,' says the writer, ' a current opinion in those days that certain plants had an antipathy to, or sympathy with, each other. However absurd such an idea may appear to us, we should take into consideration, that the opinions of the ancients may not have been faithfully handed down to us, or that their works may admit of a somewhat different construction. We find Phillips observes that all the plants which they recommend to be sown or planted together are of very opposite natures, and there may be more reason in the system pursued by the ancients than is generally allowed; for plants drawing the same juice from the earth must naturally weaken each other, whereas those requiring different nutriment may in some degree assist each other, each feeding upon juices that are prejudicial to plants of the other species. In this there is great truth.'

How easy it is to laugh at the wisdom of the ancients; yet in most things we have to come round to their opinions in the long run. Gardeners nowadays are quite alive to the affinities of plants, and their predilection for certain soils and situations; and in planting onions, if they do not grow savory with them, care should be taken that they have good rich loamy soil, and are well weeded and watered. This was probably the secret of their successful cultivation among the Romans. We do not know when the onion and its allies were first introduced into this country, but probably it is one of the benefits we derive from the Roman occupation of Britain. Garlic is first mentioned in 1548, and the leek in 1562. Shakespeare makes it the badge of the Welsh after the Battle of Crecy, and their fondness for the onion tribe is noticed by Worlidge, who says: 'I have seen the greater part of a garden planted with leeks, and a part of the remainder with onions and garlic.' Perhaps it is to this diet that the Welshman owes his pugnacity.

CHAPTER XVIII

PULSE AND CABBAGE

BEANS and peas are familiar to everybody as vegetables, and are in use all the year round, but few people are aware that they have been in cultivation perhaps longer than any other vegetable in Europe, and that many curious notions regarding both—especially beans—have been handed down to us from hoar antiquity. Beans are supposed to have been brought from Egypt; yet the Egyptian priests regarded it as a crime even to look at them. Pythagoras commanded his followers to abstain from them, professing to believe that man was formed from them; and Lucian introduces a philosopher in hell, saying that to eat beans and to eat our father's head were equal crimes. The Romans at one time believed that the souls of the dead resided in beans; yet they had a solemn feast in which beans were offered in honour of Carna, the consort of Janus, who is said to have enjoyed a little bacon with them: hence our bean-feasts date from very remote times. The Athenians used sodden beans in their feasts to Apollo. Black and white beans were used to record the votes of the people in choosing their magistrates, etc. A white bean signified absolution; a black, condemnation, which is apparently the origin of the custom of blackballing an opponent.

Beans and peas are both found among the relics of the

Swiss Lake dwellings, and are named among the provision conveyed to David when he was hiding from his son Absalom. The botanical name of the bean, *Faba*, is said to be derived from *phago* (to eat), or *paba* (to feed), and it has undoubtedly formed a favourite food from time immemorial; but notwithstanding the many centuries during which it has been cultivated, only two species—the common garden or broad bean, and the horse bean—are known. The kidney bean (*Phaseolus*)—so named from *phaselus* (a little boat), because of the shape of the pods—seems to have come to us from two widely different sources. The dwarf kidney bean, commonly known as the French bean, is a native of India, but is mentioned as being generally cultivated in England in 1597, whilst the scarlet runner was introduced from South America in 1633, and was first cultivated by the celebrated gardener Tradescant, at Lambeth; but for nearly a century it was grown almost wholly for its flowers, which formed the chief ornament in all nosegays, and its pods or legumes were only occasionally used as a vegetable until the eighteenth century, when they were brought into notice by Miller, of Chelsea. They are not, however, as nutritious as the broad bean, which contains 57 per cent. of nutritive matter.*

* The traveller Navarette speaks of a paste of kidney beans eaten by every one in China from the emperor to the meanest peasant. The juice is extracted from the beans, which are pressed into cakes like large cheeses as white as snow. This paste is eaten either raw or fried with fish, herbs, and other things, or smoked and mixed with carraway seeds, which is said to be best of all. Navarette marvels at the vast quantity of this food, known as Teu Fu, and says, 'that Chinese who has Teu Fu, herbs, and rice, needs no other sustenance. It is a great help in case of want, and is good for carriage.'

The small black beans called *fricollis*, which are in such great demand all over Mexico, are doubtless a kind of kidney bean. Immense fields of this bean are cultivated, and they are eaten at every meal, being relished alike by native and foreigner. There is another sort of bean, called the snail flower (*Phaseolus Caracalla*), from a Celtic word meaning a hood, which was also brought by the Portuguese from South America. Nor must we omit to mention the locust bean, supposed to have been the food of John the Baptist in the wilderness, although, if procurable, the genuine locusts would be quite as likely to have formed the diet of the recluse as the bean, seeing they are eaten with relish by the natives of all the countries which they devastate, as well as by all domestic animals. The locust bean, called St. John's bread, is the fruit of the handsome carob or carouba tree, which grows abundantly in Palestine and other Eastern countries, where the pods are turned to many uses, the husks being used for feeding cattle, and are supposed to be those referred to in the parable of the Prodigal Son. A juice expressed from the pods after the beans are taken out, is used, with other ingredients, for making sherbet; the pulp is also eaten, and the leaves and bark of the tree are used for tanning skins. Of late years the dried pods have been imported into this country and used for feeding cattle.

Lentils, which are also leguminous plants, have long formed an article of diet in Egypt, and in many parts of Europe, but have only recently been introduced into England as a vegetable; they are, however, now much esteemed, especially in soups. Lentils were largely used in Greece, and were reputed to soften the temper and dispose the mind to study; but the Romans, on the contrary, said they made men lazy, hence the name from *lentus* (slow). Haricot beans, which are much more extensively used on the Continent than here, are the ripe beans of the white French bean, but in Italy a dish is frequently served which at first seemed to us to resemble the haricot bean, although much smaller : this, however, we found to be the seed of the white lupin, which is grown in large quantities, and respecting which a legend is told. It is said that, when the Holy Family were journeying to Egypt, being pursued, they hid themselves in a field of lupins, but the seeds rattled and almost betrayed them, whereupon they cursed the plant, declaring that henceforth men should eat of them and not be satisfied; and they are certainly unsatisfying, although pleasant eating.

Peas, which are more esteemed than beans at the present time, have almost as ancient a pedigree, having probably been brought from Egypt or Syria. Nevertheless, they do not appear to have been cultivated in England so early as the bean, for, in the reign of Queen Elizabeth, Fuller says, they were brought from Holland and were fit dainties for ladies—they came so far and cost so dear. There is an entry in the privy purse expenses of Henry VIII.: "Paied to a man in rewarde for bringing peascodds to the King's grace iiij*s*. viii*d*.

The chick pea, which is cultivated in South Europe, especially in Spain, does not boil soft, but is used to garnish savoury dishes, and always forms part of the universal Spanish dish called an *olla*, which is composed of bacon, cabbage, pumpkin, and chick peas, called *garvanzos*. This pea, when parched, is much esteemed, and is supposed to be that which formed the parched pulse which was the common provision of the Hebrew soldiers : it was also probably that which was supplied to Daniel, Shadrach, Meshech, and Abednego instead of meat. Parched pulse seems also to have formed a part of the ordinary food of the common people of ancient Rome.

A curious property is noticed as belonging to the chickling vetch, a leguminous plant, which in the last century was used for making bread, until forbidden by the Government. Mixed with half flour it is good and harmless, but eaten alone it produces paralysis of the limbs, and swine fed upon it become very fat, but quite unable to stand. The Italians, however, still eat it mixed with three-parts of flour. There is a bean called the chestnut bean, dis-covered by Mr. Cunningham growing on a tree in New South Wales, which when roasted, is said to resemble chestnuts.

There is a kind of bean which, although not used in cookery, must yet be noticed here, it is that known as the Kuara bean, growing on a beautiful tree in Abyssinia and many other parts of Africa. This tree, known as *Erythrina*, produces a beautiful spike of scarlet flowers, succeeded by pods containing several little scarlet beans with a black spot, which vary so little in weight, that under the name of *carats* they have been used from time immemorial as the standard weight for gold and gems, especially diamonds.

A curious fact regarding leguminous plants is mentioned in Rhind's 'History of the Vegetable Kingdom,' which is that they generate so much carbonic acid gas, especially when flowering, that in mining districts the overseers have to guard against the deadly gas sinking into the pits and causing the death of the miners, by especial ventilation during the bean season. We do not remember to have seen anything of the kind mentioned elsewhere, and it is perhaps an exploded idea. Of late years green peas tinned, have been largely imported from France, and are excellent eating, but some in bottles, preserved in England, are still better; we also get from America, Boston baked beans, and *succotash*, which is Indian corn mixed with beans, and very good as a winter vegetable.

The vegetable which was in universal use before the potato was known, still holds its place as second in public estimation; this is cabbage, which in its wild state appears to be indigenous in England, as well as on the Continent of Europe, but in its cultivated form came to us first, we are told, through the Romans, although the many varieties of this useful plant which are now sold in our markets and served on our tables are of later introduction, and come from various countries. According to Candolle, the wild cabbage of the Mediterranean is the parent of all our varieties.

Dr. Lindley divides cabbage into five classes, the first of which includes kail as grown in Scotch kailyards—that is, cabbage in which the leaves are loose and do not turn into a head.—In the second class we find Brussels sprouts; in the third, common cabbage, savoys, etc.; in the fourth, cauliflower and brocoli; in the fifth, kohl-rabi.

According to Columella, cabbage was a favourite food with Roman freemen, and was sufficiently abundant to be given also to slaves. Cromwell's soldiers are credited with its introduction into Scotland, but we can hardly believe that it was unknown to Scotland at so late a date. The close-hearted variety was imported from Holland, until Sir

Anthony Ashley brought it into cultivation in England. It is said that a cabbage is sculptured at the feet of this gentleman on his monument in Wimborne Minster, Dorset, but according to all accounts he was not altogether an admirable personage, although he rendered a great benefit to the gardeners of this country by the introduction of the cabbage, which in some form serves as food for rich and poor all the year round.

Sir Anthony Ashley brought his cabbage, it is said, in more forms than one, from *Cales* (Cadiz), where he held a command and grew rich by taking unlawful possession of other men's goods, and especially by appropriating some jewels entrusted to him by a lady; hence he is said to have got more by *Cales* (Cadiz) than by *Cale* (cabbage). This, perhaps, may be the origin of our term to *cabbage*. A curious cabbage is found in the Channel Islands. It grows to 8 or even 16 feet in height, and throws out branches from the central stem, which is so hard and woody that walking-sticks are made of it, and it is used as rafters for cottage roofs. Then there is the Portugal cabbage, the mid-ribs of which are cooked like seakale.*

Among the curious kinds of cabbage must also be reckoned the kohl-rabi, which is something between—or, rather, a *combination* of—the cabbage and the turnip, the stem of the cabbage swelling out just above the roots, and forming a round, turnip-like mass, which in this country is only grown—and that very sparingly—as food for cattle ; but which, among the Dutch at the Cape, as well as on the

* The staple food of Russian peasants consists of black rye-bread and cabbage broth thickened with oatmeal, to which salt fish is sometimes added.

Continent of Europe, especially in Germany, is greatly esteemed as a vegetable, and, when properly cooked, is very delicious. Both parts are used : the green leaves are cooked like spinach, and put round the dish, whilst the turnip part is cut into strips, boiled tender, and placed in the centre, thus forming an ornamental and very appetising addition to the dinner-table, which might be advantageously introduced into England ; but the prejudices of our cooks are not easily overcome. It is hard to convince them that what 'furriners' and cattle eat, can be good for Englishmen, although we are glad to see in the greengrocers' shops everywhere now, the large and very delicious cow cabbage, one of which is sufficient for a dozen men. Perhaps, some day the kohl-rabi also may appear on the market, instead of being, as at present, occasionally exhibited at agricultural shows as good food for cattle, in which exhibits, size is the great recommendation ; whereas for cooking purposes, the smaller plants are preferable, and they should, of course, be taken when both leaves and bulb are young and tender.

Next to ordinary cabbage, the savoy ranks as a favourite for winter use, and is best when seen with frost shining on its outer wrinkled leaves : whilst the different varieties of cauliflower and brocoli now appear in the market all the year round, the latter being sent up to Covent Garden during the winter from Cornwall, where it has become a great source of profit since the railway has allowed of its rapid transmission to London. The favourite manure employed for the brocoli fields is old rags, which are sent over by the shipload from Ireland, and stacked for use, being spread over the fields as required, without further manipulation—a practice which appears open to objection on sanitary grounds, although we have never heard any complaint on that score. Certainly the brocoli seems to thrive luxuriantly amidst the old coats of 'Paddy from Cork.'

Seakale (*Crambe maritima*) grows wild on our sea coasts, and we are told in Rhind's 'History of the Vegetable Kingdom' that bundles of it were seen in the Chichester market in 1753. Since that time it has been cultivated with care, and has now become one of the most delicate and highly-prized of our winter vegetables. Grown in darkness under pots made for the purpose, and covered up warmly, it comes to table white and tender, just at the time most needed; but its price makes it a luxury, so that it can never become a poor man's vegetable. A very good substitute for it may, however, be found in the sprouting brocoli, the tender stems and purple flowers of which in the early spring are almost equal in flavour to asparagus.

Cabbage of all kinds is highly nutritious and wholesome, and was prescribed by Hippocrates in cases of colic, but unless cooked fresh it is indigestible, and the smell of the water in which it is boiled is very offensive : this, however, may be obviated by boiling a crust of bread with it.

Sauerkraut, which may be looked upon as a German national dish, is made by pressing layers of cabbage and salt in a vessel. An acid fermentation ensues, which is completed in a few days; the vessel is then covered tightly, and the sauerkraut kept for use as required.

Spinach as a vegetable is more eaten and esteemed in London than in the provinces, but it has been known for centuries, and was cultivated by the monks as early as 1351. Its name is supposed to denote the country from which it was derived, that is *hispanach*, or Spanish plant. Two sorts appear in the market, a summer and a winter spinach; but there is a wild plant known as Good King Henry, which both here and on the Continent is frequently eaten as spinach, which it much resembles, although rather coarser and tougher. It is, however, an excellent substitute, especially in mountainous regions where the cultivated plant is unattainable. Nettles used also to be boiled and eaten in the spring as a substitute for spinach, and are even now sometimes used medicinally by our peasantry.

There are two other favourite vegetables which must be mentioned, although they do not belong to the cabbage tribe. These are asparagus and artichokes, both maritime plants, and both supposed to have come to us from the shores of the Mediterranean, where they grow wild. The wild asparagus is still often served at table in Venice, but it is strong in flavour and less succulent than the cultivated plant. There are two sorts of this delicious vegetable, one pinkish-white and the other green; the latter is certainly to be preferred, although the pink is earliest in the market, being often forced. It is grown largely in France and the Channel Islands as well as in Cornwall, and is ready for table long before the green variety—which is that chiefly grown in England—can be produced, which is a great advantage, as it prolongs the season of a vegetable almost universally esteemed, but which was formerly unattainable before the middle of April or beginning of May. Some of the asparagus now cultivated is of immense size, but hardly equals that grown by the ancient Romans, of which, according to Pliny, three stalks would weigh a pound.

Roman cooks dried asparagus, and when wanted threw them into hot water and boiled them for a few minutes, when they became fresh and green.

Artichokes, unlike asparagus, have rather declined in public estimation of late years, although they are still largely cultivated on the Continent. The flavour is excellent, but the price at which they are sold renders them unfit for the tables of the people, who scarcely know them, and generally look upon the underground, or Jerusalem arti-choke, as the only plant of the name. Artichokes appear to have been highly esteemed during the reign of Henry VIII., in whose privy purse expenses the following entry occurs : 'Paied to a servant of Maister Tresorer in rewarde for bringing archecokks to the king's grace to Yorke place iiij*s*. iiij*d*.

Mushrooms, which have always been so highly esteemed, were formerly known only in the wild state, but of late years their cultivation has been attempted with great success, and they are becoming every year more abundant, tons being sent to market that have been grown in prepared beds.

In France and Germany many strange and highly-coloured mushrooms, which we should reject, are freely eaten, but they are always inspected before being allowed to be offered for sale, and I am informed that an onion is always boiled with them, and if this becomes black, the whole contents of the pot is thrown away as poisonous. It is certain that we often reject as unwholesome and dangerous many varieties of mushroom which might be eaten with impunity, but the frequent illnesses and sometimes fatal cases of poisoning which have from time to time occurred through deleterious fungi, render people over-cautious in eating those which are really wholesome and highly nutritious. Among these may be reckoned the puff-balls, which were formerly regarded as very poisonous, but are now known to be delicious and wholesome when gathered young, cut into slices and fried, but when they are at all yellow inside they should not be eaten. It was formerly believed that all mushrooms grown under a fig-tree, well manured and watered, were wholesome.

Truffles, so highly belauded by all cooks for their excellent flavour, are underground mushrooms, found by the help of dogs or pigs. They grow principally under elms, and were as much prized by the Romans as by modern cooks. Anciently they were served with meat, gravy, wine, skirrets, pepper, and honey, but Avicenna says they were peeled, cut in pieces, cooked in salt and water, and dished up with oil, benzoin, and spices. Leo Africanus says the Arabs cook them in milk. They are now chiefly used as a flavouring in various dishes. The giant mushroom, known as the vegetable beefsteak, is by many looked upon as equal in flavour to real beefsteak.

CHAPTER XIX

HAVING now passed in review most of the vegetables commonly seen on an English dinner-table, it remains only to mention two or three plants grown chiefly for salads, which on the Continent form an indispensable adjunct to the dinner-table, and although less commonly used in England, are still in great request during the summer months.

First and foremost among salad plants is the lettuce, of which there are two principal varieties, the cabbage and the cos; of these the latter is the crispest and best, but the little tender cabbage lettuce is the first to appear in the market, and was doubtless that earliest cultivated in England, as the name of cos applied to the other variety shows that it came to us originally from Cos or some of the neighbouring Greek islands. There is a variety called Bath cos, which is perhaps best of all, and is distinguished by a brownish tinge on the leaves and stalks.

When lettuces are scarce and almost unattainable, their place is supplied by endive, of which also two varieties appear in the market, one with very much divided feathery leaves, and the other, in which the leaves are longer and plain. Both these are bleached for the table, and, with the addition of what is known as small salad, that is, mustard and cress, and that very wholesome plant the watercress, compose an excellent salad during the winter and spring months. During this time also the delicious celery is in season, and forms a very appetising addition to the luncheon or dinner-table, being especially esteemed as an adjunct to bread and cheese. Radishes also and beetroot frequently form ingredients in a winter salad, which abroad is often composed of sliced potato dressed like cucumber, with oil and vinegar.

Celery is sometimes stewed as a vegetable, and of late has been much recommended as a cure for rheumatism, and a variety known as celeriac, of which the root only is eaten, has long been cultivated in Germany for stewing. This has recently been introduced into England, but is still only rarely used.

The composition of a salad is a matter of great nicety, and is seldom left to the taste of an ordinary cook. Abroad the great bowl is set before the mistress of the house, who proceeds to dress it with oil and vinegar, salt, pepper, and mustard. In England less oil and a greater variety of condiment is used, such as is well expressed in the poetical recipe of Sidney Smith,—

> ' Two large potatoes, pass'd through kitchen sieve,
> Smoothness and softness to the salad give;
> Of mordent mustard add a single spoon,
> Distrust the condiment that bites too soon ;
> But deem it not, thou man of herbs, a fault
> To add a double quantity of salt :
> Four times the spoon with oil of Lucca crown,
> And twice with vinegar procured from " town " ;
> True flavour needs it, and your poet begs
> The pounded yellow of two well-boiled eggs.

Q

Let onion's atoms lurk within the bowl,
And scarce suspected, animate the whole;
And lastly, in the flavour'd compound toss
A magic spoonful of anchovy sauce.
Oh! great and glorious, and herbaceous treat,
'Twould tempt the dying anchorite to eat.
Back to the world he'd turn his weary soul,
And plunge his fingers in the salad-bowl.'

Truly an excellent *dressing;* but curiously enough the salad itself is omitted altogether. And here I would hint to those not much accustomed to continental fashions, that whenever the salad makes its appearance, whether at hotel or private table, they may be sure that the feast, as far as meats are concerned, is ended, and if they have not already satisfied their appetite, they must content themselves with the dish (usually roast fowl) which accompanies the salad, for they will get nothing afterwards excepting pastry and dessert.

Of the numerous useful pot-herbs known to cooks, each deserves a special notice, for most of them have medicinal as well as culinary virtues; but it is impossible to do more than name two or three of the principal. Parsley is perhaps that in most universal use, for not only is it employed in numerous seasonings and soups, but it is also largely used in garnishing. It was used by the Greeks, and is said to have been introduced into England in the sixteenth century, but was probably known much earlier.

Sage, known now chiefly in association with onions as a seasoning for ducks, geese, and roast pork, was formerly much in vogue as a medicine in the form of tea, and the leaves were also pressed in curd, which, under the name of sage-cheese, was highly esteemed, as well as another cheese, that in which lemon-thyme took the place of sage. Herb-cheese was a Roman delicacy, and one flavoured with parsley seeds is said to have been greatly relished later by Charlemagne, who had first been regaled upon it by a bishop on a fast-day, and enjoyed it so much that he afterwards ordered a supply of these cheeses to be sent to him annually; and, lest the cheesemonger should send them without the due proportion of seeds, he commanded that they should be cut in two and afterwards skewered together.

Thyme is perhaps best known by name from Shake-speare's song, 'I know a bank whereon the wild thyme grows,' but it is highly esteemed for its flavour in seasoning, although a very small quantity suffices.

Mint, so much associated in the popular idea with lamb, is one of a large variety of plants of the same species, most of which are highly valued in many countries for their medicinal virtues. Peppermint is known everywhere, and the menthol, which of late has been so much used for neuralgia, is pre-pared from a mint, but that which we use in sauce for lamb, is the spearmint.

Marjoram, chervil, basil, and marigold were much used formerly in seasonings, but, like the sorrels, burnet, and garden rocket, which were salad plants in the last century, are seldom seen now. Fennel, also, is little used except as a garnishing, and occasionally as a flavouring in fish sauces, for fashion reigns in food as much as in dress, and the epicures of to-day would turn up their noses at some of the most highly esteemed delicacies of Apicius, whilst the latter would probably scorn the cookery of the most renowned French chef of to-day. We may, however, be thankful that the gluttony of Rome and of ancient Egypt is no longer the fashion. We eat, it is true, often more than hunger requires, but certainly do not indulge in the excesses recorded by ancient historians, although in Russia and Scandinavia it is still the custom to introduce a variety of dishes as a preliminary stimulant to the appetite before dinner. In Russia salt fish, cheese, and brandy serve this purpose; but in Norway and Sweden a greater variety is introduced. Among ourselves, perhaps, oysters may be considered in the same light; and even soups are regarded as a preparation for more solid food. Oysters, however, must now be classed among luxuries, and soups in England are far too rare. We know nothing of the excellent bouillons and vegetable soups which form the invariable prelude to more substantial dishes on the Continent. If an English housewife wants soup she buys an ox-tail, or a pound or two of lean beef, or a calf's head, and the soup thus produced is of course too strong and expensive for family consumption; whereas abroad a very small piece of meat, or none at all, and plenty of vegetables, compose a wholesome and appetising soup at a very small cost.

Our national culinary tastes at present are perhaps too simple. The tables of the wealthy are, of course, supplied with delicacies; but among the middle classes and poor there is a tendency to fancy the plainest of food the most wholesome and economical. A leg of mutton roasted on Sunday, and perhaps only half done, appears on the table cold the greater part of the week, and is finished up on Friday or Saturday in a watery and repellant hash; whereas the same amount of meat, well cooked, with plenty of vegetables, or made into pies or pasties, would make many

savoury, appetising, and wholesome dishes, acceptable alike
to the elders and children of the household; and the bone
crushed and boiled, with the addition of sundry vegetables,
peas, lentils, or a tin of tomatoes, would make a splendid
soup. Certainly we have much to learn in the way of
economical, wholesome, and savoury cookery; and it is
sincerely to be hoped that the various schools of cookery,
which seem to be slowly arousing an interest among
mistresses, will succeed also in inducing servants to study
cooking as an art far more worthy of study for them than
the piano, French, or embroidery,—an art which, when they
get married, will enable them to draw their husbands and
sons from the public-house and club, for however cynical
the saying may appear, it is yet true that 'a man's heart lies
in the region of the stomach.'

I have not attempted in this little book to lay down any
hygienic rules as to diet, for I am convinced that in the
present day too much attention is paid to what is called the
digestibility of food. A healthy stomach ought to be able
to eat with relish, of any well-cooked meat in moderation,
and the extreme care now taken to give children everything
wholesome and nutritious, is tending to produce a nation of
valetudinarians in the near future. Sir Henry Thompson
has well said : ' The wholesomeness of a food consists solely
in its adaptability to the individual, and this relation is
governed mainly by the influences of his age, activity,
surroundings, and temperament or personal peculiarities.'
I have known people to experience indigestion and nausea
after eating boiled mutton, who could eat roast pork with
impunity.

Whilst carefully avoiding the gluttony and extravagance

of the ancients, we need not fall into the opposite extreme, and deem meagreness and bad cooking, household virtues. We need not live to eat, but since we must eat to live, we may as well see that our necessary food is good and appetising.

RECIPES, OLD AND NEW

·' By rosting that which our Forefathers boiled,
   And boiling what they rosted much is spoiled.'

' An ill Cooke cannot licke his owne fingers.'

THE old recipes which follow are taken chiefly from family recipe-books dating back to the last century, and also from two old books without date or title page, but known as 'The Experienced English Housekeeper,' and 'The Frugal Housewife.' The frugality of the latter may be doubted, if we are to judge by the quantity and quality of the comestibles recommended, as an instance of which I would refer to the *Battaglia Pie* (p. 267), but even this is eclipsed by some in the other old book, as for instance, a goose pie which is to be made by stuffing a good fat goose with a large fowl, and that again with an ox tongue; and for a turkey pie it is recommended to have two large capons to *fill up the corners*. Certainly both the family parties and family appetites of the last century, must have been much larger than those of the present day.

It may be of interest also to notice that in a list of things in season appended to the old cookery-book referred to, 'The Experienced English Housekeeper,' we find mention made of hothouse cucumbers in January, forced strawberries in March, cherries and apricots in April, whilst among the fruits and vegetables are many scarcely known now, such as *services*, which are the fruit of the service tree, and under the name of *sorbes*, are still eaten in Italy, but never appear now upon English tables.

Then, among vegetables we get cardoons, chervil, tarragoons, scorzonera, skerrits, salsify, sorrel, chard-beet, burnet, tansey, tarragonel mint, butnet, hyssop, tragopogon, purslane, recombole, finscha, corn salad, etc., etc., a great many of which will read as Greek to modern ears, although we have some others in their places which, if not new, are more abundant than in the days of our great-grandmothers.

To the old recipes I have added others of more modern date, supplied by friends who have tried and found them good. Some of these come from the Cape of Good Hope and from Scotland, and a few are culled from the very excellent 'Domestic Cookery,' by a lady, published in 1810, and also two or three Portuguese dishes from Mrs. Addison's 'Economical Cookery Book,' which is not so well known as it deserves to be.

BREAD, CAKES, PASTRY.

Whole-meal Bread.—To 5 lbs. of meal take 1 oz. carbonate of soda, ¾ oz. tartaric acid, 3 pints water. Dissolve the soda in 2½ pints of water, and mix thoroughly with the meal in a glazed pan; let it stand an hour or so; then dissolve the tartaric acid in the remaining ½ pint of water, and mix as quickly as possible; put on and under tins, and into the oven immediately—oven rather sharp heat. We have been favoured with the above recipe by a London baker.

Unfermented Bread.—Take fine flour 5 lbs., bicarbonate of soda 1 oz., pure tartaric acid 1 oz., water 1 quart, salt ½ oz. Mix the bicarbonate of soda and salt with the flour, and put the tartaric acid into the·water, and then blend the whole in the usual way of making dough; bake in tins, or without. Bread thus made has an agreeable taste, keeps much longer than fermented bread, is more digestible, and less liable to turn sour or mouldy.

French Bread.—With a quartern of fine flour mix the yolks of 3 and whites of 2 eggs beaten and strained, a little salt, ½ pint of good yeast (not bitter), and as much milk made a little warm as will work into a thin light dough; stir it about, but don't knead it. Have ready three quart wooden dishes, divide the dough among them, set to rise, then turn them out into the oven, which must be quick. Rasp when done.

Rolls and Muffins, or any sort of bread, may be made to taste new when two or three days old, by dipping them into water and baking afresh; or a stale loaf may be pulled to pieces, dipped a moment into milk, and the pieces baked a light brown. This is called *pulled bread;* in French, *croûtons.*

Baking Powder.—An equal quantity in bulk of tartaric acid, carbonate of soda, and ground rice or cornflour. Mix thoroughly, and rub through a wire sieve. One teaspoonful to be used to each pound of dry ingredients used in your cake, pudding, etc.

The most primitive of bread is still made and eaten by young travellers and colonists remote from civilisation.

Apropos of which bread, I have seen a letter from the Transvaal, in which the writer says :—'We all know plumduff (minus the plums) is better 1000 miles off than on the table, and *rösterkook* of mealie meal is a thing to contemplate—something to dwell upon, when so heavy that G—— took one in his hand and wanted to know if anyone wanted a dog killed : he knew he could brain him with it, leave alone the choking. For anyone suffering from indigestion, I could recommend our fare. It would be kill or cure !' Transvaal *rösterkook* would seem to be even worse than Australian damper; but I have been assured by another traveller that if made of wheat-meal, with a small quantity of sheep's-tail fat or dripping, the *rösterkook*, i.e., *gridiron cake*, is not to be despised. It is also good cooked on hot stones.

Scone Loaf (Scotch recipe).—2 teacupfuls of flour, 1 teaspoonful of salt, 1 teaspoonful of cream of tartar, ½ teaspoonful of carbonate of soda, a little milk. Mix all well with a spoon, not touching it with the hand, and bake in a moderately quick oven for half an hour.

Tea Cakes.—1 lb. flour, 2 teaspoonfuls of baking powder, 3 oz. butter, pinch of salt. Mix; cut with glass or tin shape, and bake twenty minutes in a quick oven.

Cornish Heavy Cake.—2 lbs. flour, ½ lb. lard, 1 lb. currants, ¼ lb. candied peel, a pinch of salt. Mix well all together, and roll out to the thickness of an inch, slash it into squares on the top, and bake in a very quick oven for ten minutes, or longer if required.

Loaf Cake.—3 lbs. of flour, 2 lbs. of butter, 2 lbs. of sugar, white of 9 eggs, small pint of yeast, some citron, 2 nutmegs, 1 lb. of raisins, and a scant half-teaspoonful of soda. Rub the flour and butter together, then add warm milk, enough to make a soft dough. This should be done at night. In the morning early add the whites of the eggs and sugar beaten together, the fruit, soda dissolved, and let it rise again. When risen, put it in the pans and let it stand about twenty minutes before baking.

Excellent Sponge Cake.—Take 7 eggs, the weight of 6 in sugar and of 4 in flour, half the rind of 1 lemon chopped very fine. The eggs to be well beaten, the yolks and whites separately; the sugar must be mixed in first, and then the flour to be well stirred till put into the oven, and baked about an hour. The oven must not be too hot.

Aberdeen Shortbread.—1 lb. flour, 8 oz. sifted sugar, 12 oz. butter, 4 oz. ground rice, 4 oz. candied orange or citron. Work the butter and sugar to a cream with the hand, add the ground rice and peel, then the flour; knead it smooth and roll it out ½ inch thick. Cut the peel very fine, and the paste into rounds or oblongs. Bake in a slow oven till pale brown.

Cornflour Cake.—Beat 2 oz. of butter to a cream, add 2 to 4 oz. (according to taste) of pounded loaf-sugar, and mix well; break in 2 eggs and beat all well together; stir in lightly ¼ lb. cornflour and 1 teaspoonful baking powder, and beat well together for five minutes; then pour the mixture into a greased cake tin, and put it into the oven immediately; bake for half an hour—the heat should rise to 240 degrees. When done, turn the cake out of the tin and slant it against a plate until cold.

Almond Cakes.—The whites of 2 eggs well beaten, 2 oz. of sweet almonds and 1 oz. of bitter, blanched and pounded, 1 lb. loaf sugar; mix all together and pound in a mortar; roll into small balls, and prick each in three places with a feather. Place the balls on paper far apart, and bake in a slow oven.

Rye Muffins.—With sweet milk—¾ of a cup of rye meal, ¾ of a cup of flour, ½ teaspoonful of soda, 1 teaspoonful of cream of tartar, 1 teaspoonful of sugar, 1 saltspoon of salt, 1 egg beaten and mixed with ½ cup of sweet milk. Put the ingredients together in the order mentioned, and then drop small spoonfuls into hot fat. Cook until done when tried with a fork. With sour milk—1 pint of sour milk, ½ cup of molasses, 1 saltspoonful of salt, the same of cinnamon, 1 teaspoonful of soda, and 2 eggs. Add enough rye flour to make a batter that will drop well from the spoon, and then fry in hot lard. These muffins are good eaten plain with an acid jelly or strong apple sauce ; the old-fashioned way was to eat them with cider, but the apple sauce is the best accompaniment.

Doughnuts.—This is an old Dutch recipe, which has been in use for more than a hundred years. Beat a cup of butter into 2 cups of sugar. Add ½ teaspoonful of salt, 2 eggs well beaten, and 2 cups of milk. Put in flour enough to make a stiff batter. Now add a cup of yeast, and continue stirring in flour till the dough is as stiff as you can stir it. Lay the mass over, sprinkle it with flour, and set it to rise. It will take from fifteen to eighteen hours. Then turn on a moulding board and roll out. Cut in balls 1½ inch in diameter. Slip a raisin in the centre of each one as you cut it out—make a sharp gash with a knife for the purpose, closing the edges by wetting them, otherwise the raisin will fry out in the fat. Let the cut-out nuts stand for half an hour, then fry in hot fat for ten minutes. When they are fried, drain them from all fat and roll them in powdered sugar. Epicures soak them in Santa Cruz rum, and heap them with ice cream for a dessert dish.

Buns (old recipe).—Take 2 lbs. flour, 1 pint of ale-yeast with a little sack, and 3 eggs beaten; knead all together with a little warm milk, nutmeg, and salt. Lay it before the fire till it rise very light. Then knead into it a pound of fresh butter and a pound of round carraway comfits, and bake them in a quick oven on floured papers, in what shape you please.

Queencakes (old recipe).—Take 1 lb. of sugar sifted, pour in yolks and whites of 2 eggs, ½ lb. of butter, a little rosewater, 6 spoonfuls of warm cream, 1 lb. of currants, and as much flour as will make it up. Stir well together, and put in your patty-pans, being well buttered. Bake them in an oven almost as hot as for bread for half an hour; then take them out and glaze them, and let them stand but a little after the glazing is on, to rise.

A Spanish Cake (old recipe).—Take 12 eggs, ¾ lb. of the best moist sugar, mill them in a chocolate-mill till they are all of a lather; then mix in 1 lb. of flour, ½ lb. of pounded almonds, 2 oz. of candied orange-peel, 2 oz. of citron, 4 large spoonfuls of orange or rose water, ½ oz. of cinnamon, and a glass of sack. It is best baked in a slow oven.

Fine Almond Cakes (old recipe).—Take 1 lb. of Jordan almonds, blanch them, beat them very fine with a little orange-flower water, to keep them from oiling; then take 1¼ lb. of fine sugar, boil it to a high candy, and put in your almonds. Then take 2 fresh lemons, grate off the rind very thin, and put as much juice as to make it of a quick taste; put this mixture into glasses, set it in a stove, stirring often that it may not candy; so when it is a little dry, part it into small cakes upon sheets of paper or tin to harden.

Saffron Cakes (old recipe).—Take ½ peck of the finest flour, 1 lb. of butter, and 1 pint of cream or good milk; set the milk on the fire, put in the butter and a good deal of sugar; then strain saffron to your taste and liking into the milk; take 7 or 8 eggs, with 2 yolks (?), and 7 or 8 spoonfuls of yeast; put the milk to it when almost cold, with salt and coriander seeds; knead all together, make up in reasonable sized cakes, and bake in a quick oven.

Maccaroons (old recipe).—Take 1 lb. of almonds, let them be scalded, blanched, and thrown into cold water, then dry them in a cloth and pound them in a mortar; moisten them with orange-flower water, or the white of an egg, lest they turn to an oil; then take an equal quantity of fine powdered sugar, with 3 or 4 whites of eggs; beat all well together, and shape them on wafer paper with a spoon. Bake on tin plates in a gentle oven.

Gingerbread Nuts.—Dissolve over the fire 1 lb. of treacle, ½ lb. of sugar, and ¼ lb. of butter. When the butter is melted let it stand till nearly cold, then add 1¼ lb. of flour, ½ oz. of ginger, some carraways, and any other spice you please. Mix the ingredients well together, and bake them on tins in an oven of moderate heat.

Jumballs (old recipe).—½ lb. of butter, the same quantity of white sugar, 1 lb. of flour, 3 oz. of almonds, 3 eggs, and a little lemon peel. Melt the butter in a pan, beat the sugar into it, break the yolks of the eggs into it, pound the almonds after they are blanched, and put with the flour and lemon peel into the pan, mix together, and make of the mixture coiled snakes, which bake. From ‘Out in the Forty-five,’ a tale of the last century. *N.B.*— The rolled ginger cakes called jumballs in London are not the old English sweetmeat of that name.

Gumballs (another old recipe).—Take 1 lb. of butter, lay it all night in rosewater. When you use it take it out and rub it in 1 lb. of flour, then take 3 eggs with 2 of the whites and a good spoonful of barm. Mix it into a paste. Roule it up in sugar, and tye it up in knots to your fancy. Go bake it on tin pans.

Almond Jumballs (old recipe).—Blanch ½ lb. of almonds, and beat them with a spoonfull of rosewater. Then take 1 lb. of sugar finely beaten, and sift a spoonfull of flower and the whites of 2 eggs, beat in by degrees to your almonds, and when 'tis well mixt, put it on your fire in a skillett; lett it boyle, but be sure you keep stirring it all the while or else it will burn. Then take it off and put it in a mortar again, and beat it till it comes to a perfect paste. Then rowl it out in long rowls and turn it in what formes you please. Bake them on wafer-paper in your oven, and when they rise take them out and lett them stand a little while, then putt them in again and lett them stand till they are enough. Lett not the oven be too hott. You must put in some coriander seed; put the flower in last.

Jumballs of Apricocks or Plums (old recipe).—Bruise the fairest apricocks in a dish and sett it on your fire, turn it and stirr it till it is as stiff as dow (dough). Then rowl it in balls and lett it lie all night. Then work some sifted sugar with your apricock paste, then lay it out in pretty fanceys and dry them on paper in a stove.

A Rich Currant Cake (old recipe).—To a quartern and a half of fine flour add 6 lbs. of currants well picked, washed, and dried, 1 oz. of cloves and mace, a little cinnamon, 2 grated nutmegs, 1 lb. of white sugar, some candied lemon, orange, and citron cut in thin pieces; 1 pint of sweet wine, a little orange-flower or rosewater, 1 pint of yeast, 1 quart of cream, 2 lbs. of butter melted, and poured into the middle of the flour. Then strew some flour over the butter and let it stand half an hour before the fire. After which

R

knead it well together, and put it before the fire to make it
rise.   Work it up very well; put the mixture into a round
tin, and bake two hours and a half in a gentle oven.

A Lenten Dish: Furmity, Frumenty, or Fromenty (old
recipe and excellent).—3 pints of prepared wheat boiled
in 6 quarts of milk, together with 1 lb. of raisins and 1 lb.
of currants, until the fruit is a little tender; meanwhile beat
up 5 eggs and make a stiff batter of flour and milk; pour
this batter gradually into the saucepan and stir till it begins
to thicken, then take off the fire and add a pinch of salt,
half a nutmeg (grated), and sweeten to taste; pour into
dishes, and eat cold.   *N.B.*—Do not stone the raisins.
To prepare the wheat, take a pint of wheat, thoroughly
cleaned, soak it all night in water, then put it in a large
basin filled with cold water; tie a cloth over; put it in a
pot of boiling water up to the rim of the basin, and let it
boil many hours, till the wheat swells and forms a white
pudding in the basin.

Oatmeal Flummery (very old recipe).—Put oatmeal (as
much as you want) into a broad deep pan, cover it with
water, stir it together and let it stand twelve hours; then
pour off that water clear, and put on a good deal of fresh;
shift it again in twelve hours, and so on in twelve more.
Then pour off that water clear, and strain the oatmeal
through a coarse hair sieve, pour it into a saucepan, keeping
it stirring all the time with a stick till it boils and becomes
very thick.   Then pour it into dishes.   When cold, turn it
into plates, and eat it with what you please, either wine
and sugar, or milk.   It eats very well with cyder and sugar.
You may observe to put a great deal of water to the oatmeal, and when you pour off the last water, put on just

enough fresh to strain the oatmeal well. Some let it stand forty-eight hours, some three days, shifting the water every twelve hours; but that is as you like it for sweetness or tartness. Groats once cut do better than oatmeal. Mind to stir it together when you put in fresh water.

Plumb Pottage (old recipe).—Take a leg of beef and a neck of mutton; put it into a gallon of water; let it boyle till all the goodness is out. Then take it off the fire and strain it, and when 'tis cold take off all the fat. The next day grate the crumb of a sixpenny loaf and let it steep in a little of your liquor. Set your liquor on the fire and put in 2 nutmegs cut into quarters, with a pretty deal of whole mace, 3 or 4 cloves, and a little cinnamon. Put in 2 lbs. of currants picked and washed, 2 lbs. of raisins of the sun, 2 lbs. of prunes, and ½ lb. of dates stoned. Put in the bread with your fruit, and when they are well boyld together take it off the fire. Sweeten to your taste and put in it a bottle of claret, a pint of sack or vinegar. Garnish with grated bread crumbs browned, and a heap of plumped raisins here and there.*

Quaking Pudding (old recipe).—Put on your fire 1 pint of milk and 1 pint of cream, mix 1 spoonfull of milk to 3 spoonfulls of flower, 6 eggs yolk and white, a little grated nutmeg, a little mace with some suet; beat it well together, pour your boyling cream and milk into it; stir it together, then butter your dish, fill him to the brim and tye a cloth close over him, boyle him an hour and quarter, then take him out, and pour over him melted butter and sack, strew sugar over him, serve him to the table.

---

* This is probably the plum-porridge with which the "Man in the South" is reported to have "burnt his mouth," and may also be regarded as the origin of our famous Christmas plum-pudding.

To make a Tansie (old recipe).—Break 18 eggs and put away the white; put to them 1 quart of cream, 1 pint of the juice of spinage, 1 spoonfull of the juice of tansie, the crumbs of a penny loaf; mix it together, and put a piece of butter in your skillet, put your tansie into it, keep stirring it over the fire till it is as thick as hasty pudding, then put a piece of butter in a frying-pan, and put in your tansie with a spoon, spread it abroad handsome, and turn it with a pye-plate once or twice, frying him crimpt,.but not burn him; let it be an inch thick. If the colour be not to your mind, heate a fire-shovel, hold it over it, and make it what colour you will, and serve it to the table with sweet oranges and sugar.

To make Cheesecakes (old recipe).—Take 1 quart of cream and 1 gallon of milk, run it tender as you do cold cheese (*i.e.*, make of it a light curd with rennet), when 'tis come, brake it and draw the whey clean from it; work your curd with a spoon through a hair sieve, put to it ¾ lb. of butter, and as much sugar as will sweeten it, with the yolk of 6 eggs, and a little grated nutmeg and a drop of rosewater: work it well, and mix 1 lb. of currants, washed and picked, amongst it; put it into your paste, bake it half an hour, then take them out and serve them to the table.

To make Rice Cheesecakes (old recipe).—Boil 2 quarts of cream or milk with a little whole mace and cinnamon, then take off the fire, remove the spice, and put in ½ lb. of rice flour, and place it on the fire again to boil, stirring it together; then take it off, and beat the yolks of 24 eggs, set it on the fire again, and keep stirring till it is as thick as curds; add ½ lb. of blanched almonds pounded, and sweeten to your palate; or, if you chuse, you may put in ½ lb. of currants, well picked, and rubbed in a clean cloth.

Lemon Cheesecakes (old recipe).—Take 2 large lemon peels, boil and pound them well together in a mortar, with about 6 oz. of loaf-sugar and the yolks of 6 eggs; mix all well together, and fill your patty-pans about half full. Orange cheesecakes you may do the same way, but be careful to boil the peels in two or three waters to get out the bitterness.

To make a Custard (old recipe).—Boil 1 quart of cream or milk, with a stick of cinnamon, a large mace, and a quartered nutmeg; when half cold, mix with it the yolks of 8 eggs and 4 whites beaten well, some sack, sugar, and orange-flower water. Set it on the fire, and stir it till a white froth rises; skim that off, then strain it, and fill your custard cups, and let them just boil up in the oven, or if you boil the eggs in the cream all together, then you may put it in your custard cups overnight, and they will be fit for use.

To make Oatmeal Pudding (old recipe).—To ½ pint of oatmeal, bruised, put ½ pint of milk, boyling hot. Let it stand all night, put to it 1 lb. of suet, ½ lb. of raisins, and as many currants, 5 eggs, three of the whites, a handful of grated bread, a little nutmeg, some salt, a little sugar, and a glass of white wine. Boyle it three hours.

Our Own Plum Pudding.—1 lb. of best beef suet chopped very fine, 1 lb. best raisins stoned and cut in half, 1 lb. of currants well washed and dried, ½ lb. of flour, ½ lb. of finely-crumbled bread crumbs, ½ lb. mixed candied peel finely shred, ½ lb. of white sugar pounded and sifted, a little lemon peel grated, small teaspoonful of mixed spice and half a nutmeg, the juice of half a lemon, 3 eggs well beaten, and a ¼ pint of brandy. Mix all the dry materials together thoroughly with a wooden spoon, then add the eggs, brandy, and lemon, with enough cold water to make a rather stiff compound. Put into well-buttered basins, cover with buttered paper and a well-floured cloth, and boil for eight or nine hours. We generally make a treble quantity at Christmas, boiling all the puddings the same time—nine hours, hang the basins in the kitchen (not to touch the wall), and they will keep for months. When wanted for use, boil an hour, taking care not to allow the water to rise to the top of the basin, or covering the basin with another well-wetted and floured cloth.

Norfolk or Hard Dumpling.—Take 1 lb. flour and mix it with cold water by degrees till it is a stiff dough, putting in a pinch of salt. Knead it well for at least five minutes, then cut it into pieces about the size of an orange. It should be stiff enough to shrink up when cut, as dough does when it is risen. Work each piece round in the hollow of the hand till it forms a smooth ball, cutting off the small knob it is worked up with. Put the dumplings into plenty of boiling water, and boil for twenty minutes. Serve with well-dredged and brown dripping, or with butter or treacle.

Light or Suffolk Dumplings.—Take a portion of bread dough which is ready for baking; cut it into pieces the size of an orange; knead or work them up into smooth round balls and boil from twenty to thirty minutes; or they may be made by adding a teaspoonful of baking powder and a pinch of salt to 1 lb. of flour worked into balls and boiled as above. The gravy to be served with them is made of the dripping from a well-basted and dredged joint, to which more flour is added, boiling it till well browned; it must be served very hot.

Good Fritters (old recipe).—Mix ½ pint of good cream

very thick with flour, beat 6 eggs, leaving out 4 whites ; add 6 spoonfuls of sack, and strain them into the cream ; put in a little grated nutmeg, ginger, cinnamon, and salt ; then put in another ½ pint of cream, and beat the batter near an hour ; pare and slice your apples thin ; dip every piece in the batter, and throw them into a pan with boiling lard.

Pancakes (old recipe).—Take 1 pint of thick cream, 6 spoonfuls of sack, and ½ pint of fine flour, 6 eggs (but only 3 whites), 1 grated nutmeg, ¼ lb. melted butter, a very little salt, and some sugar ; fry them thin in a dry pan.

Crumply Pudding.—1 quart of milk, 4 tablespoonfuls of flour, 2 eggs, ¼ lb. of moist sugar, and a little finely-chopped suet. Grease a mould, stick it with raisins, orange and lemon peel, and citron ; make the flour into a smooth paste with the milk, and add the sugar. Pour this into the mould, and on the top place sufficient chopped suet to cover it. Bake in the oven until the suet looks brown and set. Turn out of the mould, and serve very hot.—*Mrs. Addison.*

Sicilian Pudding.—Melt ¼ lb. of fresh butter and let it cool gradually, then pour it on the yolks of 2 eggs and the white of 1 ; add ¼ lb. pounded sugar, and flavour with almond. Then line a dish with good puff paste, and put a layer of one or two kinds of preserves in it, pouring the above mixture over all, and bake it ; when it is just baked, spread over it the whites of 2 eggs, whipped to a solid froth, and sift some finely-powdered sugar over it till it looks quite white ; let it stand for a few minutes in a cool oven or before a fire to harden, and then stick spikes of blanched almonds all over it.—*Weekly Scotsman.*

Alderman's Pudding.—6 oz. bread crumbs, 4 oz. sugar, 4 oz. suet, 1 lemon rind, 1 egg, 1 tablespoonful brandy.

Chop the suet finely, add the bread crumbs and sugar, grate over the lemon rind. In a separate basin beat the egg till very light, add it to the mixture in the basin. Pour over the brandy, and mix all well together. Grease a mould with butter, pour in the mixture, cover the mould with a sheet of paper. Place the mould in a saucepan half full of boiling water, and let the water boil for one hour and twenty minutes. Turn out the pudding on to a hot dish, and pour round a jam or wine sauce.— *Weekly Scotsman.*

Scotch Pudding.—1 teacupful of suet, and the same quantity of sugar and currants, 1½ teacupful each of flour and milk, 1½ tablespoonful of ground rice, 1 teaspoonful of soda, and the same quantity of spice. Mix well together, and put in a basin with a plate on the top, in boiling water, not to cover the basin. Boil two hours.— *Cape Recipe.*

Brown Betty.—Fill a pie-dish with alternate layers of bread crumbs dotted with butter and slightly sprinkled with spice, and sharp-flavoured apples cut thin and strewn with sugar. Let the top layer be of crumbs, and then bake a nice light brown.

Brentwood Pudding.—3 oz. bread crumbs, 3 oz. butter, 3 oz. sugar, the yolks of 3 eggs, the juice of a lemon and half the peel grated. Put a layer of jam or marmalade at the bottom of a pie-dish, over which pour the above ingredients well mixed. Bake forty minutes. Take it out at the end of thirty minutes and pour over it the whites of the eggs beaten to a stiff froth with lump-sugar, and then return it to the oven for ten minutes. Good hot or cold.

On Paste making.—The art of paste making is a mystery to which some cooks never attain: they have, as it is termed, a heavy hand, and, do what thay will, their pastry is never light. The varieties of paste and modes of making are numerous. There is short paste, flaky or puff paste, French paste, and the raised crust used for pork and other meat and game pies. Sifted sugar is generally used in short crust, which, of course, renders it unfit for use with meat. The ingredients for a good crust are, $\frac{3}{4}$ lb. of butter to 1 lb. of flour, 1 tablespoonful of sifted sugar, and $\frac{1}{3}$ pint of water; or less butter may be used, with the addition of the yolks of 2 eggs and $\frac{1}{4}$ pint of milk instead of water. For the best puff paste equal parts of flour and butter are used, part of the butter being rubbed into the flour and the rest spread in layers on the crust, which should be rolled out several times, a very slight sprinkling of flour being put over the butter as spread, which, when rolled out, serves to separate the layers and make it light and flaky. Some cooks beat the paste with a rolling pin; some set it aside for some hours in a cold cellar, or on a marble slab; whilst others roll it out quickly and put it in the oven at once. We have tasted excellent pastry made in all these ways, and also when clarified dripping, or half butter half lard has been used instead of all butter. For common household pastry, 8 oz. of butter and lard, or clarified dripping, to 1 lb. of flour is quite sufficient. To make raised crust, boil $\frac{1}{4}$ lb. of lard, or clarified dripping, in $1\frac{1}{2}$ gills of water, and pour it hot on to 1 lb. of flour, to which a good pinch of salt has been added. Mix into a stiff paste, pinch off enough of it to make the lid, and keep it hot. Flour your board and work the paste into a ball, then with the knuckles of your right hand press a hole in the centre, and mould the paste into a round or oval shape, taking care to keep it a proper thickness. Having put in the meat, well seasoned, join the lid to the pie, which raise lightly with both hands so as to keep it a good high shape, cut round the edge of the lid with a sharp knife, and make the trimmings into leaves to ornament the pie; and having placed these on, with a rose in the centre, put the pie on a floured baking-sheet, and brush it over with yolk of egg. The crust of the pie should be cool and set, before putting it into the oven, which should be a moderate heat. Some people use a tin mould, but it is much better raised by the hand; in order to succeed, the crust must be moulded whilst hot, and it also requires quick manipulation.

Paste for Venison Pasties (old recipe).—Take 4 lbs. of butter to $\frac{1}{2}$ peck of flour; rub it all into your flour, but not too small; then make it into a paste, and beat it with a rolling-pin for an hour before you use it. If you please you may beat 3 or 4 eggs, and put them in your paste when you mix it.

An Umble Pie (old recipe).—Take the umbles of a buck, boil them and chop them as small as meat for minced pies, put to them as much beef suet, 8 apples, $\frac{1}{2}$ lb. of sugar, $1\frac{1}{2}$ lb. of currants, a little salt, some mace, cloves, nutmeg, and a little pepper; then mix them together, and put it into a paste; add $\frac{1}{2}$ pint of sack, the juce of 1 lemon and orange, close the pie, and when it is baked serve it up.

A Lumber Pie (old recipe).—Take $1\frac{1}{2}$ lb. of fillet of veal, mince it with the same quantity of beef suet, season it with sweet spice, 5 pippins, 1 handful of spinach, a hard lettuce, thyme, and parsley; mix it with a penny loaf grated, and the yolks of 2 or 3 eggs, sack and orange-flower water, $1\frac{1}{2}$ lb. of currants and preserves, with a caudle.

A Battaglia Pie (old recipe).—Take 4 small chickens, squab pigeons, and 4 sucking rabbits, cut them in pieces, and season them with savoury spice; lay them in the pie with 4 sweetbreads sliced, as many sheep's tongues and shivered palates, 2 pair of lamb sweetbreads, 20 or 30 cocks' combs, with savoury balls and oysters; lay on butter, and close the pie with a lear.

Minced Pie (old recipe).—Shred 1 lb. of neat's tongue parboiled, with 2 lbs. of beef suet, 5 pippins, and a green lemon peel; season it with 1 oz. of spice, a little salt, 1 lb. of sugar, 2 lbs. of currants, ½ pint of sack, a little brandy, the juice of a lemon, ¼ lb. of citron, lemon, and orange peel; mix these together, and fill the pie.

A Lamb Pie with Currants (old recipe).—Take a leg and a loin of lamb, cut the flesh into small pieces, and season with a little salt, cloves, mace, and nutmeg; then lay the lamb in your paste, with as many currants as you think proper, and some Lisbon sugar; a few raisins, stoned and chopped small, and some forced meat balls, yolks of hard eggs, with artichoke bottoms, or potatoes boiled and cut in dice, with candied orange and lemon peel in slices; put butter on the top, and a little water; then close your pie. Bake it gently; when it is baked, take off the top and put in your caudle, made of gravy from the bones, some white wine and juice of lemon; thicken it with the yolks of 2 eggs and a bit of butter. When you pour in your caudle, let it be hot, and shake it well in the pie; then serve it, having laid on the cover.

Note.—If you observe too much fat swimming on the liquor of your pie, take it off before you pour in your caudle.

Eel Pie (old recipe).—Cut, wash, and season them with sweet seasoning and a handful of currants; butter and close it. Some omit the currants.

MEATS, ETC.—OLD RECIPES.

For Roasting Beef.—If a sirloin or rump, you must not salt it, but lay it a good way from the fire; baste it once or twice with water and salt, then with butter; flour it, and keep basting it with its own dripping. When the smoak of it draws to the fire it is near enough done. If the ribs, sprinkle them with a little salt half an hour before you lay it down; dry and flour it, then butter a piece of paper very thick, and fasten it on to the beef; put the buttered side next the meat.

For Roasting Lamb or Mutton.—The loin and the saddle must be done as the beef, but the skin should be raised and skewered on again to prevent it from scorching. A quarter of an hour before you take it up, take off the skin, dust on some flour, baste with butter, and sprinkle on a little salt. Garnish with scraped horse radish, and serve with potatoes, brocoli, French beans, watercresses, pickled cabbage, etc. The shoulder requires onion sauce.

To Roast Mutton, Venison Fashion.—Take a hind quarter of fat mutton, and cut it like a haunch; lay it in a pan with the back side down; pour a bottle of red wine over it, and let it lie twenty-four hours; then spit it and baste it with the same liquor, and butter all the time it is roasting at a good quick fire; two hours and a half will do it. Have a little good gravy in a boat, and currant jelly in another. A good fat neck of mutton eats finely done thus.

A Shoulder or Leg of Mutton Stuffed.—Stuff with mutton suet, salt, pepper, nutmeg, grated bread, and yolks of eggs; then stick it all over with cloves and roast it. When about half done, cut off some of the under side of the fleshy end in little bits; put these into a pipkin with a pint of oysters, liquor and all, a little salt and mace, and ½ pint of hot water; stew them till half the liquor is wasted, then put in a piece of butter rolled in flour, shake all together, and when the mutton is done take it up; pour the sauce over it and send to table.

To Roll a Breast of Mutton.—First bone the mutton, then make a savoury forced meat for it, and wash it over with the batter of eggs, then spread the forced meat on it, roll it in a collar, and bind it with packthread, then roast it; put under it a regalia of cucumbers.

To Roast Veal.—Paper the udder of the fillet, and the back of the loin to prevent scorching; lay the meat at some distance from the fire at first, baste it well with butter and dust it with flour, then draw it nearer the fire, and a little before you take it up baste it again. The breast must be roasted with the caul on, and the sweet-bread skewered on the back side. It is proper to have a toast nicely baked laid in the dish with the loin. Garnish with lemon and barberries. Most people stuff the fillet and shoulder thus: Take about 1 lb. of grated bread, ½ lb. of suet, some parsley shred fine, thyme, marjoram or savory, a small onion, a little grated nutmeg, lemon peel, pepper and salt, and mix well together with whites and yolks of eggs; put half in the udder, and the rest in the holes from which the bones were taken.

To Roast Pork.—Pork requires more cooking than other

meat, and it is best to sprinkle it with a little salt the night before you use it, except on the rind, which must never be salted. The best way to roast a leg is to parboil, then take off the skin and lay it down; baste it with butter; then take a little pepper and salt, a little sage shred fine, bread crumbs, and a little nutmeg. Throw these all over it whilst it is roasting; then put a little drawn gravy into the dish with the crumbs that drop from it. Some stuff the knuckle with sage and onions, and serve with apple sauce. This is called a mock goose.

To Roast a Pig.—Spit your pig, and lay it down to a clear fire. Put into the belly a few sage leaves, a little pepper and salt, a small crust of bread, and a bit of butter; sew it up, and flour well. When the skin is crisp put two plates into the dripping-pan to save the gravy which comes from it. Put ¼ lb. of butter in a clean coarse cloth, and rub all over till the flour is quite taken off; then take it up into your dish, take the sage, etc., out of the belly, and chop it small. Cut off the head, open it, and take out the brains, which chop, and put the sage and brains into ½ pint of good gravy, with a piece of butter rolled in flour; then cut your pig down the back, and lay it flat on the dish. Cut off the two ears, and lay one on each shoulder; put the head between the shoulders, pour the gravy out of the plates into your sauce and then into the dish; garnish with lemon, and if you please, pap sauce in a basin.

To Roast a Hare.—Truss your hare, and then make a pudding thus: ¼ lb. of beef suet minced fine, as much bread crumbs, the liver chopped fine, parsley and lemon peel shred fine, seasoned with pepper, salt, and nutmeg. Moisten with an egg, and put it into the hare's belly. Let your dripping-pan be very clean; put into it 1 quart of milk and 6 oz. of butter, and baste it with this till the whole is used. About five minutes before you take it up dust on a little flour, and baste with fresh butter that it may be well frothed. Put a little gravy in the dish and the rest in a boat; garnish with lemon.

To Roast a Green Goose with Green Sauce.—Roast your goose nicely; in the meantime make your sauce thus : Take ½ pint of the juice of sorrel, 1 spoonful of white wine, a little grated nutmeg, and some grated bread. Boil this over a gentle fire, and sweeten with pounded sugar to your taste; garnish with lemon.

The German Way of Dressing Fowls.—Take a turkey or fowl, stuff the breast with what forcemeat you like, fill the body with roasted chestnuts peeled, and lay it down to roast. Take ½ pint of good gravy, with a little piece of butter rolled in flour; boil these together with some small turnips and sausages, cut in slices, and fried or boiled; garnish with chestnuts. You may dress ducks the same way.

To Roast Quails.—Truss them, and stuff with beef suet and sweet herbs shred very fine, and seasoned with a little spice. When warm baste with salt and water, then dredge them, and baste with butter. For sauce, dissolve an anchovy in good gravy, with 2 or 3 shallots shred very fine, and the juice of a Seville orange. Dish them up in this sauce, and garnish with fried bread crumbs and lemon.

To Roast Plovers.—Green plovers are roasted as you do woodcocks. Lay them upon toast, and put good gravy sauce in the dish. Grey plovers are roasted or stewed thus: Make a forcemeat of artichoke bottoms cut small, seasoned with pepper, salt, and nutmeg. Stuff and put the birds into a saucepan with a good gravy just to cover them, a glass of white wine, and a blade of mace; cover them close, and stew them softly till they are tender; then take up your plovers into a dish, put in a piece of butter rolled in flour to thicken your sauce; let it boil till smooth, squeeze in a little lemon, scum it clean, and pour over the birds; garnish with orange.

To Roast Culf's Liver.—Lard it well with large slices of bacon, fasten it on a spit, roast it at a gentle fire, and serve with good gravy or melted butter.

To Roast an Eel.—Scour the eel well with salt; skin him almost to the tail; then gut, wash, and dry him. Take ¼ lb. of suet shred fine, sweet herbs, and a shallot; mix together with salt, pepper, and nutmeg; scotch your eel on both sides, wash it with yolks of eggs, lay some seasoning over it, and stuff the belly with it, then draw the skin over it, and tie it to the spit; baste with butter, and make a sauce of anchovies and melted butter. Any other river or sea fish that are large enough may be dressed in the same way.

For Boiling Meats we need not give old recipes, as they are the same as the modern, but this mode of cooking seems to have been extended to things which we should not dream of boiling nowadays, such as geese and ducks, woodcocks and snipes, pheasants and partridges, the latter being served with celery or mushroom sauce, or with melted butter, flavoured with parsley, lemon, and the livers of the birds.

To Fry Beefsteaks.—Take rump steaks, beat them very well with a roller, fry them in ½ pint of ale that is not bitter, and whilst they are frying, for your sauce, cut a large onion small, a very little thyme, some parsley shred small, some grated nutmeg, and a little pepper and salt; roll all together in a piece of butter, and then in a little flour, put this into the stew-pan, and shake all together. When the steaks are tender, and the sauce of a fine thickness, dish them up.

To Fry Sausages with Apples.—Take ½ lb. of sausages and 6 apples, slice 4 about as thick as a crown, cut the other 2 in quarters, fry them with the sausages of a fine light brown, and lay the sausages in the middle of the dish, with the apples round; garnish with the quartered apples. Stewed cabbage and sausages fried is a good dish; then heat cold peas pudding in the pan, when it is quite hot, heap it in the middle of the dish, and lay the sausages all round edgeways and one in the middle at length.

To make Scotch Collops.—Dip slices of lean veal in the yolks of eggs that have been beaten up with melted butter, a little salt, some grated nutmeg, and grated lemon peel. Fry them quick, shake them all the time to keep the butter from oiling. Then put to them some beef gravy and some mushrooms, or forced meat balls. Garnish with sausages and sliced lemon, and slices of fried bacon.

To Stew Beef Collops.—Cut raw beef, as veal is cut for Scotch collops. Put the collops into a stew-pan with a little water, a glass of white wine, a shallot, a little dried marjoram rubbed to powder, some salt and pepper, and a slice or two of fat bacon. Set this over a quick fire till the pan be full of gravy, which will be in a little time, add to it a little mushroom juice; serve it up hot, garnished with sliced lemon or small pickles and red cabbage.

To Stew a Hare.—Beat it well with a rolling-pin in its

S

own blood, cut it into little bits and fry them. Then put the hare into the stew-pan with a quart of strong gravy, pepper and salt, and let it stew till tender. Thicken it with butter and flour. Serve it up in its gravy, with sippets and lemon sliced for garnish.

To Jug a Hare.—Having skinned your hare, turn the blood into a jug; then cut the hare in pieces, but do not wash it; cut ¾ lb. of fat bacon into thin slices; pour upon the blood about 1 pint of strong old pale beer; put into the jug 1 middling-sized onion, stuck with 3 or 4 cloves and 1 bunch of sweet herbs, and having seasoned the hare with pepper, salt, nutmeg, and lemon peel grated, put in the meat, a layer of hare and a layer of bacon; then stop the jug close, so that the steam be kept in entirely; put the jug into a kettle of water over the fire, and let it stew three hours, then strain off the liquor, and having thickened it with burnt butter, serve it up hot, garnished with lemon juice.

To Stew Ducks.—Draw and clean your ducks well, and put them into a stew-pan with strong beef gravy, a glass of red wine, a little whole pepper, an onion, an anchovy, and some lemon peel; when well stewed, thicken the gravy with butter and flour, and serve all up together, garnished with shallots.

To Spitchcock Eels.—You must split a large eel down the back, and joint the bones, cut it in two or three pieces, melt a little butter, put in a little vinegar and salt; let your eel lay in it two or three minutes, then take the pieces out, roll them in bread crumbs, and broil them of a fine brown. Let your sauce be plain butter, with the juice of a lemon, or good gravy with an anchovy in it.

To Broil Eggs.—First put your salamander into the fire,

then cut a slice round a quartern loaf, toast it brown and butter it, lay it on a dish, and set it before the fire; poach 7 eggs just enough to set the whites, take them out carefully and lay them on your toast, brown them with the salamander, grate some nutmeg over them, and squeeze Seville orange over all. Garnish with orange cut in slices.

To Hash Mutton.—Take mutton half roasted, and cut it in pieces as big as half a crown; then put into a sauce-pan ½ pint of red wine, as much strong broth or gravy, 1 anchovy, 1 shallot, a little whole pepper, some nutmeg grated, and salt to taste; let these stew a little, then put in the meat and a few capers and samphire shred; when it is hot through, thicken it up with a piece of butter rolled in flour; have toasted sippets ready to lay on the dish, and pour the meat on them. Garnish with lemon.

To Mince Veal.—Take underdone veal and shred as fine as possible, then take some beef gravy, dissolve in it the quantity of a hazel nut of cavear to ½ lb. of meat; put into the gravy the minced veal, and let it boil not above a minute, pour it into a soup plate or dish upon sippets of toasted bread, and garnish with pickled cucumbers, or with slices of broiled bacon.

To Dress a Mock Turtle.—Take a calf's head with the skin on, cut off the horny part in thin slices, put in the brains and the giblets of a goose well boiled; have ready between 1 quart and 3 pints of strong mutton or veal gravy, with 1 pint of Madeira wine, 1 large teaspoonful of cayenne pepper, half the peel of a large lemon shred very fine, a little salt, the juice of 2 lemons; stew all these together till the meat is very tender, which will be in about an hour and a half; then have ready the shell of a turtle edged with a paste of flour and water hardened in the oven; put in the ingredients, and set it in the oven to brown, and when that is done garnish the top with yolks of hard-boiled eggs and forced meat balls.

To Hash Cold Fowl.—Cut up your fowl into small pieces, put them in a stew-pan with a blade or two of mace, and a little shred lemon peel; dredge on a little flour and throw in some gravy; when it begins to simmer, put in a few pickled mushrooms, and a lump of butter rolled in flour; when it boils give it a toss or two, and pour into the dish. Garnish with sliced lemon and barberries.

To Fricassee Pigeons.—Prepare some pigeons, quarter and fry them; take some green pease and fry them also till they be like to burst, then pour boiling water upon them, and season the liquor with pepper, salt, onions, garlic, parsley, and vinegar; thicken with yolks of eggs.

For Stewing Ducks whole.—Wash your ducks, then put them in a stew-pan, with strong broth, anchovy, lemon peel, whole pepper, an onion, mace, and red wine; when well stewed put in a piece of butter and some grated bread to thicken it; lay forcemeat balls and crisped bacon round them.   Garnish with shallots.

To Fricassee Cold Roast Beef.—Cut your beef into very thin slices, then shred a handful of parsley very small, cut an onion into pieces, and put them together into a stew-pan with a piece of butter and a good quantity of strong broth; season with pepper and salt and let it stew gently a quarter of an hour; and beat the yolks of 4 eggs in some claret, and a spoonful of vinegar, and put it to your meat, stirring it till it grows thick; rub your meat with a shallot before you serve it up.

Ragoo of Cock's Combs, Cock's Kidneys, and Fat Livers.—
Take a stew-pan, put in some butter, a bunch of sweet
herbs, some mushrooms and truffles, put it for a minute
over the fire, flour it, moisten it with broth, season with salt
and pepper, let it stew a little, then put in the cock's
combs, kidneys, fat livers, and sweet herbs ; let your ragoo
be palatable, thicken it with the yolks of eggs, serve it for
a dáinty dish.

To make a fine White Soup.—Take a leg of beef and a
knuckle of veal, and let them boil at least four hours, then
beat 1 lb. of sweet almonds very fine and mix them with
some of the broth, then serve with the almonds in it, and
sippets of fried bread.

Gravy Soup.—Cut 1 lb. of mutton, 1 lb. of veal, and 1
lb. of beef into little pieces, put it into 7 or 8 quarts of
water, with an old fowl beat to pieces, 1 onion, 1 carrot,
some white pepper and salt, a little bunch of herbs, 2 blades
of mace, and 3 or 4 cloves, some celery, cabbage, endive,
turnip, and lettuce. Let it stew over a slow fire till half is
wasted, then strain it off for use.

For making Veal Rolls.—Lay some slices of veal on
some slices of bacon of the same size, then lay some green
forcemeat upon that. Roll them, tie them, and roast them,
rub them with the yolks of eggs, flour them and baste them
with butter. When done enough lay them in a dish, and
have ready some gravy, morels, truffles, and mushrooms ;
garnish with lemon.

A FEW MODERN RECIPES—TRIED AND APPROVED.

To Dress Springbok.—Take the leg, lard it well with
strips of bacon or salted tail of the Africander sheep

(which has a tail sometimes 25 lbs. in weight), put butter on it and dredge with flour, roast it well, basting frequently. Serve with it quince or guava jelly.

The South African Hunter's Greatest Delicacy while Camping Out.—The liver of the bok just killed, either grilled on a gridiron or roasted on large flat stones made red hot in a wood fire. Eaten with *hunter's sauce*, and a little pepper and salt if obtainable.

Stewed Springbok.—Take the chine only, sever the bones at each joint, put into a camp-kettle with water and some butter or dripping, simmer gently till all the water has evaporated, then keep stirring it well in the rich gravy, dredge in a little flour, and add pepper and salt. To be served with quince jelly and a dish of rice or stamped maize.

This mode of cooking would be equally applicable to chamois, and in the Tyrol they serve with it Verona fruits, which consist of all kinds of fruit partly pickled and partly preserved, so as to be very hot and very sweet. Dried peaches stewed make an excellent condiment to eat with springbok or other game.

Frehkedel.—Mince any kind of meat, take some stale bread that has been soaked in milk, and mix with 2 or 3 eggs, flavour with spices and salt, make into balls; keep the white of 1 egg and roll the balls in it, then strew over them grated bread or biscuit crumbs, and fry a light brown.

Garlic Pork (Portuguese Christmas Dish).—Cut up fresh streaky pork into small pieces, rub them with salt, pound a few cloves of garlic, a bunch of sweet herbs, and some Chili peppers. Pack closely in a stone jar, adding sufficient vinegar to cover them. This should be done a week before required for use, but will keep for months. When wanted, take as much meat as may be necessary, drain it and fry a light brown. Serve each piece on toast. A cut orange is always sent to table with this dish, a few drops of the juice being a great improvement.—*Mrs. Addison.*

Fricasseed Calves' Feet.—Soak them three hours, simmer them in equal proportions of milk and water until they are sufficiently tender to remove the meat from the bones; cut into good-sized pieces, dip them in yolk of egg, cover with fine bread crumbs, pepper and salt them, fry a beautiful brown, and serve with white sauce.

A Fricandelle.—Chop some remains of veal or any other cold meat, fat and lean together; season it with pepper and salt to your taste. Put grated bread crumbs to it in proportion to the quantity of meat—about 1 teacupful generally suffices; add 1 oz. of butter, 1 egg, and a little good gravy. Mix these ingredients well together, and press them firmly into a basin or mould, which must be previously buttered. Boil for half an hour, turn it out of the mould, and send it to table with a little brown gravy over it.

Minced Collops.—Fresh meat chopped very fine and put into a pan in which a piece of suet has been allowed to melt to a brown gravy. Let the whole stew gently for about ten minutes, turning the meat occasionally; then cover the meat with boiling water (not cold), and let it stew for an hour longer, adding salt and pepper just before dishing. Garnish with hard-boiled eggs and bits of brown toast.

Hashed Venison.—The meat should be cut in slices. Have ready some good, well-flavoured gravy; place in the stew-pan a little butter and flour, and simmer and stir till brown; add to this the gravy strained, and a little Harvey sauce or port wine. Let the venison be placed in the gravy only long enough to be thoroughly *hot*, as if *boiled* it will be *spoiled*.

Meat Omelette.—A very small piece of cold steak will make, with 3 eggs, a meat omelette which will be sufficient for four persons. The meat must be carefully trimmed of all stringy portions, and chopped very fine. Crumb a slice of bread into a teacup, and fill it with milk. Beat the yolks and whites of the eggs separately; add to the yolks the soaked crumbs, then the whites; season the meat well with salt and pepper; put a good lump of butter in the pan, and fry a light brown as with other omelettes.

Ham and Potatoes.—Beat the yolks of 2 eggs into a little melted butter (about 2 oz.), cut some thin slices of cooked ham, dip them in it; butter a dish or pan, and lay in it a layer of cold boiled and sliced potatoes, sprinkle them with pepper and salt, then put a layer of the pieces of ham, another of potatoes, and so on till the dish be full, finishing with the potatoes. Pour over this ½ pint of cream; stand the dish in the oven and bake quickly.

Poached Eggs (*French*).—Put into a saucepan some minced ham, butter, a little stock, the juice of a lemon, and bind all with a little flour; add salt and pepper to taste; when the mixture is on the boil, and just before serving, break the eggs into it, taking care not to break the yolks. Serve on buttered toast.

Cock-a-Leekie.—Take an old cock and a gallon of good stock; a good bunch or two of leeks cut into lengths of about 1 inch; simmer the fowl and half the leeks in the stock gently for half an hour, then add the rest of the leeks and simmer for three or four hours. Skim and season to taste. Take out the fowl, carve it in joints, placing them in the tureen, then pour the soup—which should be quite thick of leeks—over, and serve. When possible, make your cock-a-leekie ot an old grouse or blackcock.

To Dress a Haggis.—Get a butcher to send you the stomach of a sheep, and the liver, heart, and lungs; see that the bag, or paunch as it is called, is well cleaned, scald it, and put it to soak all night in a weak brine. The day you get it boil the liver, etc., for an hour and a half. Next day cut away all superfluities, and put all the rest through a mincing machine, with ½ lb. of suet; put these in a basin and mix with them ½ lb. of oatmeal, pepper and salt to taste, a good deal of the former being used. An onion or two finely cut is by many considered an improvement. A pint of the liquor in which the heart, etc., was boiled is added, and the whole well mixed. Take the bag out ot soak and put in the above mixture, which should leave sufficient space in the bag for the expansion of the ingredients; sew up the opening. Have ready a large pot of boiling water, into which plunge the haggis; as it swells prick it here and there to prevent bursting. Boil for three hours, then serve very hot.

> " Fair fa' your honest, sonsie face,
> Great chieftain o' the puddin race!
> Aboon them a' ye tak' your place,
> Painch, tripe, or thairm :
> Weel are ye worthy o' a grace
> As lang's my arm."—*Burns.*

Hot-Pot.—Hot-pot is made of mutton chops placed in a deep dish (known as a hot-pot dish), with a good layer ot potatoes cut in pieces, some onion chopped fine, pepper,

and salt; then another layer of chops, and more potatoes.
The potatoes at the top are left whole. Add a little water,
and bake in a moderate oven for three or four hours.
Kidneys, oysters, and anchovies are a great improvement.
It may be made of cooked meat, but it is not quite so good.

Calf's Head Hashed (*à la Poulette*).—Cut the remnants of
a boiled head into uniform pieces the size of half an apple.
Melt in a sauce-pan 1 oz. or 2 oz. of butter, according to the
quantity of meat to be hashed; amalgamate with it 1 or 2
tablespoonfuls of flour, then stir in ½ pint, more or less, of
white stock. Stir well, then add a few button mushrooms,
white pepper and salt to taste, and let the sauce boil for ten
minutes. Put the sauce-pan by the side of the fire, and lay
the pieces of calf's head in it; let them get hot slowly, but
not boil. Just before serving stir in, off the fire, the yolks
of 2 eggs, beaten up with the juice of a lemon, and strained;
also a small quantity of either tarragon or parsley very finely
minced.

Eel Pie.—Skin and wash 1 lb. of eels, cut them into
pieces, make a seasoning of bread crumbs, shallot, chopped
parsley, a little sauce, pepper, salt, and nutmeg, with the
juice of half a lemon; place some of this at the bottom of
the dish, then the eels, then the remainder of the seasoning,
adding a little butter; cover with good puff paste, and bake
for an hour.

Curried Lobster.—Take a tin of lobster, strain off the
liquor, cut the lobster in small pieces; mix 2 tablespoonfuls
of curry powder, 1 dessertspoonful of flour, and a pinch of
salt; add this to a sliced onion fried in butter until brown,
then stir in a wineglassful of milk, the juice of a lemon, and
the lobster, and let all simmer gently for a few minutes.

Oyster Patties.—Make some rich puff paste, and bake a light brown in patty-pans, keeping an opening in the centre by inserting a piece of bread, which remove when done; take as many oysters as required, remove the beards, and cut each into four pieces; just scald them in their own liquor, and make a sauce of 2 oz. of butter, 3 tablespoonfuls of cream, a little flour, lemon juice, pounded mace, and cayenne; warm, but do not let it boil. Place a little of the mixture in each patty, put on the cover, and return to the oven to make very hot before serving.

To make a Devil.—Cut up thin slices of any cold meat, fowl, or kidney, lay them in a shallow dish, and pour over them the following:—1 tablespoonful of powdered mustard, 2 teaspoonfuls of Worcestershire sauce and mushroom ketchup, 1 teaspoonful of Chili vinegar, $\frac{1}{2}$ teaspoonful of cayenne, 1 teaspoonful of salad oil, or a small piece of butter if there is no fat in the meat, 1 teaspoonful of lemon juice, and 1 wineglassful of claret. Set the dish in the oven and stir the meat about in the same for a quarter of an hour.

Egg Balls for Soups.—Procure some hard-boiled yolks of eggs, then moisten with some raw yolk, till you can roll the mixture into a ball. Roll up into balls the size of small marbles, dip into flour, and throw into boiling water till set, then drain and throw them into the soup before serving. Some chopped parsley can be mixed with the egg.

Bredie (a South African Dish).—Take about 1 lb. of small ribs of mutton, fry with onion, put in a few bits of chili and salt, then add your vegetables, either cauliflower, cabbage, green beans, or anything you may fancy. These must be chopped fine, and allowed to steam with the meat till done. It must be eaten with rice, as it is too rich without.

Cabbage Bredie (a Cape Dish).—Take a fine white drum-head cabbage; scoop out in the centre as much as will leave a space as large as a good sized shaddock; fill this with a mixture of fresh meat (not cooked) minced fine, a tomato peeled, a little lemon peel chopped fine, a small onion or a few shallots, some bread crumbs, pepper, salt, and a teaspoonful of butter, adding also a portion of the cabbage taken out; tie it up in a cloth, and boil gently for an hour; serve hot.

Bean Bredie (African Dish).—Stew fresh meat cut small with green French beans till all the water is evaporated, or nearly, adding a little pepper and salt, and serve very hot.

Soles au gratin (a French Dish).—Put into a buttered stew-pan some gravy or butter, mushrooms, a *little* shallot, garlic, and parsley, all chopped *fine*, a little salt and pepper, half a glass of white wine, and some raspings. All must boil together for five minutes. Place the filleted soles in a pie-dish; pour all the above upon them, and cook them in the oven for three-quarters of an hour; serve in the dish as they are. Mushrooms may be dispensed with, and onions used instead of garlic.

Veal Balls (a French Dish).—Take some small and thin bits of tender veal cutlet; lay on each piece a little finely-chopped parsley, onion, or shallot, pepper and salt, and a little sausage-meat; roll up each, and tie with small string; then roll each ball lightly in flour; fry them in hot butter or lard until they are a nice brown, then add a little gravy or water, and some mushrooms; stew gently for fully half an hour.

Roman Pudding.—Boil a rabbit till quite tender; take the meat off the bones and cut it rather small; mix with it

2 oz. boiled maccaroni, 2 oz. grated cheese, 1 small onion chopped fine, ½ pint of milk, pepper and salt. Place in a pie-dish, and bake with a little butter on the top for an hour.—*Mrs. Addison.*

Maccaroni Pie.—Any kind of cold meat minced, pepper, salt, and a little Worcester sauce, an onion cut small, and half a cupful of stock. Place all at the bottom of a pie-dish, fill it up with boiled maccaroni, strew the top with grated cheese or bread crumbs and some little dabs of butter. Bake in a brisk oven till the maccaroni begins to turn colour.

Portuguese Stewed Chicken.—Cut into small joints a nice fowl, put it in a pan of cold water for an hour, dry well on a cloth. Flour each piece, and fry in a frying-pan a nice brown. Cut up some Spanish onions and tomatoes and fry them in a sauce-pan, add the fowl, a little water, pepper and salt, spice and sweet herbs. Simmer gently until cooked. Serve with toasted sippets round the dish.

Stewed Rabbit.—Joint and wash an Ostend rabbit, drain it; slice two Spanish onions, take a sauce-pan, place a layer of onions at the bottom, then a layer of rabbit, sprinkle over the rabbit a seasoning of flour, pepper, and salt; then put another layer of onions and another of rabbit, finishing up with onions. Place the sauce-pan over the fire, and when hot draw it aside and let it simmer gently for two hours or more. Or the rabbit, etc., may be placed in a covered jar and allowed to cook in the oven.

Potted Eggs.—The yolks of 3 eggs boiled hard, 1 oz. of butter, 1 tablespoonful of anchovy sauce. Mix together, braid it well; flavour to taste with nutmeg, cayenne, and pepper.

Cheese Puddings.—¼ lb. of cheese grated and nearly ½ gill

of cream, 2 eggs, ½ oz. of oiled butter. Mix all together as for a pudding, and bake in a quick oven for a quarter of an hour or twenty minutes. It may be baked in small tins or pans.

Cheese Straws.—Equal quantities of grated cheese, butter, and flour. Mix butter and flour together in a bowl with a little cayenne and salt. Add the cheese. When well mixed, roll it out thin and cut into strips, which place on a tin and bake in a moderate oven till pale brown.

Parmesan Omelette.—Beat up 3 eggs, with pepper and salt to taste, and a tablespoonful of Parmesan cheese grated. Put a piece of butter the size of an egg into an omelet pan. As soon as it is melted pour in the eggs, etc., and holding the handle of the pan with one hand, stir the omelet with the other by means of a flat spoon. The moment the omelet begins to set, cease stirring, but keep shaking the pan for a moment or so, and then with the spoon double up the omelet; keep on shaking the pan until the underside is of a good colour. Turn on a hot dish, coloured side uppermost, and serve quickly.

Savoury Dish.—3 kidneys, 7 or more mushrooms, 3 eggs, 2 rashers of bacon, potatoes. Skin the kidneys, sprinkle them with seed onions, stew the mushrooms, boil the eggs hard. When ready place them each in the dish, the kidneys in the centre, and between each a piece of the bacon, the mushrooms round the kidneys. Peel the potatoes, and between each put a slice of egg. Pour some gravy with the liquor from the mushrooms over the kidneys, warm in the oven, and serve hot.

Scotch Woodcock.—Take 2 slices of toasted bread ½-inch thick, butter on both sides; 4 or 5 anchovies, washed, scraped, and chopped fine, put them between the toast. The yolks of 2 eggs beaten up and ¼ pint of cream, which put over the fire to thicken, but not boil; pour it over the toast, which must be kept hot and sent to table quickly.

Welsh Cheese.—The inside of a roll to be soaked in boiled milk. Add ¼ lb. of grated cheese (Cheddar best), the yolks of 2 eggs, the whites to be beaten separately and added just before putting in the oven. Bake twenty minutes in a *tin dish* in a quick oven.

Babotie (a Cape Dish).—Take a leg of mutton and mince it very fine, add to the bones and sinews a pint of water, and let it simmer slowly for half an hour, then soak a thick slice of white bread in the hot broth, and when cool mix it with the meat, to which add 6 eggs well beaten; take 2 large white onions, chop them very fine with 3 or 4 slices of garlic and some salt, fry them in butter until nice and brown, then stir in a tablespoonful of good Indian curry powder. Mix the whole well together, put into a pie-dish or cups, putting a lemon leaf and a small lump of butter into each mug; then put in the meat mixture, and rub over the top an egg beaten up with a little milk, then cover the top with some lemon leaves, and let it bake for an hour. 3 eggs will do, and dripping may be substituted for butter. Serve with rice.

To Cure Hams.—1 lb. of bay salt, ½ lb. of common salt, 2 oz. saltpetre, 1 oz. black pepper ground; mix and pound these together. Rub the hams with it and let them lie four days, then put 1½ lb. of treacle over them, turning them every day for three weeks for a small ham, or a month if large; then soak twenty-four hours in cold water and hang up to dry.

This is sufficient for hams of 20 lbs. weight, and they will be fit to cook at any time without further soaking, unless kept for a year, when they should be soaked a day.

I regret that I cannot give any French or Italian recipes for the cooking of frogs and snails. In England snails are considered best soaked in salt and water and then cooked, being pulled out with a pin like periwinkles, and eaten with pepper and vinegar. The Romans preferred them grilled; but for the cure of consumption they should be boiled in milk. I have found one curious old English recipe, which I subjoin, for—

Syrrop of Snailes.—Putt house snailes in a baskett, put fennell in the bottom, middle, and top of them, cover them very close; lett them stand twenty-four hours, wipe them very cleane with a coarse cloath, prick them with a bodkin, and stop their mouths with Lisbon sugar, put them in a sieve with their mouths downwards, and sprinkle a little rosewater all over them. Let them stand till the sugar is dissolved and the syrrop drops clear in a dish; take it off for present use without boyleing. For to keep, putt it on the fire, lett it just boyl, scum it very clean, take if off the fire, and keep it till the next day, then bottle it.

VEGETABLES, FRUIT, ETC., ETC.

Tomato Soup.—1 pint tin of tomatoes, or 4 large raw ones cut up fine, add 1 quart of boiling water, and let them boil a quarter of an hour; then add 1 teaspoonful of carbonate of soda, when it will foam immediately; add 1 pint of sweet milk, with salt and pepper, and about 1 oz. of butter; when this boils, add a few plain biscuits rolled fine. An enamelled sauce-pan must be used.

Scotch Kail or Greens, as eaten in Scotland, are first boiled in slightly salted water; when they are tender the water is drained away, and the kail left in the pot; this is mashed with a potato masher; a good sprinkling of pepper is put in, and then half a cupful of good cream is added and the whole stirred well, allowed to heat up over the fire, and served hot with some crisp oatcakes, and a delicious dish it is.

To Dress Kohl-Rabi (Dutch recipe).—Cut off the green leaves and boil till quite tender, chop up and rub through a sieve; add a little butter, and put back into the stewing-pan, which allow to stand on the side of the stove to keep hot; then slice the kohl-rabi, boil it, and add a little butter, put it into a dish, the white in the centre, and the green round it.

Fricassee of Parsnips.—Boil in milk till they are soft, then cut them lengthways into pieces 2 or 3 inches long, and simmer in a white sauce, made of 2 spoonfuls of broth, a little mace, $\frac{1}{2}$ cupful of cream, a bit of butter, and some flour, pepper, and salt.

Mushroom Powder (old recipe).—Take 1 peck of good mushrooms, wash them very clean, and rub them with a flanel cloath; then put them into a stew-pan, with 1 handfull of salt, 2 or 3 onions, and $\frac{1}{4}$ oz. of cloves, $\frac{1}{4}$ oz. of whole pepper, 2 nutmegs cut, $\frac{1}{4}$ oz. of mace, a sprigg of rosemary, 7 or 8 bay leaves, 3 oz. of fresh butter; let all these stew together till the liquor be dried up, then put them into a broad pan, and set them in the oven after household bread, which done three or four times will dry them enough to rub them to powder or to pound them; keep in a bottle close stopt. Broad mushrooms is best, but scrape out the inside or red.

T

To Dress Artichokes (French fashion).—Boil them till tender, then put them in a dish, cover with white sauce, adding a thick layer of Parmesan cheese; brown lightly in the oven, or with a salamander, and serve.

To Preserve Oranges (old and tried recipe).—Pare them very thin and rub them with salt, lay them in water for twenty-four hours; then boil till they are very tender, and put them in fresh cold water for two days. For 6 oranges, take 3 lbs. of loaf-sugar and 3 pints of water, boil and scum it well, and when cold put in the oranges, and set them by for four or five days, then boil them till they are clear; keep them a few days, and then boil them again, and be sure to have syrup enough to cover them.

Orange Preserve (Cape recipe).—Rasp the outer rind, and make incisions lengthways with a knife at equal distances round the orange; put the oranges into a dish and cover them with water; change the water every day for three or four days, squeezing the oranges a little to get out as many of the pips as possible; boil in fresh water until tender, and press them; make a syrup of equal weight of fruit, water, and sugar, and boil till it becomes almost a jelly; let the syrup cover the fruit. If it becomes thin, boil again.

To make Lemon Pickle.—Cut 6 lemons into 8 pieces each, put on them 1 lb. of salt, 6 cloves of garlic, 2 oz. of horse-radish sliced, of cloves, mace, nutmeg, and cayenne $\frac{1}{4}$ oz. each, and 2 oz. of flour of mustard; put to them 2 quarts of vinegar; boil a quarter of an hour in a well-tinned sauce-pan; set it by in a closely covered jar and stir daily for six weeks; then put it in small bottles.

Orange Marmalade Pudding.—¼ lb. finely chopped suet, ¼ lb. grated bread crumbs, ¼ lb. moist sugar, 2 tablespoonfuls marmalade, 2 eggs well beaten; mix all well together, put into a buttered basin, and boil five hours. Serve with wine or lemon sauce.

Quickly Made Jelly.—Soak 1 oz. gelatine in ½ pint of cold water for ten minutes; add ½ pint of boiling water, stir until the gelatine is dissolved, add 2 glasses of sherry, 1½ lb. sugar, lemon, and lemon peel; boil all together for five minutes, take off the fire, stir in a few drops of cochineal, and pour into a wetted mould.

Small Cocoanut Puddings.—Dissolve 2 oz. of butter, add to it 2 oz. of grated cocoanut, 4 oz. of moist sugar, the grated rind of ½ lemon, and 2 eggs; beat this mixture well together, then add the juice of ½ lemon; put the mixture in patty-pans, and bake for half an hour.

To make an Apple Tansey (old recipe).—Cut 3 or 4 pippins into thin slices, and fry them in good butter, then beat 4 eggs with 6 spoonfuls of cream, a little rosewater, sugar and nutmeg, stir them together, and pour it over the apples; let it fry a little, and turn with a pie-plate. Garnish with lemon, and sugar strewed over it.

For making a Gooseberry Tansey (old recipe).—Fry 1 quart of gooseberries till tender in fresh butter, mash them, then beat 7 or 8 eggs, 4 or 5 whites, 1 lb. of sugar, 3 spoonfuls of sack, as much cream, a penny loaf grated, and 3 spoonfuls of flour; mix all these together, and put the gooseberries out of the pan to them; stir all well together, and put them into a sauce-pan to thicken, then put fresh butter into the frying-pan, fry them brown, and strew sugar on the top.

Quince Cakes (old recipe).—Take 1 lb. of the best yellow quince. Pare, quarter, and boyle till they are very tender, then bruise them in a mortar, and put them in a broad dish, and sett them on a chafing dish of coles. Put to them their weight in sugar, and keep them stirring till the sugar is dissolved, lay them on plates in what shape you please, and strew some sugar over them in your stove, turning them as they dry. Grate sugar over them; paper and box them.

To make a Jelly of Pippins and Codlins (old recipe).—Take 6 pippins and codlins, pare and slice them in a quart of spring water, boil till it comes to a pint, strain and add to the clear 1 lb. of sugar, boil it till it will jelly, skim it clean as it boils; this jelly is proper to put a little on the top of any red or white preserve.

To Candy Cherries.—Get them before they are full ripe, stone them, and having boiled your fine sugar to a height, pour it on them, gently moving them, and so let them stand till almost cold, then take them out and dry them by the fire.

To Candy Barberries and Grapes.—Take preserved barberries, wash off the syrup in water, and sift fine sugar on them, and let them be dried in the stove, turning them from time to time till they are dry enough. Preserved grapes may also be candied the same way.

To Candy Apricots.—You must slit them on the side of the stone, and put fine sugar on them, then lay them one by one in a dish, and bake them in a pretty hot oven; then take them out of the dish, and dry them on glass plates in an oven for three or four days.

To Preserve Cherries, with leaves and stalks green.—

Take morel cherries, dip the stalks and leaves in the best vinegar boiling hot, stick the sprigs upright in a sieve till they are dry; in the meantime boil some double-refined sugar to syrup, and dip the cherries, stalks, and leaves into the syrup, and just let them scald; lay them on a sieve, and boil the syrup to candy height, then dip the cherries, leaves, stalks, and all; then stick the branches in sieves, and dry them as you do other sweetmeats. They are pretty in a dessert.

To Preserve Fruit Green all the year.—Gather your fruit when three-parts ripe, on a very dry day, when the sun shines on them; then take earthen pots and put them in, cover the pots with corks, or bung them up that no air can get in; dig a place in the earth a yard deep, set the pots therein, and cover them with the earth very close, and keep them for use. When you take any out, cover them as at first.

To Pickle Cucumbers to resemble Mangoes.—Peel, cut them in halves, throw away the seeds, and lay the cucumbers in salt for a day. Then wipe them dry, fill them with mustard seed, peeled shallots, garlic, small slips of horse-radish and mace, and tie them round with twine; put them into jars, pour boiling vinegar over, and cover up close till cold, then tie them down with leather, and a bladder over that.

To keep Lettuce Green all the year.—Put them into a pot with vinegar, salt, pepper, and bay leaves; keep them very closely covered, and when required they may be used either in salads or soups.

To Pickle Mushrooms (old recipe).—Take button mushrooms and throw them in a pan of salt and water, wipe them with flannel, then boyle them quickly for a quarter of an hour; let them drain in a sieve till cold.   Make a pickle of best white wine vinegar, some Rhenish wine, whole pepper and ginger cut in slices, boyle and let stand till cold, then put your mushrooms in with a little mace; tye them down close, and pour over them a little of the best oyle.

INDEX

INDEX

U

www.ingramcontent.com/pod-product-compliance
Lightning Source LLC
Chambersburg PA
CBHW060553030726
47498CB00005B/1374